London
for less

"The
guidebook
that pays
for itself –
in one day"

TEXT BY
BEN WEBSTER

KU-216-134

PUBLISHER

Metropolis International
(UK) Limited
222 Kensal Road
London W10 5BN
England

Tel:+44-(0)20-8964-4242

Fax:+44-(0)20-8964-4141

E-mail:
metropolis@for-less.com

Web site: www.for-less.com

TITLES

Publisher Information

LONDON FOR LESS

First published in Great Britain in 1997 by Metropolis
International (UK) Limited, a member of the London
Tourist Board. Second edition 1998. Third edition
2000/2001.

Discounts by Metropolis International (UK) Limited.
Text by Ben Webster.
Principal photography by Debra Sweeney.

ISBN 1-842490-01-X

COPYRIGHT

Copyright © Metropolis International (UK) Limited,
1997, 1998, 2000/2001.

for less, *for less* logos and *for less* guidebooks are
trademarks of Metropolis International (UK) Limited.

All rights reserved. No part of this book may be
reproduced or utilized in any form or by any means,
electronic or mechanical, including photocopying,
recording or by any information storage retrieval
system, without permission in writing from the
publishers.

DISCLAIMER

Assessments of attractions, hotels, museums and so
forth are based on the author's impressions and
therefore contain an element of subjective opinion
which may not reflect the opinion of the publishers.

The contents of this publication are believed to be
correct at the time of printing, however, details such
as prices will change over time. We would advise you to
call ahead to confirm important information.

Care has been taken in the preparation of this
guidebook, however, the publisher cannot accept
responsibility for errors or inaccuracies that may
occur.

The publisher will not be held responsible for any loss,
damage, injury, expense or inconvenience sustained by
any person, howsoever caused, as a result of
information or advice contained in this guide except
insofar as the law prevents the exclusion of such
liability.

Contents

for less guidebooks . . .

GUIDEBOOKS

London for less
New York for less
Paris for less

Unlike "budget guides", the series of stylish *for less* guidebooks enable <u>every</u> visitor, however much they anticipate spending, to save money at all the <u>best</u> places.

The *for less* guidebooks have 288 pages of information, plus a full range of discounts at top attractions, hotels, tours, restaurants, shops and entertainment venues.

WHAT THE PAPERS SAY...

'Less is definitely more with *London for less*'
The Washington Post, USA

'This discount program can save travelers from 10% to 70% at participating hotels, major attractions and museums, plays, concerts, tours, rental cars and restaurants'
The Los Angeles Times, USA

'A typical individual traveler can recover the purchase in savings in one afternoon and a typical family may save more than $100 per day'
Britainews, British Tourist Authority, Britain

Easy-to-use, informative, vividly written, packed with photos and maps, these comprehensive guidebooks are available for New York, London and Paris.

Maps

Fold-out street and underground maps come with each guidebook, with all the main attractions clearly located. They link to hundreds of mini-maps inside the book.

Discount Cards

The *for less* discount card that comes with each guidebook gives up to 4 people great savings at hundreds of places in each city.

WEB SITE

For the most up-to-date information about the *for less* titles as well as practical information about the cities you are planning to travel to, visit our Web site at www.for-less.com.

... *for less* Compact Guides

Slim enough to fit in your pocket, the *for less* Compact Guides combine quality text with discounts at top attractions, making them ideal for a shorter trip.

The area-by-area format and extensive information enable even first-time visitors to

get the most out of their visit.

The series covers a number of destinations in Europe and the United States, and the list is constantly growing.

Compact Guides can be purchased from all good bookstores. Many of the titles are available in French, Spanish, German and Dutch, as well as English.

Maps

Each guide comes with a detailed fold-out street and underground/ Metro (subway) map. All the main tourist attractions are clearly located, making it easy for visitors to find their way around. Linked to the main map are hundreds of mini-maps in the guidebook.

Discount Coupons

Visitors can obtain "2-for-1" discounts at an impressive range of top attractions and museums, simply by handing in the relevant voucher printed at the back of the guide. In this way, holders of *for less* Compact Guides can enjoy incredible savings at unmissable sights.

New titles are regularly added to the **compact guide** series. Check our web site **www.for-less.com** to find out about the latest ones.

DID YOU KNOW ... ?

More than one million people from over 30 different countries have saved money using *for less* guidebooks.

How to Use *London for less*

London for less has been created to enable visitors to save money by obtaining discounts at the best places in London. All discounts are applicable for up to four people for up to eight consecutive days. Each page is colour coded as follows:

Attractions and Museums	Tours
Hotels	Restaurants
Shops	Performing Arts

Before you use the card, you must validate it by following the instructions printed underneath it on the inside front cover. The card should always be presented when you request the bill (check) and before payment is made.

Discounts apply whatever method of payment you choose, however, **London for less** cannot be used in conjunction with other offers or discounts, such as family admission tickets.

Throughout this book, you will find the *London for less* logo. Every time it appears, it indicates that you are entitled to a discount.

Use of the card or vouchers must conform to the instructions on pages 7 and 8 and to the specific instructions set out in each entry.

All organizations offering discounts in this guidebook have a contract with the publisher to give genuine discounts to holders of valid *for less* cards and/or vouchers.

Care has been taken to ensure that discounts are only offered at reputable establishments, however, the publisher and/or its agents cannot accept responsibility for the quality of merchandise or service provided, nor for errors or inaccuracies in this guidebook.

The publisher and/or its agents will not be responsible if any establishment breaches its contract (although it will attempt to secure compliance) or if any establishment changes ownership and the new owners refuse to honour the contract.

For post-publication updates and amendments to the discounts offered you should consult our website at www.for-less.com.

CREDIT CARD SYMBOLS USED

AM = AMEX
VS = VISA
MC = MASTERCARD
DC = DINERS CLUB
DS = DISCOVER

How to Obtain Discounts...

ATTRACTIONS AND MUSEUMS

To obtain discounts at attractions or museums you must either show your card or hand in a voucher

which you will find at the back of the book. When you hand in the voucher you should circle the number of people in your party and also show your *for less* card.

At most attractions, discounts are available off the adult, child, senior and student prices (but not off family tickets). Children are usually defined as under 12, seniors as over 65. An index of attractions, museums and galleries that offer *London for less* discounts is on page 260.

Tower of London

HOTELS

For details of how to book hotels see page 32.

TOURS AND TRANSPORTATION

London for less offers you discounts on transfers into London from Heathrow, Gatwick and Stansted airports (see page 18). *London for less* also offers large savings on coach tours (pages 238-244), car rental (page 225), open-top bus tours (page 236), walking tours (page 237) and river trips (page 237).

Open-top bus tours

To obtain the discounts, you must book as instructed in each tour's entry. You cannot book through a

travel agent, hotel concierge or other intermediary.

RESTAURANTS

London for less entitles you to a flat 25% off the total bill (check), including food and beverages, at 65 restaurants in London, listed on

The Pavilion restaurant

. . . How to Obtain Discounts

pages 262-264. The vouchers on page 285 entitle you to discounts at any Bella Pasta or Pizza Piazza restaurant.

Mackenzie's

The price indicated is not a fixed or minimum price. It is only a guide to the average cost of a meal. It is based on a typical two-course meal for one person without an alcoholic drink. You are entitled to the discount however much you spend.

So that the service (tip) is not reduced by the discount, it is recommended that you tip on the total amount of the bill, before the discount is applied. A standard tip in London is 10-15% of the bill.

SHOPS

London for less offers a 20% discount at 40 shops, listed on page 262. To obtain the discount, simply show the card before you pay for the goods. Discounts on goods already reduced in price or on sale are at the discretion of the shop's management.

English National Ballet

PERFORMING ARTS

London for less offers you discounts on tickets for West End theatre productions (see page 206). Unfortunately, we cannot guarantee that you will be able to obtain discounts for particular performances, as certain shows are frequently sold out.

FOREIGN CURRENCY EXCHANGE

With the vouchers on page 273, you can change money commission free at branches of Travelex listed on page 253. Their rates are competitive and you will save 100% on the transaction charge.

West End shows

Introduction

Introduction to London . . .

'When a man is tired of London, he is tired of life; for there is in London all that life can afford.'
– Dr. Samuel Johnson

Each of the world's great cities has breathtaking monuments from its heyday: Istanbul has its Blue Mosque, New York its skyscrapers, Rome its classical

and renaissance architecture. But only London has emerged from each era in its 2,000 years of history more magnificent, more varied and more richly endowed with the treasures of a long and proud civilization.

The unique appeal of London includes the splendid collections of the **British Museum** and the **National Gallery**, famous department stores like **Harrods** and **Liberty**, and 'must-

The Tower of London

see' attractions such as **Madame Tussaud's** and the **Tower of London**.

REFLECTIONS

'London: a nation, not a city.' – Benjamin Disraeli, Prime Minister (1874-80)

With its multiplicity of traditions and customs – from the pomp and ceremony of the **Changing of the Guard** at Buckingham Palace to the youthful vigour of the **Notting Hill Carnival** – London is a multicoloured tapestry of living history.

This happy marriage of old and new is most striking in **the City**, London's financial district and the site of the original Roman town. Gleaming office blocks surround the 1,000-year-old Tower of London.

The City is Europe's financial centre, with many billions of pounds traded each day on the various exchanges: London has more Japanese banks than Tokyo and more American banks than New York.

On most maps, it is impossible to see the seams of

London's patchwork of urban 'villages'. Yet many of these areas retain a good deal of the distinctive character they enjoyed before they were engulfed by the city's growth. **Chelsea**, with its chic boutiques and bars, as well as its streets of elegant terraced homes, is a world apart from the exotic cafés and shops of **Notting Hill's** ethnic melting pot.

The City from the Thames

To help you make sense of London's vastness, the eight

. . . Introduction to London . . .

most important areas have each been given their own chapter in this guide and their boundaries are shown on the fold-out map.

London is an extraordinarily cosmopolitan city, with large Asian, Afro-Caribbean, Arab, Jewish and Chinese communities. It has a knack of adopting the best of each culture, with restaurants and shops from more than one hundred different countries.

While various ethnic groups have settled in different areas – Afro-Caribbeans in Notting Hill, Arabs in Bayswater and Jews in Golders Green – no place has become the exclusive preserve of one culture. London, by and large, enjoys broad-minded racial harmony.

Tower Bridge

Pigeons in Trafalgar Square

Although Greater London stretches over more than 600 square miles, nearly all the major sights are within a compact area. The 100-year-old **Tube** network, which is constantly being overhauled, makes travel across the traffic-snarled city fast and simple. None of the main attractions is more than a ten-minute walk from a tube station.

REFLECTIONS

'Oh, London is a fine town,
A very famous city,
Where all the streets are
paved with gold,
And all the maidens
pretty.' – George Colman
(1797)

London may have seven million inhabitants (not to mention 28 million visitors each year), but it is still possible to find, and enjoy, peaceful solitude. After fighting through the army of shoppers on **Oxford Street** or braving the British Museum's huge summer crowds, you can soothe jangled nerves with a stroll through one of London's many parks and gardens. Apart from the vast expanses of **Hyde Park/Kensington Gardens** and **Regent's Park**, there are dozens of smaller gardens and grassy squares.

Charles and the late Diana on a visit to Parliament

Britain's **royal family**, which has in the past decade become a daily soap opera, is perhaps the country's top tourist attraction. Though they have a string of sumptuous palaces across England, the royals spend much of their time in the capital.

. . . Introduction to London . . .

Some of their homes are open to visitors. **Buckingham Palace** (pages 50-51) can be visited during August and September, when the Queen holidays in Scotland. From May to December, you can tour **Kensington Palace** (page 194), formerly the home of the late Diana, Princess of Wales.

A London Police Officer

There are several other former royal residences scattered across London. They include the mighty Tower of London (pages 136-137) on the river at the eastern edge of the City and Henry VIII's **Hampton Court Palace** (pages 216-217) several miles upstream to the west. **Windsor Castle** (pages 218-219), which was ravaged by fire in 1992 but is now being restored, requires a day trip.

REFLECTIONS

'London Swings Again... the seat of a thriving indigenous film industry, the nerve center of pop music...a center of gastronomy and fashion that outclasses Paris.'
– *Vanity Fair*
(March 1997)

Many visitors feel bound, like pilgrims, to visit London's world-renowned religious and cultural monuments such as **St. Paul's Cathedral** (pages 134-135), **Westminster Abbey** (pages 52-53) and the **British Museum** (pages 168-169). While these are undeniably impressive, the city abounds with beautiful churches and fine museums.

One of the great pleasures of London is straying off the crowded tourist trail to find 'secret' treasures tucked away, like the tiny **Sir John Soane's Museum** (page 140), with its wonderfully eclectic art collection, or the picturesque tranquillity of **Little Venice** (page 187).

Big Ben

An aerial view of Westminster

You will quickly learn that the cliché about English reserve is unfounded. Most Londoners have busy working and social lives, but, in general, they are friendly and helpful if you can get them to stop for a moment. It's true that no one talks on the Tube, but few will cold-shoulder your efforts to strike up conversation.

. . . Introduction to London

Another myth about London, or rather England, is that it rains all the time. This is not true, as London has less rainfall than either Paris or New York. It enjoys warm summers, which are rarely unpleasantly hot. The winters are reasonably mild, and even in the coldest month, January, the average temperature is almost always over 6°C (43°F).

Parliament from the Thames

From the visitor's point of view, London enjoys another great advantage: personal safety. It has one of the lowest violent crime rates of any capital city in the world.

Anyone visiting London will be struck by the number of young tourists. They are drawn from around the world by the hundreds of fascinating micro-cultures, each with its own music, clothes and clubs.

The rise of **'Britpop'**, spear-headed by the London-based bands Oasis and Blur, has created a new mood reminiscent of the Swinging Sixties and the heyday of the Beatles. In fact, London has become so trendy that the American magazine *Newsweek* dubbed London "the coolest city on the planet". By comparison, youth culture in other European cities can seem dull and uniform.

REFLECTIONS

'Cause in sleepy London town / There's just no place for a street fighting man!' – The Rolling Stones

Since the turn of the new century, London has enjoyed a spate of exciting new developments alongside thoughtful refurbishment of existing structures. The river has been a focus for many of the new plans, and the **BA London Eye** (page 157), the **Tate Modern** (page 156) and the **Millennium Bridge** (page 160) are just some of the new attractions to be seen along the central stretch of the Thames. The **British Museum**, the **National Portrait Gallery** (page 79) and the **V & A** (page 112) are among the established favourites that have received new wings, re-fits or other improvements to herald the 21st century.

Britpop band 'Oasis'

Whenever you visit London, in addition to the perennial attractions, special events will be taking place. The **Boat Show** in January, the **Chelsea Flower Show** in May, the **Wimbledon Lawn Tennis Championships** in June or July, the **Notting Hill Carnival** in August and the **Lord Mayor's Show** in November are just some of the highlights (see pages 246-247 for the calendar of events).

London: Area by Area . . .

WESTMINSTER

For centuries, this historic area has been the centre of political and royal power. Dozens of London's grandest buildings and monuments, including the Houses of Parliament, Nelson's Column, Westminster Abbey, 10 Downing Street and the Queen's London home, Buckingham Palace, are found in this area. It is the most popular tourist area but is also a working part of London with dozens of government offices.

WEST END

Always bustling with people, the West End is London's entertainment and theatre district. There are dozens of pavement cafés, lively pubs and trendy clubs drawing in massive evening crowds. Covent Garden offers daytime street entertainment, while Soho's bars and sex shops ply their trade into the small hours. Hundreds of restaurants serve every kind of cuisine. In Chinatown, centred on Gerrard Street, you will find a wide choice of Chinese food. Oxford Street and Regent Street form London's busiest shopping district.

MAYFAIR AND ST. JAMES'S

Once the home of Britain's aristocracy, this exclusive area now contains many of London's up-market clubs, art galleries and luxury hotels. Designer stores can be found on Bond Street. It is bordered by three royal parks, Hyde Park, Green Park and St. James's Park.

SOUTH KENSINGTON AND CHELSEA

Three magnificent museums – the Victoria and Albert, the Natural History and the Science – are the principal attractions in South Kensington. Harrods, the famous department store, and other luxury shops line Knightsbridge. Chelsea's King's Road, on the cutting edge of fashion since the 1960s, has many popular shops, bars and restaurants.

. . . London: Area by Area

CITY OF LONDON

London's financial district boasts some of the capital's finest historic buildings, including St. Paul's Cathedral, the Tower of London and Tower Bridge. The medieval street pattern remains, though the skyline is now dominated by office blocks like the NatWest Tower and futuristic new buildings like Lloyd's of London. The City becomes a ghost town in the evening and at weekends when the 300,000 office workers have gone home.

SOUTH OF THE RIVER

The once dilapidated southern river frontage has sprung to life in recent years, with impressive developments such as London Bridge City and Butler's Wharf. Shakespeare's reconstructed Globe Theatre has joined the South Bank arts centre in attracting both tourists and Londoners across the river, and the world's biggest observation wheel, the BA London Eye, has begun a five-year stint to mark the third millennium. Another riverside attraction is the warship HMS *Belfast* , and just a stroll away lies London's most bloodthirsty museum, the London Dungeon.

BLOOMSBURY AND MARYLEBONE

The British Museum sets the tone for Bloomsbury, a neighbourhood replete with cultural and literary associations. Its leafy squares and the smart 18th-century streets around Portland Place are full of architectural gems. Further west, there are two hugely popular attractions: Madame Tussaud's and the London Planetarium.

BAYSWATER AND NOTTING HILL

Bayswater contains many of London's tourist hotels, with Queensway and Whiteley's shopping mall staying open until late in the evening. Portobello Market is the star attraction of Notting Hill, a trendy residential area packed with interesting little restaurants, modern art galleries and seriously hip bars.

Before You Go . . .

WHEN TO GO

Tourists visit London all year round, but the high season is from June to September. Attractions are most crowded in July and August, during the school summer holidays.

There are special events nearly every weekend and on holidays throughout the year (see pages 246-247).

London's climate is generally mild, with average daytime temperatures ranging from a low of 10°C (50°F) in winter to a high of 20°C (70°F) in the summer. Summer and winter extremes are rare, as is air-conditioning in London buildings.

VISAS AND ENTRY REQUIREMENTS

All visitors require a valid passport to enter the United

Virgin Atlantic Airways

Kingdom, except European Union (EU) citizens who can show their identity card instead. Visas are not needed by visitors from the EU, the United States, Canada, New Zealand or Australia. Citizens of all other countries should check visa requirements with the local British embassy before they leave home.

For import restrictions on duty-free goods, see page 250. Following a change in the quarantine laws, animals with a valid "pet passport" attesting to their health can travel to Britain from Western Europe and other rabies-free countries. Pets from the Americas, Asia and Africa still have to under go a six month quarantine period.

MONEY

The currency is Sterling: 100 pence (p) equals one pound (£). Most major credit cards, especially MasterCard and Visa, are widely accepted in London. Many of the automatic teller machines offer cash advances on credit and debit cards. Only a few major stores accept Sterling

Travelex foreign currency exchange

traveller's cheques as a cash alternative. For commission-free (i.e. no transaction charge) currency and travellers cheque exchange at Travelex see page 253 and the vouchers on page 273.

. . . Before You Go

London is an expensive city, and the average daily tourist budget, excluding accommodation but including entrance prices, meals, transportation and entertainment, is approximately £50 per person.

HEALTH AND INSURANCE

There is little risk of contracting an infectious disease

in Britain. Citizens of EU countries are entitled to free National Health Service (NHS) treatment, though they must provide the appropriate form showing that their country has a reciprocal arrangement.

Citizens of other countries get free on-the-spot treatment at accident and emergency units at NHS hospitals, but must

A West End theatre

pay for all other medical services. Health insurance is, therefore, advisable for visitors. Pharmacists can only dispense a limited range of drugs without a doctor's prescription.

PACKING FOR LONDON

A warm coat is needed in winter and a jacket is advisable in summer, when there are occasional cold, wet days. An umbrella is useful throughout the year.

Electricity is 240 volts (at 50 hz) with unique, square, three-pin plugs. Most travellers will need an adaptor and sometimes an electric current converter. Shaver sockets in hotels conform to the international standard.

BOOKING A HOTEL ROOM IN ADVANCE

London hotels tend to be fairly expensive and fill up quickly in high season. You should therefore book as far ahead as possible. With **London for less** you can

A bedroom at the Dorchester Hotel

obtain specially discounted rates at 42 hotels listed on pages 33 to 46. For booking information, see page 32.

BOOKING THEATRE TICKETS IN ADVANCE

It is a good idea to book seats well in advance for the more popular London shows. The **London for less** ticket line (page 206), which is operated by Ticketmaster, takes 24-hour credit card bookings for all West End shows. Remember to ask which shows offer **London for less** discounts and check if there is a booking fee.

Arriving in London . . .

GETTING FROM THE AIRPORT

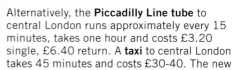 The **Airbus** is a frequent link between all four Heathrow terminals and the centre of London. The red double-decker buses go to King's Cross via popular hotel areas such as Bayswater, Marble Arch, Euston and Russell Square. There are more than 30 journeys daily from 5.30am to 9.45pm, and the journey time is 1 hour 45 minutes. You can get £1 off a single ticket (normal price £7) and £2 off a return ticket (normal price £10) with the voucher on page 273.

Berkeleys Hotel Connections transfers passengers to and from central London hotels. Operating from all Heathrow terminals, the service can

be booked on the website (*www.berkeleys.co.uk*) or by telephone (☎ *01442 298507*). One trip to or from Heathrow costs £14, and this price is reduced by £2 with the voucher on page 273 (mention **London for less** when booking, and present voucher when you board the coach).

Berkeleys Hotel Connections serves all three main London airports

Alternatively, the **Piccadilly Line tube** to central London runs approximately every 15 minutes, takes one hour and costs £3.20 single, £6.40 return. A **taxi** to central London takes 45 minutes and costs £30-40. The new **Heathrow Express** (☎ *0845 6001515*) leaves every 15 minutes from platforms 6 and 7 at Paddington Station and takes about 15 minutes. Tickets are £12 (£22 return).

 The **Airbus** runs between Gatwick Airport and Victoria Rail and Coach Stations, with a journey time of 1 hour 20 minutes. The distinctive red coaches are air-conditioned, with plenty of luggage space, and run hourly from 5.15am to 9.50pm. You can get £1 off a single ticket (normal price £7) and £2 off a return ticket (normal price £10) with the voucher on page 273.

Berkeleys Hotel Connections operates alongside the Gatwick Express to transfer passengers from the airport to their London hotels. For booking, see under Heathrow Airport (above). One trip to or from Gatwick costs £20, and this price is reduced by £2 with the voucher on page 273 (mention **London for less** when booking, and present voucher when you board the coach).

Alternatively, the **Gatwick Express** train to Victoria leaves every 15 minutes and takes 30 minutes, with tickets costing £10.20 (single) and £20.40 (return). A **taxi** to central London will cost up to £60.

. . . Arriving in London

for less **The Airbus** runs between Stansted Airport and Victoria Rail and Coach Stations, with a journey time of 1 hour 40 minutes. There is a service every half hour from 4.15am to 12.15am. The double-decker buses are air-conditioned, with plenty of luggage space and coach-style seating. You can get £1 off a single ticket (normal price £7) and £2 off a return ticket (normal price £10) with the voucher on page 273.

Alternatively, the **train** to London Liverpool Street leaves every 30 minutes, takes 45 minutes and costs £10 single, £20 return. If you take a **taxi**, it will cost close to £100!

A London black cab

GETTING AROUND LONDON

If time is at a premium, you can avoid time-consuming travel and concentrate your sightseeing each day on a particular area. To help you do this, ***London for less*** is organized into areas.

Although credit cards are widely accepted in London you will need cash for transportation, entrance prices and food. You can change money at Travelex branches at Heathrow and Gatwick (see page 253 for a listing of branches and page 273 for vouchers).

for less **Bus and coach tours** – Taking a guided tour on an open-top double-decker bus is the best way to orient yourself and see most of the capital's major sites. Several companies operate bus tours, including London Pride, which offers a 50% discount to *for less* card holders (page 236). If you would prefer a more luxurious overview of the city you can take a Frames Rickards guided coach tour (pages 238-244).

The Underground (tube) – The tube is the easiest way to get around London. Trains run every three to ten minutes, depending on the time of day. Travelcards, either for a single day, for a weekend or for a whole week, offer unlimited travel on tubes, buses and trains within central London, and can be bought at any tube station (page 258).

Double-decker buses – The ordinary red double-decker buses, which operate hundreds of routes around London, can be complicated for visitors to understand. The Travelcard works on the buses too.

A London double-decker bus

Taxis – A ride in one of London's famous black cabs is a unique experience. However, even short journeys will usually cost you at least £5. You are most likely to need a cab after midnight, when the tube stops running. Unfortunately, at this time it can be hard to find one that is available.

Planning Your Trip . . .

IF YOU HAVE ONE DAY

This itinerary will give you a flavour of London life and afford a glimpse of the riches of English culture.

Sightseeing – Head for Trafalgar Square, from where you can walk down Whitehall to the Houses of Parliament (pages 54-55) and Westminster Abbey (pages 52-53). A stroll through St. James's Park (page 198) brings you to the Queen's London residence, Buckingham Palace (pages 50-51).

St. Paul's Cathedral

Unless you are a dedicated royal watcher, it's not worth queuing to go inside when it is open in August and September. After lunch head east – preferably on an open top double-decker bus (see below and page 236) – to the Tower of London (pages 136-137) and St. Paul's Cathedral (pages 134-135). From there, head down to the River Thames and walk along Victoria Embankment, back towards Westminster. Waterloo Bridge, on a curve in the river, offers the finest views of London.

A river trip

Double-decker bus tour – Starting and finishing at Piccadilly Circus, the 90-minute tours usually cover two huge loops around the west and east of the city. Tickets are valid for 24 hours and allow you to hop on and off to visit attractions (see page 236 for discount).

Lunch in a pub – Most pubs in central London serve food at lunchtime and usually offer traditional English dishes, like shepherd's pie and rhubarb crumble.

Afternoon tea – Several of the up-market hotels and shops offer special afternoon teas (sandwiches, cakes, scones

A typical London pub

and different varieties of tea), usually available from lunchtime until early evening. The crème de la crème is tea at the Ritz or the Dorchester (pages 256-257), costing over £20.

West End show – Many of Broadway's biggest hits start life in London, the world's theatre capital. Andrew Lloyd Webber has a string of long-running hit musicals

INSIDER'S TIP

Double-decker tour buses come either open-topped or covered – check the weather before boarding.

. . . Planning Your Trip

but there are also dozens of other theatres showing new plays or inventive revivals. For discounts on tickets for West End shows see page 206.

IF YOU HAVE TWO DAYS

Spreading the previous itinerary over two days will be far more relaxing. The extra day should allow you to spend an afternoon exploring a major museum or historical site, such as the British Museum (pages 168-169). A late afternoon walk through the peaceful tree-lined paths of Hyde Park will help recharge your batteries.

The British Museum

IF YOU HAVE THREE OR FOUR DAYS

Harrods

A trip to the South Kensington museums (pages 112-115) will take up most of a day, but can be combined with shopping at nearby Harrods (page 116) and walking in the gardens beside Kensington Palace (page 194).

London's renowned street markets (page 252) offer bargains galore and the chance to buy exotic and quirky goods.

DON'T MISS

On Fridays and Saturdays Portobello market in West London has antiques, jewellery, trendy clothing and stores that sell food from around the world (page 186).

IF YOU HAVE ONE WEEK

A week allows you to go in search of hidden London: the hundreds of smaller museums, historic buildings and characterful streets that are glossed over by tourist brochures. Here are some ideas:

1. Highgate Cemetery (page 211), which inspired Bram Stoker's *Dracula*, contains the tombs of hundreds of intellectuals and artists, including Karl Marx, Michael Faraday and George Eliot.

2. The City of London, which has 36 churches (many built by Wren) and a number of ancient guild and livery company buildings (Apothecaries' Hall is the most impressive: inquire at the tourist office beside St. Paul's).

Hampton Court Palace

3. A guided walk around one of London's many historic neighbourhoods, such as the Bloomsbury literary walk, the East End Jack the Ripper walk or the London of Sherlock Holmes (see page 237).

4. A day-trip by river boat from Westminster Pier to Greenwich (page 237) or Hampton Court Palace.

If You Do One Thing . . .

These ten ideas may not be the most famous or popular destinations, but they are an honest selection of personal favourites.

If you visit one attraction:

*Tower of London
(page 136)*

If you go to one art gallery:

*Wallace Collection
(page 173)*

If you walk in one park:

*Holland Park
(page 120)*

If you go to one nightclub:

*Ronnie Scott's
(page 205)*

If you dine at one traditional
English restaurant:

*Veronica's
(page 189)*

If you take one tour:

*London Pride open-top bus
(page 236)*

If you go to one store:

*Liberty
(page 89)*

If you visit one museum
(apart from the British):

*Victoria & Albert (V & A)
(page 112)*

If you make one excursion:

*Boat trip to Greenwich
(page 214 & 237)*

If you visit one church:

*St. Paul's Cathedral
(page 134)*

History of London

History . . .

London began life in 43AD, when the **Emperor Claudius** decided to establish a far-flung outpost of the Roman empire beside the River Thames. Roman Londinium stood in the vicinity of the present day financial district known as the City.

The Romans stayed for almost 400 years and, during their occupation, London became a thriving port.

In the 5th century, the Teutonic Saxons took control of the settlement, which was attacked repeatedly over the next few centuries by marauding Vikings. **King Alfred the Great** built up London's fortifications in the 9th century, but governed his kingdom from Winchester, 50 miles to the south.

Head recovered from Temple of Mithras (Museum of London)

It was not until **William the Conqueror** invaded Britain in 1066 that London gained a great ruler. William was the first monarch to be crowned at Westminster Abbey, where most subsequent coronations have taken place. He made London his capital and strengthened its defences, building the White Tower, a key riverside fortress, which remains the centrepiece of the Tower of London to this day.

REFLECTIONS

'London, thou art the flower of cities all!/ Gemme of all joy, jasper of jocunditie.' – William Dunbar (1501)

'This blessed plot, this earth, this realm, this England.' – *Richard II*, William Shakespeare (1595)

The city's merchants thrived during the Middle Ages, developing a trading empire that stretched across Europe. Unfortunately, many of the fine religious buildings erected with the profits were destroyed during **Henry VIII's** Protestant Reformation of the 1530s. In recompense, his turbulent reign saw the construction of Hampton Court Palace a few miles up river.

Queen Elizabeth I (National Portrait Gallery)

It was during the reign of **Elizabeth I** (1558-1603) that London first emerged as a great cultural capital. Several theatres, such as the Rose and the Globe, were built to show new plays by Shakespeare and others.

. . . History . . .

London experienced massive population growth in the 16th century and, by 1600, it had more than 200,000

16th-century view of London with the Globe and Rose theatres, old London Bridge and old St. Paul's

inhabitants. As a result, the densely packed streets along the main thoroughfare of the Thames became overcrowded and filthy.

The physical decay of London was mirrored by the moral decay of the monarchy under **Charles I** (1625-1649). When the English Civil War broke out, ordinary Londoners – who detested the extravagance of the royal court – supported **Oliver Cromwell** instead. The war culminated in the beheading of **Charles I** in Whitehall in 1649.

However, the city's merchants rapidly became disillusioned with Cromwell, who reneged on promises of democratic reform and assumed the quasi-royal title of Lord Protector. As a result, two years after Cromwell's death in 1658, **Charles II** was welcomed back to the throne. Cromwell's body was disinterred and his head spiked on the roof of Westminster Hall.

In 1665, the Great Plague blighted the city's slums, claiming 75,000 lives. The following year, the Great Fire broke out, destroying two-thirds of the city, including 87 churches.

The Great Fire of London

The fire allowed planners and architects like Sir Christopher Wren to redesign much of the city, and dozens of beautiful churches were built as the cornerstones of blossoming London neighbourhoods. Wren's masterpiece, St. Paul's Cathedral, rose majestically above the revitalised city.

REFLECTIONS

'Pish! A woman might pisse it out.' – Lord Mayor of London on seeing the beginning of the Great Fire of 1666

. . . History . . .

During the 18th century, London grew rapidly as the nobility moved out of the cramped city to spacious, elegant mansions further west. London's intellectual life flourished in the Georgian era, with the opening of the British Museum (1759) and the establishment of learned societies, such as the Royal Academy (1768).

Crystal Palace built in Hyde Park for the Great Exhibition (1851)

With the construction of the West India Dock to the east of the city in 1802, London became the largest port in the world. 19th-century London saw unprecedented development, with a dozen bridges built across the Thames and a complex railway network laid out with termini ringing the city.

During the reign of **Queen Victoria**, who ruled for 63 years from 1837 to her death in 1901, a quarter of the world's land mass was governed from London. The imperial pride of Victorian London was expressed in Hyde Park's hugely successful Great Exhibition (1851), the profits from which left an enduring legacy of museums and cultural institutions in South Kensington.

REFLECTIONS

'The capital [London] is become an overgrown monster.'
– Scottish novelist Tobias Smollett (1771)

By 1901, London's population had topped 6.5 million and its suburbs stretched ten miles in each direction from the city centre.

St. Paul's during the Blitz

During the First World War (1914-18), London suffered its first aerial bombardment, but it was nothing to compare with the catastrophic destruction wrought by the Blitz in the Second World War (1939-45). More than 30,000 people were killed by bombs and many historic buildings, including the Houses of Parliament and Westminster Abbey, were either damaged or destroyed. Miraculously, St. Paul's Cathedral survived almost unscathed, while the surrounding streets were levelled to the ground.

In the 45 years since the coronation of **Queen Elizabeth II**, London has grown upwards, with

. . . History

thousands of new office blocks and high-rise flats. Fortunately, much of the capital's distinctive architecture has been spared and a few striking buildings, such as Canary Wharf Tower and the Lloyd's Building, have been added.

In the 1950s, mass immigration from Britain's former colonies helped give London its fascinating ethnic mix. Some areas, such as Notting Hill and parts of Camden, became ghettos, but in recent years they have been transformed into lively, colourful areas.

Despite the steady erosion of the British Empire throughout the 20th century, London has retained its importance. It is, for example, one of the world's leading financial centres.

Windsor Castle

During the twelve years Margaret Thatcher was Prime Minister (1979-1992), London experienced an economic boom, but lost its governing authority, when she abolished the socialist Greater London Council in 1986.

The problems that have beset the Royal Family, with all three of the Queen's married children getting divorced, were symbolized by the terrible fire at Windsor Castle in 1992. However, the Queen has striven to maintain royal dignity and continues to represent the nation at historic ceremonies, such as the opening of the Channel Tunnel in 1994. Once worlds apart, London and Paris are now connected by a three-hour express train.

The launch of the National Lottery in 1994 raised hundreds of millions of pounds for charitable causes, including London's great arts institutions, such as the Royal Opera House and the Tate. A gigantic millennium exhibition, to rival the Great Exhibition of 1851, saw in the new century and began a series of new developments and refurbishments, some of which are ongoing.

The sense of prosperity and optimism which has prevailed since the turn of 2000 has been reinforced by the election of a new mayor, Ken Livingston, and the reinstating of a city council. At the time of writing, it is still to be seen whether such a move will really make a noticeable difference to the lives of Londoners in an already very hopeful and forward-thinking climate.

REFLECTIONS

'The Thames is liquid history.'– British politician John Burns to an American who had compared the Thames disparagingly with the Mississippi (1943)

BA London Eye

Timeline . . .

ROMAN

43 AD Roman Emperor Claudius invades Britain and establishes Londinium as a key port and garrison. He builds the first London Bridge across the Thames, 50 metres east of today's London Bridge.

61 The Iceni people, led by their queen Boadicea, massacre the Romans and burn down the town.

200 The Romans construct massive fortifications around a rebuilt London.

410 Emperor Honorius withdraws the last Roman troops, leaving London at the mercy of Saxon pirates. London is abandoned for the next two centuries.

SAXON

604 The Saxons control most of England and develop the area immediately to the west of the Roman walls, known as Ludenwic. The chronicler Bede records the building of the first St. Paul's Cathedral.

VIKING

871 After decades of raiding, the Vikings establish London as their winter base.

886 Alfred the Great, the Saxon Christian King of Wessex, defeats the Vikings. He rebuilds London's walls and turns the city into a major trading centre.

984 The Vikings start trying to re-conquer London, finally succeeding in 1013.

1016 The Viking leader Canute becomes King of all-England and pronounces London the national capital, in place of Winchester.

1042 London expands westwards after Edward the Confessor becomes king. He moves his court and church upstream to Thorney Island and builds a magnificent palace so he can oversee construction of his 'West Minster', later Westminster Abbey.

NORMAN

1066 William the Conqueror defeats King Harold at the Battle of Hastings. He crowns himself William I at Westminster Abbey, a tradition followed ever since. He grants the city a charter guaranteeing its semi-autonomy.

1290 The Jews are expelled from London and are not allowed to return for 400 years.

1348-50 The Black Death, or bubonic plague, wipes out half the capital's 50,000 population.

1381 The Peasants' Revolt, in which hundreds of clerics and merchants are lynched, is only quelled when the peasants' leader, Wat Tyler, is stabbed to death by Mayor William Walworth at Smithfield.

. . . Timeline . . .

1300-1400 English culture continues to blossom, with Geoffrey Chaucer (1340-1400) producing the first truly great work of literature in English with the publication of *The Canterbury Tales*.

1477 William Caxton, working in Westminster, publishes the first printed book in England.

1485 Henry VII initiates 120 years of Tudor rule, during which London enjoys rapid growth, more than doubling in population to 200,000 by 1600.

1533 Henry VIII breaks with the Catholic church and commences the dissolution of the monasteries.

1566 The Royal Exchange is founded, establishing London as a leading market for world trade.

1574 The City of London bans theatres, forcing companies to decamp to the south bank of the Thames. In 1599, the Burbages build the Globe, where Shakespeare premières many of his plays.

1605 Guy Fawkes's Gunpowder Plot to blow up Parliament is thwarted.

1643 The power struggle between Charles I and Parliament erupts into Civil War. Londoners successfully defend the capital against royalists.

1649 Charles is beheaded. Oliver Cromwell rules Britain as a Commonwealth.

1660 The monarchy is restored, Charles II is crowned.

1665 The Great Plague kills over 75,000.

1666 The Great Fire destroys two-thirds of the City, including 87 churches, 13,200 houses and St. Paul's Cathedral.

1675 The foundation stone of Sir Christopher Wren's new St. Paul's Cathedral is laid.

1710 London has a population of 575,000 and is the largest city in western Europe.

1751 An Act of Parliament restricts gin retailing which had led to alcoholism of epidemic proportions in London's overcrowded slums.

1759 The British Museum opens.

1801 First census reveals a population of 959,000.

1802 West India Dock opens in marshes to the east of the City; the huge docks serve ships from the rapidly expanding British Empire.

. . . Timeline

1816 Architect John Nash begins laying out grand terraces and circuses. Much of London as we know it today is built during the 19th century.

1833 Construction of London's rail network begins.

VICTORIAN

1837 Queen Victoria is crowned, aged 18, and rules for 63 years until her death in 1901.

1851 The Great Exhibition, held in Hyde Park, attracts six million visitors and funds the construction of South Kensington's museums, as well as the Royal Albert Hall.

1890 The first electric 'tube' line (part of the present Northern Line) opens in tunnels excavated far below ground level.

EDWARDIAN

1914 Outbreak of World War I, during which London experiences its first aerial attacks from Zeppelin airships.

INTER-WAR YEARS

1936 Edward VIII abdicates to marry American divorcée Wallis Simpson.

1939 Outbreak of the Second World War. Aerial bombardment, known as the Blitz, destroys 130,000 houses and kills 30,000.

POST-WAR LONDON

1950s The post-war demand for manpower leads to mass immigration from Britain's colonies.

1956 The Clean Air Act is passed to rid London of its infamous smog.

1965 The Greater London Council is established.

1977 The tube is extended to Heathrow Airport, making London the world's first capital city to have such a link.

1981 The 600-foot (180-metre) NatWest Tower, then Britain's tallest building, opens.

1986 Prime Minister Margaret Thatcher abolishes the Greater London Council.

1990 Worst riots in many decades as thousands gather in Trafalgar Square to protest over the new Poll Tax. London's population stands at seven million, with an additional 28 million annual visitors.

1995 Huge public celebrations outside Buckingham Palace and in Hyde Park mark the 50th anniversary of the Allies' Victory in Europe.

1997 British General election: victory of Labour Party.

2000 Election of mayor and new assembly for London.

Booking a Hotel Room

BHRC desk at Heathrow Airport

In association with the British Hotel Reservation Centre (BHRC), *London for less* offers you the possibility of obtaining up to 50% off the published room rates at selected London hotels.

In order to obtain the published discount, you must book your rooms through the BHRC, either by fax on +44-(0)20-7828-6439, by telephone on +44-(0)20-7828-0601 or by e-mail on londonforless@bhrc.co.uk. Bookings made directly with hotels or through other booking agents (such as tour operators, tourist authorities or travel agents) will <u>not</u> be eligible for the *London for less* discount.

Because of the nature of the hotel business, we cannot promise that using *London for less* will give you the best rates: sometimes special promotions will undercut our rates. Moreover, when hotels are busy our best rates may not be available. You are therefore advised to book as far ahead as possible.

The £ symbols by each hotel's entry indicate the standard double room rates, <u>before</u> the *London for less* discount. £=under £60, ££=£61-90, £££=£91-120, ££££=£121-150, £££££=over £150. To find out what rate you can obtain with *London for less*, you must contact the BHRC. Breakfast is included where mentioned.

BHRC desk at Victoria Station

As long as your card is valid on the first night that you intend to stay in the hotel you can stay as long as you like at the discounted rate (subject to room availability).

The number of stars under each hotel's name indicate its quality:

★★ : At least half the bedrooms have en suite bath/shower rooms and may also have phones and TVs.

★★★ : Full reception services, more formal restaurant and bar arrangements, bedrooms all have en suite facilities, mostly with baths.

★★★★ : More spacious accommodation offering high standards of comfort and food. The range of services should include porterage, room service, formal reception and often a selection of restaurants.

HOTEL FACILITIES

 Shower

 Bath

 Minibar

 Tea / coffee making

 Room service

 24-hour room service

 Radio

 TV

 Satellite / cable TV

 Direct dial telephone

Wake-up call

Hairdryer

Trouser press

 Room safe

 Non-smoking rooms

 Air conditioned rooms

 Laundry service

Babysitting service

 Elevator / lift

Disabled facilities

Secretarial services

Fitness centre

Swimming pool

Grange Rochester Hotel

★★★★

**69 Vincent Square
Westminster**

The Rochester is housed in a handsome Victorian building overlooking a quiet square. All bedrooms boast hand-carved rosewood furniture and marble finished bathrooms. The rate includes breakfast. *(70 rooms)*

PRICE CATEGORY

£££££

Millennium Britannia

★★★★

**44 Grosvenor Square
Mayfair**

A traditional business hotel in the heart of fashionable Mayfair, within easy reach of the financial and commercial City. There is a 24-hour business centre, and a wide range of conference facilities. *(180 rooms)*

PRICE CATEGORY

£££££

Mayflower Hotel

★★★

**26-28 Trebovir Road
Knightsbridge**

The Mayflower is a delightful, family-run hotel located close to the Knightsbridge and South Kensington shopping areas. It prides itself on attentive, friendly service. All rooms have a private bathroom. *(48 rooms)*

PRICE CATEGORY

££

PRICE CATEGORY

£££££

PRICE CATEGORY

£££££

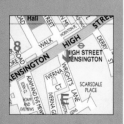

PRICE CATEGORY

£££££

Millennium Knightsbridge

★★★★

**17 Sloane Square
Knightsbridge**

Located in the heart of Knightsbridge, this is one of London's most stylish hotels. All rooms have individually controlled air conditioning, minibar, in-house movies, Play Station and modem connection. *(222 rooms)*

Grange Strathmore Hotel

★★★★

**41 Queen's Gate Gardens
South Kensington**

Once the London residence of the Earl of Strathmore, this hotel blends Victorian grandeur with contemporary luxury. It is located close to Knightsbridge tube station. Breakfast is included in the rate. *(77 rooms)*

Copthorne Tara

★★★★

**Wright's Lane
South Kensington**

The award-winning Copthorne Tara has an enviable reputation for its high standard of comfort and friendly service. A modern hotel, it is situated in a quiet corner of fashionable Knightsbridge. *(834 rooms)*

Rydges Kensington Plaza Hotel

★★★

**61 Gloucester Road
South Kensington**

Renovated in 1992, this Victorian hotel has bedrooms furnished and equipped to a high standard. The Mongolian Barbecue restaurant offers interesting good value meals. The room rate includes breakfast. *(60 rooms)*

PRICE CATEGORY

££££

 # Millennium Bailey's Hotel

★★★★

**140 Gloucester Road
South Kensington**

Established in 1876, Millennium Bailey's has recently been restored to its original glory. The bedrooms are decorated in soft colours and have excellent facilities. It has a popular bar and bistro. *(211 rooms)*

PRICE CATEGORY

£££££

 # Grange Adelphi Hotel

★★★

**127-129 Cromwell Road
South Kensington**

Each of the Adelphi's bedrooms is decorated to a high standard with elegant rosewood furnishings. The hotel has a conservatory restaurant, a coffee shop and a lounge bar. *(70 rooms)*

PRICE CATEGORY

££££

The Amber Hotel

★★★

101 Lexham Gardens
South Kensington

PRICE CATEGORY

£££

The Amber has a quiet location in the heart of Kensington. It boasts a private garden and room service. The rate includes a buffet-style breakfast with a complimentary newspaper. *(40 rooms)*

Barkston Gardens Hotel

★★★

34-44 Barkston Gardens
South Kensington

PRICE CATEGORY

£££

Built at the turn-of-the-century and still retaining much of its original splendour, this hotel is located in a quiet street close to Earl's Court tube station. It has a restaurant, lounge and well-appointed rooms. *(82 rooms)*

The Cranley

★★★

10-12 Bina Gardens
South Kensington

PRICE CATEGORY

£££££

Located in the heart of South Kensington, close to the museums and to Harrods, the Cranley is a small, exclusive hotel. Each bedroom is unique, with luxurious antique furnishings and exquisite décor. *(37 rooms)*

The Burns Park Hotel

★ ★ ★

**18-26 Barkston Gardens
South Kensington**

Situated in a quiet, attractive square in South Kensington, the Burns Park features elegant bedrooms designed and furnished to a high standard. It has an intimate bar and a pleasant restaurant. *(106 rooms)*

PRICE CATEGORY

££££

The Paragon Hotel

★ ★ ★

**47 Lillie Road
South Kensington**

This large, imposing, modern hotel is located close to the Earl's Court tube station. Its rooms are well-furnished, with excellent facilities. There is an all-day coffee shop (with evening carvery) and a pub. *(501 rooms)*

PRICE CATEGORY

£££££

Henley House Hotel

★ ★

**30 Barkston Gardens
South Kensington**

Henley House is a small and friendly hotel located close to Earl's Court tube station. It has elegant rooms, some of which overlook the garden square. Breakfast is included in the tariff. *(20 rooms)*

PRICE CATEGORY

£££

Millennium Gloucester Hotel

★★★★

**Harrington Gardens
South Kensington**

£££££

The Millennium Gloucester is a luxurious hotel in the heart of fashionable South Kensington. It is elegantly furnished and has an excellent restaurant, a fashionable café, 24-hour room service and a business centre. *(548 rooms)*

Holiday Inn Kensington

★★★★

**100 Cromwell Road
South Kensington**

£££££

The luxurious Holiday Inn Kensington is located close to Gloucester Road tube station. It has a whirlpool spa, steam room, sauna, fitness room and a private garden. Its duplex suites have spiral staircases. *(162 rooms)*

Hotel Plaza Continental

★★★

**9 Knaresborough Place
South Kensington**

££

Located between Earl's Court and Gloucester Road tube stations, the Plaza Continental has well-appointed bedrooms and, for the working visitor, a fully-equipped business centre. The rate includes breakfast. *(25 rooms)*

Beaver Hotel

★★

**57-59 Philbeach Gardens
South Kensington**

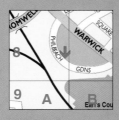

Located close to Earl's Court, the Beaver is a small hotel situated in a quiet tree-lined crescent of charming late-Victorian townhouses. A full English breakfast is included in the tariff. *(37 rooms)*

PRICE CATEGORY

££

Haddon Hall

★★

**30-40 Bedford Place
Bloomsbury**

This friendly bed and breakfast hotel is situated in the leafy surrounds of Bloomsbury, and is just moments from Covent Garden and the West End. As well as comfortable rooms, there is a television lounge to relax in. *(33 rooms)*

PRICE CATEGORY

££

Wansbeck Garden Hotel

B&B

**4-6 Bedford Place
Bloomsbury**

The Wansbeck Garden Hotel, located close to the British Museum, features an attractive walled garden and comfortably furnished rooms. The generous breakfast is included in the price. *(34 rooms)*

PRICE CATEGORY

£

Grange Holborn Hotel

★★★★★

**50-60 Southampton Row
Bloomsbury**

PRICE CATEGORY

£££££

This new deluxe hotel is ideally located where the West End meets the city. Spacious bedrooms with state of the art facilities complement the superb gymnasium and swimming pool. *(46 rooms)*

The Generator

Hostel

**Compton Place
Bloomsbury**

**Facilities
off-suite**

PRICE CATEGORY

£

The Generator offers hostel accommodation for young travellers at amazingly low prices. The building is futuristic with hard-edged decoration. Rooms are compact and bathrooms are shared. *(207 rooms)*

The Bonnington

★★★

**92 Southampton Row
Bloomsbury**

PRICE CATEGORY

££££

Established in 1911, The Bonnington is owned by the same family that opened it. Close to the British Museum, it is within walking distance of the West End. The rate includes a full English breakfast. *(215 rooms)*

Euston Plaza Hotel

★ ★ ★ ★

17-18 Upper Woburn Place
Bloomsbury

This modern hotel is designed in a Swedish style, with attractive light wood décor. Among the excellent facilities are a health centre, a pleasant bar and a popular restaurant. *(150 rooms)*

PRICE CATEGORY

£££££

 # Grange White Hall Hotel

★ ★ ★ ★

2-5 Montague Street
Marylebone

This is one of the best-appointed small luxury hotels in London. Located beside the British Museum, it has a landscaped garden. Rooms have hand-carved furniture and marble bathrooms. Rates include breakfast. *(60 rooms)*

PRICE CATEGORY

£££££

 # Holiday Inn Garden Court

★ ★ ★

57-59 Welbeck Street
Marylebone

Located in a quiet Edwardian terrace, the Holiday Inn Garden Court is ideally suited for West End shopping and entertainment. The rooms are modern and there is a popular restaurant and bar. *(138 rooms)*

PRICE CATEGORY

£££££

PRICE CATEGORY

£££££

PRICE CATEGORY

£££££

PRICE CATEGORY

££££

Grange Langham Court Hotel

★★★★

**31-35 Langham Street
Marylebone**

This historic, protected building is now a luxurious hotel with elegantly decorated bedrooms in traditional English style. Located in a quiet street close to the West End, breakfast is included in the tariff. *(60 rooms)*

Grange Fitzrovia Hotel

★★★★

**20-28 Bolsover Street
Marylebone**

Fashionably located moments from Oxford Street and the West End, this hotel provides a perfect London retreat. Many of the rooms have marble and granite bathrooms, as well as hand-carved rosewood furniture. *(90 rooms)*

Norfolk Towers Hotel

★★★

**34 Norfolk Place
Bayswater**

Located close to Paddington station, Norfolk Towers has good transportation links to the West End. It has a popular lounge bar and, in the basement, a café/bar where you can relax. *(85 rooms)*

New Linden Hotel

★★

59 Leinster Square
Bayswater

The New Linden Hotel is a five-minute walk from Queensway and Bayswater tube stations. It has friendly service and well-appointed rooms. Breakfast is included in the tariff. *(51 rooms)*

PRICE CATEGORY

£££

 # Holiday Villa London

★★★

37 Leinster Gardens
Bayswater

This comfortable hotel is an excellent base for discovering central London. It has a leisure complex with indoor swimming pool, jacuzzi and sauna. A cosy bar and restaurant serves authentic Malaysian cuisine. *(98 rooms)*

PRICE CATEGORY

££££

 # Comfort Inn, Bayswater

★★★

5-7 Princes Square
Bayswater

This newly refurbished hotel, which is situated in a garden square on the edge of fashionable Notting Hill, is also close to cosmopolitan Queensway with its restaurants, icerink and casino. The underground is nearby. *(65 rooms)*

PRICE CATEGORY

£££

PRICE CATEGORY

££££

PRICE CATEGORY

££££

PRICE CATEGORY

£££

London Guards Hotel

★★★

**36-37 Lancaster Gate
Bayswater**

The London Guards Hotel is located close to Kensington Gardens. The air-conditioned rooms have been fully refurbished, and continental breakfast is included. There is a coffee shop and licensed bar. *(40 rooms)*

Queen's Park

★★★

**48 Queensborough Terrace
Bayswater**

Situated in a peaceful Victorian terrace, close to Hyde Park, in the lively centre of Bayswater, Queen's Park has tastefully decorated and well-equipped bedrooms. It also has a pleasant restaurant. *(86 rooms)*

Quality Hotel Paddington

★★★

**8-14 Talbot Square
Bayswater**

Set in a quiet garden square, this is an elegant town house hotel located in the heart of London. Paddington main line and underground station, which services the Heathrow Express, is only a 5-minute walk away. *(70 rooms)*

 # Westminster Hotel

★★★

**16 Leinster Square
Bayswater**

PRICE CATEGORY

££££

Located in the heart of busy Bayswater, the Westminster overlooks a pretty garden square. The bedrooms are equipped with modern facilities. The hotel has a fashionable bar and rates include breakfast. *(114 rooms)*

 # Hillgate Hotel

★★★

**6-14 Pembridge Gardens
Bayswater**

PRICE CATEGORY

£££

Recently converted by linking five impressive Victorian houses, the Hillgate is situated close to Kensington Gardens. Bedrooms are well-furnished, there is a lounge and bar and breakfast is included. *(70 rooms)*

 # Berjaya Eden Park Hotel

★★★

**35-39 Inverness Terrace
Bayswater**

PRICE CATEGORY

£££

Located in a tree-lined terrace, the Eden Park recalls the elegance and charm of early Victorian England. All bedrooms are appointed to a high standard. The Tulip Bar and King's Restaurant are both popular. *(137 rooms)*

PRICE CATEGORY

£££

Blakemore Hotel

★★★

**30 Leinster Gardens
Bayswater**

Located on a quiet street close to Bayswater tube station, the Blakemore's bedrooms have recently been refurbished to a high standard. It now offers a blend of modern facilities and Victorian grandeur. *(164 rooms)*

Comfort Inn Heathrow

★★★

**Shepiston Lane
Hayes, Middlesex, UB3 1LP**

PRICE CATEGORY

£££

Within easy access of the M4, M25 and M40 and just 2 miles from Heathrow, there is a hotel shuttle service to terminals 1,2 and 3. The hotel has been completely refurbished and offers spacious accomodation. *(200 rooms)*

Quality Hotel Heathrow

★★★

**London Road
Greater London**

PRICE CATEGORY

£££

Located out of the centre of London, close to Heathrow Airport, the Quality Hotel is ideal for travellers starting their trip outside central London. It is also convenient if you have an early morning flight home. *(112 rooms)*

Westminster

Introduction . . .

From Trafalgar Square, you can see both **Buckingham Palace** (pages 50-51) and **Big Ben** (page 54), the clock tower of the **Houses of Parliament** (pages 54-55) – the twin seats of regal and political power in the United Kingdom's unique royal democracy.

Houses of Parliament and the River Thames

For a thousand years, first monarchs and then parliamentarians have wielded their power from within the area known as Westminster.

The royal court moved to Westminster in 1060, a few years before the Norman conquest of England. No buildings survive from this pre-Norman period but Westminster Hall, built by William the Conqueror's son in 1097, still stands as the vestibule of the House of Commons. In the Middle Ages, the area around Westminster Abbey deteriorated into a plague-ridden slum that was only fully cleared in the 19th century with the construction of Parliament Square and Victoria Street.

INSIDER'S TIP

The best view of the Houses of Parliament is from Westminster Bridge, from where you can see Members of Parliament having tea on the terraces.

Big Ben

Westminster was once separated by farmland from the old Roman and medieval heart of London which is a couple of miles to the east and now forms the business district known as the 'City'. Urban expansion has long since closed the gap between the two centres.

The best introduction to the area is a tour past the many grand institutions and landmarks lining the wide, triumphal avenues of Whitehall and the Mall.

You can see nearly all the major sites of Westminster by strolling a one-and-a-half-mile circuit beginning and ending in Trafalgar Square, passing along Whitehall, through Parliament Square and then on to Birdcage Walk and the Mall.

Admiralty Arch

. . . Introduction

The highlights include **Nelson's Column** on Trafalgar Square (built in 1843 to commemorate Lord Nelson's victory at the Battle of Trafalgar), 10 Downing Street (where the Prime Minister resides), **Westminster Abbey** (pages 52-53 – where Britain's kings and queens are crowned), the Houses of Parliament (with its famous clock tower Big Ben), and Queen Elizabeth II's London home, Buckingham Palace. (See pages 60-63 for details about this circuit.)

The massed bands of the Grenadier Guards

A half-mile detour along Millbank beside the Thames, brings you to the **Tate Britain** (page 58), Britain's premier collection of British art.

The imposing buildings lining Whitehall are mainly

The Houses of Parliament

occupied by government departments. Indeed, 'Whitehall' is the term used to describe the Civil Service, the public administrators who run the nation, supposedly under the direction of politicians. In the heyday of the British Empire, under Queen Victoria (who reigned from 1837-1901), a quarter of the world's land mass was governed from Whitehall.

REFLECTIONS

'Think how many
royal bones /
Sleep within this
heap of stones.'
– *On the tombs in
Westminster Abbey*,
Anonymous

There are two large residential areas close to Westminster: Belgravia to the west is one of London's most exclusive neighbourhoods, while Pimlico to the south has a mix of smart townhouses and ugly public housing.

The stuccoed terraces of Belgravia were developed from the 1820s to the 1850s by the immensely rich Grosvenor family, with Belgrave Square as the centrepiece. Gerald Grosvenor, the present Duke of Westminster, owns most of Belgravia and much of Mayfair. He is one of the world's richest men, with an estimated £2 billion fortune. Unlike Mayfair, Belgravia is still home to hundreds of the wealthiest British families and many prominent individuals, including former Prime Minister Margaret Thatcher.

Genteel Belgravia

Buckingham Palace . . .

The Palace and the Victoria Monument

ADDRESS

At the end of The Mall
☎ 020-7930-4832

GETTING THERE

Green Park, St. James's
Park or Victoria tube
stations

HOURS

Changing of the Guard
☎ 0891-505452
Apr 1-Aug 7:
Mon-Sun: 11.30am
Aug 8-Mar 31:
11.30am every other day

State Apartments
Aug-Sep: generally
9.30am-4.30pm

PRICES

Adult £10.50
Child (under 17) £5.00
(under 5 free)
Senior £8.00
Student £10.50

The main daily attraction at Buckingham Palace is the Changing of the Guard ceremony. It lasts forty minutes, starting at 11.27am, when the Queen's Guard, accompanied by a band, leaves Wellington Barracks. The soldiers march via Birdcage Walk to Buckingham Palace.

The public have only been able to visit the state rooms of Buckingham Palace since August 1993, when the Queen decided to open up her London home to raise money for the restoration of Windsor Castle, which had been badly damaged by fire a year earlier.

The palace itself can only be visited from early August to the end of September, when the royal family spends time in Scotland. Even then, times are subject to change, so it is best to call in advance.

The State Dining Room

Same-day tickets are sold on a first-come first-served basis from a booth at the edge of Green Park, facing the piazza outside the palace. The booth opens at 9am and, at peak times, queuing can take up to two hours, with a further delay until your allocated visiting time.

Built in 1702 on the site of a notorious brothel, Buckingham House was originally the London home of the Duke of Buckingham. Sixty years later, George III bought it as a family home to house his many children.

Changing of the Guard

The architect John Nash began rebuilding the house as a palace for George IV in the early 19th

. . . Buckingham Palace

century. His flamboyant redesign went way over budget and was so widely ridiculed, that the Prime Minister, the Duke of Wellington, told the Chancellor of the Exchequer to 'make a hash of Nash'. A short time later, Nash was indeed hashed and Edward Blore finished the building.

The Grand Staircase

Queen Victoria grew very attached to the new palace, remarking in her diary in 1843, "I have been so happy there".

In 1913 the front of the palace was replaced with a Portland stone façade and the famous balcony was added. The only major changes since have been the addition of a swimming pool, a cinema and the rebuilding of the bomb-damaged chapel after the Second World War.

Only 18 of the palace's 661 rooms are on show, but they include the grand halls used for state occasions.

The tour starts in the huge **Quadrangle** and then leads to the back of the palace. The **Grand Staircase**, a curled, ornamental structure built by Nash with a floral gilt balustrade, leads up to the **Green Drawing Room**. The first room entered by guests at royal functions, it contains a fine Regency chandelier featuring three weeping women.

Next is the **Throne Room**, which – disappointingly – contains only a pair of pink chairs initialled E II R for Elizabeth and P for Philip. It is here that the Queen invests those who are knighted.

The highlight of the tour is the vaulted **Picture Gallery**, which is over 150 feet (45 metres) long and contains part of the royal collection of 10,000 paintings (several times larger than that of the National Gallery).

The Picture Gallery

Two Canova sculptures are among the fine art treasures in Buckingham Palace: *Fountain Nymph* at the bottom of the Ministers' staircase and *Mars and Venus* in the 200-foot (60-metre) **Marble Hall**.

Royal memorabilia of all kinds, from paperweights to Buckingham Palace chocolates, can be bought from the souvenir shop in the garden.

INSIDERS' TIP

Avoid the inevitable queues by going on a Frames Rickards tour (page 240) or by booking in advance early in the year. Send a self-addressed envelope to The Visitor Office, Buckingham Palace, London SW1A 1AZ and ask for an application form.

REFLECTIONS

'If you expect me to put my hand to any additional expense, I'll be damned if I will.' – Prime Minister, the Duke of Wellington, on being asked by architect John Nash for more money to re-build the Palace (1828)

ADDRESS

Westminster Abbey
Broad Sanctuary
☎ 020-7222-5152

GETTING THERE

Westminster or St.
James's Park tube stations

HOURS

Mon-Fri: 9am-4.45pm
(last admission 3.00pm)
Sat: 9am-2.45pm (last
admission 1.45pm)

PRICES

Entrance to the nave
and cloisters is free.

Admission to Royal
Chapels and Poet's Corner:
Adult £5
Child £2 (under 11s free)
Senior £3
Student £3

Super Tours, conducted by
Abbey Vergers, take place
at intervals throughout the
day. Inclusive tickets cost
£8 and can be booked in
advance by calling
☎ 020-7222-7110.

Westminster Abbey . . .

The setting for coronations for nearly 1,000 years and the final resting place of many of Britain's kings and queens, Westminster Abbey is one of the nation's pre-eminent national monuments.

The majesty of the place is immediately apparent, with its beautifully restored Gothic twin towers by Nicholas Hawksmoor, 100-foot-high nave, easily the tallest in the country, and the graceful vaulted ceilings of the royal chapels.

The towers of Westminster Abbey

The Abbey embodies more English history than any other building, from William the Conqueror's journey up the aisle on horseback in 1066 to the coronation of Queen Elizabeth II in 1953. More than 3,000 of the nation's most revered figures are buried in the Abbey.

In the centre of the aisle is the **Tomb of the Unknown Soldier,** garlanded with red poppies. It commemorates the one million British soldiers who died in the First World War. Near to it, there is a slab remembering **Sir Winston Churchill**, though he is buried in a family plot in the village of Bladon. Richard II is depicted on the first pillar on the right. It is the oldest portrait of an English monarch painted from life.

The **Musicians'** and **Statesmen's Aisles** contain dozens of monuments to famous British composers and politicians. The former includes a statue of **Henry Purcell**, who was once the Abbey's organist; the latter contains the tomb of four-time Liberal Prime Minister in the Victorian period, **William Gladstone**.

Elizabeth I and her half-sister "Bloody Mary" – bitterly opposed to each other in life – are buried in the same chapel, the first in the tour of the Royal Chapels.

The **Henry VII Chapel**, built from 1503 to 1521, has a glorious vaulted ceiling. High above stand 100 saints' statues, while below lie Henry VII and James I, in black marble tombs partially hidden by a grille.

St. Edward's Chapel houses the Coronation Chair and the tombs of several medieval monarchs grouped around Edward the Confessor's shrine, which is the most sacred part of the Abbey.

. . . Westminster Abbey

Edward I's **Coronation Chair** stands beyond the tomb. This well-worn oak throne has been used for every coronation since 1300. Until 1996, it held the **Stone of Scone**, a great slab of sandstone that was used as early as the 4th century to crown kings in Ireland and later became Scotland's coronation stone. In 1296, Edward I took the stone to England. A group of Scottish nationalists stole it back on Christmas Eve, 1950. However, it was quickly recovered and returned to the Abbey. In 1996 the stone was returned to Scotland. It is now on display in Edinburgh Castle.

The Abbey's North Transept

Shakespeare's statue is the best known memorial in **Poets' Corner** – a section of the Abbey commemorating Britain's greatest writers. Geoffrey Chaucer, Jane Austen, Charles Dickens and the actor Lawrence Olivier are among those honoured. Henry Longfellow is the only American.

The **Great Cloister** can be reached via a door in the south aisle. Souvenirs can be purchased from the shop at the front of the Abbey. For a more unusual memento, visit the brass-rubbing centre in the cloisters.

for less Leading off the eastern end is the octagonal **Chapter House**, where the House of Commons met from 1257 until the reign of Henry VIII in the early 16th century. Faithfully restored in the 19th century, the Chapter House contains some of the finest examples of medieval English sculpture.

The Abbey's Chapter House

Chapter House tickets include entry to the 11th-century Pyx Chamber, containing the Abbey treasures, and the Abbey Museum, with its collection of medieval royal effigies. *(Westminster Abbey, entry through Dean's Yard and Cloister. ☎ 020-7222-5897. Apr-Sep: Mon-Sun: 9.30am-5.00pm. Oct-Mar: Mon-Sun: 10am-4pm. Adult £2.50, child £1.30 (under 5s free), senior £1.90, student £1.90. 50% discount on admission with voucher on page 275.)*

DON'T MISS

Churchill's memorial,
Poets' Corner,
Elizabeth I's tomb,
the Coronation Chair.

INSIDER'S TIP

Visit on a midweek afternoon when it is quieter.

ADDRESS

Bridge Street and
Parliament Square

House of Commons
☎ 020-7219-4272
House of Lords
☎ 020-7219-3107

GETTING THERE

Westminster or St. James's
tube stations

HOURS

Strangers' Gallery:
House of Commons:
usually Mon-Wed:
2.30pm-10pm. Thu:
11.30am-2.30pm. Fri:
9.30am-3pm.
House of Lords: Mon-Wed:
2.30pm onwards. Thu:
3pm. Sometimes Fri: 11am
onwards.

PRICES

Admission is free

State Opening of Parliament

Houses of Parliament . . .

The United Kingdom's seat of power, this fine Victorian
Gothic building contains the House of Commons (to

The Palace of Westminster

which Members of
Parliament are
democratically
elected) and the
House of Lords
(where peers either
inherit their seats or
gain them for life by
appointment).

The building is
known as the Palace of Westminster, because kings
and queens lived here from Edward the Confessor's
reign in the early 11th century until Parliament took
control in the 17th century.

The Queen opening Parliament

The old palace burnt down
in 1834. The present
building is the product of
an inspired collaboration
between Augustus Welby
Pugin and Charles Barry. A
huge clock tower, known by
the name of its largest bell,
Big Ben, dominates the
northern end of the
building. Londoners set
their watches by the chimes
of Big Ben, which are
broadcast around the globe
by the BBC World Service.

The only substantial
remnant of the medieval palace is the huge
Westminster Hall, with its grand oak hammerbeam
roof. It is where deceased members of the royal family
and senior statesmen traditionally lie in state, prior to
being buried.

Guy Fawkes, who tried to blow up the
Houses of Parliament in 1605, was tried in
Westminster Hall before being hanged,
drawn and quartered. It is also where **Oliver
Cromwell** was appointed Lord Protector in
1653, during Britain's 11 years without a
king. After the restoration of the monarchy
in 1660, Cromwell's body was disinterred
and his head placed on the roof where it
stayed for 25 years before his skull blew
down. A statue of Cromwell stands outside the hall.

. . . Houses of Parliament

The **House of Commons**, with its lines of green leather-upholstered benches, is surprisingly small. The party of government and the opposition party sit facing each other. Two red lines run along the floor between them.

Members of Parliament (MPs) are not allowed to cross these lines, which were installed to stop violent brawls and are, therefore, two swords' lengths apart. It is these lines that have inspired the English saying, "to toe the line".

The House of Commons in session

No monarch since Charles I (beheaded in 1649) has been permitted to enter the House of Commons. At the State Opening of Parliament, which takes place annually in October or November, the Queen sits in the **House of Lords**, with the door of the Commons symbolically slammed shut. The House of Lords, decorated in gold and scarlet and dominated by the gold throne, is grander than the Commons.

Proceedings in the House of Commons and the House of Lords can be watched from the **Strangers' Gallery**, but queuing up and getting through the security checks can take an hour or more. The queue starts outside St. Stephen's Gate, off Parliament Square to the rear of Westminster Abbey. On Tuesdays and Thursdays it is easier to gain entry after 4.30pm as most of the seats for Prime Minister's Question Time are booked in advance by MPs for their constituents.

Central Lobby

Past the entrance hall, a few steps from the House of Commons chamber, you reach the **Central Lobby**, where constituents are permitted to gather to petition MPs, hence the term 'to lobby' an MP.

The patch of grass opposite St. Stephen's Gate has become the unofficial TV studio of Westminster, with MPs sometimes queuing up to be interviewed with Big Ben in the background.

A television interview outside Parliament

REFLECTIONS

'It is not at all uncommon to see a member lying stretched out on one of the benches while others are debating. Some crack nuts, others eat oranges.' – Pastor Carl Moritz on the House of Lords (1782)

ADDRESS

Clive Steps,
King Charles Street
☎ 020-7930-6961

GETTING THERE

Westminster or St. James's
tube station

HOURS

Mon-Sun: 9.30am-6pm
last admission 5.15pm.
(Oct-Mar: opens 10am)

 # Cabinet War Rooms . . .

Prime Minister Winston Churchill directed operations from this secret underground bunker for the six-year duration of the Second World War.

Located in the basement of government offices, the Cabinet War Rooms were hurriedly converted on the eve of the war as emergency accommodation to protect the British Government against air attack.

The rooms were in operational use from August 27, 1939 until the Japanese surrender in September 1945.

It is hard to imagine how the entire British war effort could have been coordinated from within the cramped conditions of the bunker, which has

Churchill's hotline to the White House

barely changed since it became surplus to requirement at the end of the war.

Although it was designed to protect Britain's war leaders and included accommodation, Churchill preferred to defy the German bombers. He rarely slept in the space allotted to him in the Cabinet War Rooms, watching the Blitz of London from the roof of the building at night.

The Blitz continued for 56 terrible nights in the autumn of 1940, with hundreds of German planes bombing London's buildings every evening.

Many other buildings in the area were hit, including Westminster Abbey and the House of Commons. However, the Cabinet War Rooms proved to be an effective shelter, although it did

The Cabinet Room

have a near-miss on September 30th, when a bomb exploded just outside the entrance.

One disadvantage was that the health of many of the

. . . Cabinet War Rooms

staff, especially the secretaries and typists who spent such long hours underground, suffered due to the lack of daylight. For those who worked in the War Rooms full time, the majority of every day and night for six years was spent cooped up in the primitive, poorly-ventilated conditions.

On a tour through the honeycomb of rooms, you can see the room where the War Cabinet met more than one hundred times. Many of the most important decisions of the war were made in its narrow and gloomy confines. It is set up today just as if a meeting of the Cabinet is about to begin.

The tour passes through the **Map Room**, practically untouched since it was abandoned in 1945. Information about operations on all fronts was collected and displayed here, and it was manned night and day throughout the war.

The rooms have remained almost untouched since the end of the war

The huge world map, on which army positions were plotted with pins, paper flags and symbols, can be seen here. A stirring extract from one of Churchill's famous broadcasts can be heard in the background.

You can also see the tiny cubbyhole in which Churchill made his top-secret telephone calls to President Roosevelt at the White House.

The room which was kept for him as a bedroom, office and broadcasting suite remains just as it was during the war, when he made his memorable and morale-boosting speeches and reports about the progress of the hostilities to the listening nation.

A free audio guide is available in English, Dutch French, German, Italian,

Exterior of the Cabinet War Rooms

Spanish, Swedish, Hebrew and in a children's version. It helps enliven the tour, pointing out artefacts and describing their history.

PRICES

Adult £4.60
Child £2.30
Senior £3.40
Student £3.40

DISCOUNT

20% discount on admission with *for less* card.

Tate Britain

The Tate Britain, formerly the Tate Gallery, has a magnificent collection of post-1550 British art. There are 3,500 paintings, sculptures and prints in the collection, but only a selection of these is on display at any one time. Pick up a free plan of the gallery at the information desk just inside the main entrance.

Founded in the late 19th century by the sugar millionaire Henry Tate, the gallery has satellites in Liverpool and St. Ives, Cornwall.

Exterior of the Tate

Britain's most famous painter, **JMW Turner** (1775-1851), has a special permanent exhibition all to himself. The **Clore Gallery** contains by far the world's largest collection of Turner oil paintings, watercolours and drawings, including the celebrated *Snow Storm*.

In the 18th-century section, **William Hogarth** has a room almost all to himself, including his anti-French satire *Roast Beef of England*. Another room is full of portraits by **Sir Joshua Reynolds** and his great rival **Thomas Gainsborough**. There are several sketches and cloud studies by landscape artist **John Constable**. His *Flatford Mill* brought landscape painting closer to nature than ever before.

The visionary watercolours of poet/prophet **William Blake** include 10 of his 12 works on the myth of the Creation.

The mid-Victorian painters known as the Pre-Raphaelites, whose work is characteristically full of emotion and colour, are well-represented at the Tate. Life almost imitated art when **Millais** was painting his famous *Ophelia*, for his model almost died from lying too long in a bath of cold water. For his *Proserpine*, **Dante Gabriel Rossetti** used his mistress Jane Morris (wife of Willam Morris, the designer and poet) as a model. Being herself trapped in a loveless marriage, Morris captures Proserpine's forlorn expression.

'Ophelia' by Sir John Everett Millais

A personal audio guide to the collection is available in the Rotunda beyond the main entrance (£2).

ADDRESS

Millbank
☎ 020-7887-8008

GETTING THERE

Pimlico tube station

HOURS

Mon-Sun: 10am-5.50pm

PRICES

Admission is free

Other Attractions . . .

Half-way along Whitehall, you will pass **Horse Guards**, where two mounted sentries of the Queen's Household Cavalry and two foot soldiers are on duty between 10am and 4pm daily. The price of being in the British Army's most prestigious regiment is that you must stand motionless for a shift lasting two hours (or one hour if you're on horseback).

The Royal Household Cavalry

There is a daily Changing of the Guard ceremony, when the Queen's Life Guards leave Hyde Park Barracks on horseback and arrive at Horse Guards via Constitution Hill and the Mall. *(Tiltyard, in front of Horse Guards or in Horse Guards Parade. ☎ 09064-123411. Changing of the Guard: Mon-Sat: 11am. Sun: 10am.)*

Through the arch is **Horse Guards Parade**, a large gravelled square which until recently was a civil servants' car park but has now been cleared for pedestrians. Once a year it is filled with the royal military regalia of the Queen's Trooping of the Colour ceremony.

South from Horse Guards, on the west side of Whitehall, is the Prime Minister's official residence at **10 Downing Street.** Robert Walpole, who was the first Prime Minister to live at No.10, took up residence in 1735. No. 11 is the official residence of the

Horse Guards Parade

Chancellor of the Exchequer, and the surrounding houses also contain government offices. The street has been closed to the public with security gates since Margaret Thatcher's term in office.

Horse Guards Parade

for less The exquisite **Banqueting House** is the only part of the old Palace of Whitehall to survive a fire in 1698. Designed by Inigo Jones in 1619, it was the first purely Renaissance building in London. It affords a glimpse of the 17th-century opulence of the court of Charles I.

10 Downing Street

The main banqueting hall was originally used for royal banquets, masques and balls, which were a regular feature of Stuart court life. The highlight of the

. . . Other Attractions . . .

building is the stunning painted ceiling by Peter Paul

The Cenotaph

Rubens. *(Whitehall, ☎ 020-7839-8919. Mon-Sat: 10am-5pm. Sun: closed. Adult £3.80, child, senior, student £3. 10% discount with voucher on page 275.)*

The main banqueting hall, Banqueting House

In the middle of Whitehall stands the **Cenotaph** – the nation's chief memorial to its war dead. The royal family and all the senior politicians gather for a ceremony here on the Sunday closest to November 11, the anniversary of the end of the First World War.

Overlooking the Cenotaph is the **Foreign and Commonwealth Office**, designed by George Gilbert Scott. Once shrouded in secrecy, it is now open to the public with a free exhibition and film show about the British diplomatic service. *(Whitehall, ☎ 020-7270-1500. Mon-Fri: 10am-5pm. Admission free.)*

Parliament Square

Parliament Square, which was laid out in 1868, contains statues of famous statesmen, including Benjamin Disraeli, Abraham Lincoln and Sir Winston Churchill. The latter statue, sculpted by Ivor Roberts-Jones in 1974, has an internal electric system to protect it from pigeons.

for less A collection of relics from the old Palace of Westminster, destroyed by fire in 1834, is displayed in the **Jewel Tower**, which is opposite the Houses of Parliament on Abingdon Street. Built by

The Jewel Tower

Edward III in 1366, it houses his valuables, including his jewels, regal robes, furs and gold vessels.

The three-storey tower, once surrounded by a moat, now includes an informative exhibit entitled 'Parliament, Past and Present'. The exhibit traces the history of the British parliament, as well as the peculiar customs still observed by MPs and Lords. *(Abingdon Street, ☎ 020-7222-2219. Mon-Sun: Apr-Sep: 10am-6pm. Oct: 10am-5pm. Nov-Mar: 10am-4pm. Adult £1.50, child 80p, senior £1.10, student £1.10. 50% discount on admission with voucher on page 275.)*

. . . Other Attractions . . .

The smaller church that stands beside Westminster Abbey is **St. Margaret's Church**, where Milton, Pepys and Churchill were all
married. The first church
on the site dated from
the 12th century, but the
present St. Margaret's
was rebuilt at the
beginning of the 16th.
It's worth a visit to
compare with the
overwhelming scale of
Westminster Abbey and
for its magnificent
stained glass window. (☎
020-7222-6382. Mon-Fri:

St. Margaret's Church and Westminster Abbey

9.30am-3.30pm. Sat: 9.30am-1.30pm. Sun: open for
services only.)

The Roman Catholic **Westminster Cathedral**, a ten-minute walk from Parliament Square, is overlooked by most visitors to London, but is well worth a detour. Work began in 1895 on this neo-Byzantine building, with its distinctive striped terracotta pattern and towering 274-foot (82-metre) campanile. Its interior, however, remains only half-decorated.

St Margaret's Church

Visit All Souls Chapel, with its 100 different types of marbles from around the world, and admire the stations of the cross, sculpted in 1913 by Eric Gill. (*Victoria Street,* ☎ *020-7798-9055. Mon-Sun: 7am-7pm (Sat: from 8am). Admission free.*)

Westminster Cathedral

The **Royal Horticultural Society** has its Headquarters in nearby Vincent Square, and the ground and lower ground floors contain the newly-opened **Lindley Library**, a renowned collection of related books, periodicals, illustrations and catalogues. The library is open to the public and admission is free. (*80 Vincent Square,* ☎ *020-7821-3600. Mon-Fri: 9am-5.30pm. Admission free.*)

Westminster Cathedral

Returning to Westminster Cathedral, double back along Victoria Street and turn on to Broadway. Notice the series of sculptures by Jacob Epstein, Henry Moore

. . . Other Attractions . . .

and Eric Gill on the façade above St. James's Park tube station.

Guards Museum

for less A little to the north is Birdcage Walk, where the **Guards Museum** has a collection of ceremonial uniforms, weapons and memorabilia covering 300 years of history of the five regiments of foot guards.

The Guards Museum

In addition to their other duties, these regiments have the task of protecting the Queen. The museum contains a large toy soldier centre that is popular with children. *(Birdcage Walk, St. James's Park, ☎ 020-7930-4466. Mon-Sun: 10am-3.30pm. January: closed. Adult £2, child £1, senior £1, student £1. 50% discount on admission with voucher on page 275.)*

Guards Chapel

The **Guards' Chapel**, inside Wellington Barracks on Birdcage Walk, was the scene of one of the worst bomb strikes of the Second World War, when 121 people were killed in 1944 by a Doodlebug rocket. The remains of the 19th-century apse were included in the rebuilt chapel, which opened in 1963. *(Sun: service 11am.)*

Queen's Gallery, on the southern side of the palace grounds, is closed for restoration until 2002, after which it will house a permanent exhibition of paintings from the fabulous royal collection. There will also be gallery space for temporary exhibitions. *(Buckingham Palace Road, visitor's office ☎ 020-7839-1377.)*

The Institute of Contemporary Arts

The Queen's gold State Coach, used for coronations and jubilees, is the star attraction at the **Royal Mews**. Other carriages on display include the Glass Coach, which is used for royal weddings. *(Buckingham Palace Road, ☎ 020-7839-1377. Mon-Thu: 12noon-4pm (last admission 3.30pm). Adult £4.30, child £2.10, senior £3.30, student £4.30, family £10.70.)*

Royal Mews

. . . Other Attractions

The Mall, a broad tree-lined avenue leading from Buckingham Palace to Trafalgar Square, forms the first part of the processional route from Buckingham Palace to Westminster.

Halfway down the Mall, opposite St. James's Park, John Nash designed the cream stucco Carlton House Terrace, where the **Institute of Contemporary Arts** is located. The Institute was established in 1947 to offer artists in Britain similar exhibition facilities to those enjoyed by American artists at New York's Museum of Modern Art.

The ICA

The Institute contains a cinema, art gallery and bar, one of the few in London which stays open until 1am. *(The Mall, ☎ 020-7930-0493. Gallery: Mon-Sun: 12noon-7.30pm. Bar: Tue-Sat: 12noon-1am. Mon-Fri: Adult £1.50, child free, senior £1, student £1. Sat-Sun: Adult £2.50, child free, senior £2, student £2. Cinema: £6.50.)*

Open Spaces

St. James's Park (page 198), which was once marshy ground, has been a royal park ever since it was drained on Henry VIII's orders so that he could use it for hunting. In the 17th century, the first formal gardens with an aviary (hence **Birdcage Walk**) were created.

Dean's Yard

Charles II had clandestine meetings with his mistress, Nell Gwyn, in the park, and over the following century, St. James's Park became notorious for prostitution.

These days, the park is well-maintained. It is perfect for a picnic and is a short walk from any of the sights of Westminster. There is a pretty lake, filled with geese and ducks, with a bridge that offers superb views of both Buckingham Palace and Westminster.

At lunchtime, the park is filled with civil servants escaping their offices in Whitehall. Even the Prime Minister occasionally takes a stroll in the park.

Whitehall from St. James's Park

Dean's Yard, beside Westminster Abbey, is a secluded grassy square. It is private property belonging to the prestigious Westminster School, where playwright Ben Jonson was a pupil, but you are allowed to stroll around and view the exteriors of the surrounding medieval buildings.

Eating and Drinking

Compared with the neighbouring West End, there are relatively few restaurants and pubs in Westminster. Most are to be found at the northern end of Whitehall, on Victoria Street and around Victoria Station.

Tattershall Castle

There are a couple of floating bars and restaurants on the River Thames near the Embankment tube station. The **Tattershall Castle** pub and the **R.S. Hispaniola** restaurant are moored beside each other.

The Victoria area has several good wine bars that serve food, including **The Ebury Wine Bar** (see below) and **Carriages** (page 65).

Finnegan's Wake *(Strutton Ground, off Victoria Street)* is a newly refurbished Irish pub. It has Irish musicians performing five nights a week and Irish food, such as a Dublin Fry, is served all day. Beers include Guinness and the much-celebrated creamy ale Kilkenny.

Lord Moon of the Mall

Further west is **The Albert** *(52 Victoria Street)*, a large Victorian public house. It is richly decorated and has a magnificent staircase. Lots of MPs drink here and a Division Bell rings in the restaurant to signal important votes for which they must return to the House of Commons. Portraits of Prime Ministers, from the Marquis of Salisbury to Tony Blair, hang on the staircase. The portrait of Mrs Thatcher was unveiled by the Iron Lady herself. Food is served in the bar from 11am to 10.30pm. The carvery restaurant is open from 12noon to 10pm.

Lord Moon of the Mall *(at the Trafalgar Square end of Whitehall)* is an attractive, spacious pub.

The Ebury Wine Bar

Modern British / Wine Bar

139 Ebury Street
☎ **020-7730-5447**

Average meal: £15-20
for less discount: 25%
AM/VS/MC/DC

HOURS

Mon-Sat: 11am-11pm
Sun: 12noon-10.30pm

The Ebury Wine Bar serves good food at wine bar prices. It is well known for its bar snacks, pre-theatre suppers and à la carte menu. The restaurant has a great atmosphere and is popular with people of all ages.

 **Carriages**

Modern British / Wine Bar

43 Buckingham Palace Road
☎ 020-7834-0119

Average meal: £10-15
for less discount: 25%
AM/VS/MC/DC

HOURS

Mon-Fri: 11.30am-11pm
Sat-Sun: closed

Carriages is located opposite the Royal Mews. It offers
bar snacks throughout the day and an innovative menu
for lunch and dinner. Delicious afternoon teas are served
during the summer.

 Dino and Gianna

Italian / International

36 Vauxhall Bridge Road
☎ 020-7630-8400

Average meal: £5-10
for less discount: 25%
AM/VS/MC/DC

HOURS

Mon-Sat: 12noon11pm
Sun: 12noon-8pm

This friendly, family-run Italian restaurant offers good
value. It can be busy at lunchtime, but in the evening it
is relaxed. It is a great place to eat after a visit to the
Tate or a walk along the Thames.

 Bella Pasta

Italian

152 Victoria Street
☎ 020-7828-7664

Average meal: £5-10
for less discount: 25%
(present voucher on page 285)
AM/VS/MC

HOURS

Mon-Thu: 10am-11pm.
Fri-Sat:
11.30am-12midnight
Sun: 12noon-11pm

Bella Pasta offers quality food with an emphasis on pizza
and pasta dishes. All of their restaurants have a pleasant,
continental atmosphere. It is ideal either for a relaxed
lunch or a romantic evening meal.

HOURS

Mon-Fri: 12.30pm-
2.30pm, 6.30pm-10pm
Sat-Sun: 6.30pm-10pm

HOURS

Mon-Fri: 12noon-3pm,
5pm-11pm
Sat: 12noon-11pm
Sun: 5pm-10.30pm

HOURS

Mon-Fri: 12.30pm-2pm,
7pm-11.15pm
Sat: 7pm-11.15pm
Sun: closed

The Pavilion

French / Continental

**Rochester Hotel,
69 Vincent Square**
☎ 020-7828-6611

Average meal: £10-15
for less discount: 25%
AM/VS/MC/DC

The Pavilion offers fine continental cuisine in elegant
surroundings. Its light and airy conservatory is an
excellent venue for a relaxed dinner. Discounts are also
available at the Rochester's Bar and Brasserie.

Psistaria

Greek

82 Wilton Road
☎ 020-7821-7504

Average meal: £10-15
for less discount: 25%
AM/VS/MC/DC

Psistaria offers Greek Cypriot food at good prices. Its
reputation is based on its grilled meats and seafood.
Entertainment includes live music and belly dancing.
No discount is available at the wine bar downstairs.

Pomegranates

International

94 Grosvenor Road
☎ 020-7828-6560

Average meal: £15-20
for less discount: 25%
AM/VS/MC/DC

Pomegranates gives you a gastronomic tour of the world.
Exotic dishes from afar are offered alongside traditional
British fare. The food is complemented by an excellent,
adventurous wine list.

Introduction . . .

The **West End**, London's entertainment district, is packed with restaurants, bars, theatres, cinemas and nightclubs, not to mention thousands of shops.

The focal point is **Leicester Square** (pronounced 'Lester'), one of the few places in London where you will still find crowds of pleasure-seekers at 2am. Four

of London's biggest-screen cinemas are located around Leicester Square, where many Hollywood movies have their British première. The square is also home to some of the largest nightclubs, including the **Hippodrome,** on the corner of Charing Cross Road, and **Equinox**, on the north side.

The main thoroughfare from Leicester Square to **Piccadilly Circus** leads past the **Trocadero** (page 75), a popular

Piccadilly Circus

entertainment centre with virtual reality games and rides and an assortment of gift shops.

Piccadilly Circus is one of London's busiest traffic junctions and, with its huge electronic billboards, is London's version of New York's Times Square. At its centre is the statue of **Eros**, the steps of which are a popular meeting spot.

Branching off from the Circus is **Shaftesbury Avenue**, which is lined with beautiful theatres and is London's more compact equivalent of Broadway. Sandwiched between Shaftesbury Avenue and Leicester Square is **Chinatown**, occupying only a handful of streets but containing dozens of Chinese restaurants (see page 82) and oriental shops.

REFLECTIONS

'In Soho, the people work hard and drink hard – tremendously hard' – Soho Vicar, Rev. Cardwell (1900)

North of Shaftesbury Avenue lies **Soho,** a strange mix of seediness and stylishness, with strip and peep shows sprinkled among classy restaurants and bars. The latter are frequented by

Theatres on Shaftesbury Avenue

fashion-obsessed folk from the many nearby advertising agencies and film companies.

The area is similar in some respects to New York's Soho, though the names have quiet different origins. While New York's Soho is an abbreviation of 'South of Houston Street', London's Soho dates back to the

. . . Introduction

16th century, when the area was Henry VIII's royal hunting ground. 'So-Ho' was the cry of the hunter who had spotted a hare or some other quarry.

Liberty department store

In the 17th century, the district was dotted with the mansions of dukes and earls, but the aristocrats eventually moved out, making way for immigrants and refugees. Even before the richer inhabitants left, Soho had acquired a reputation for tolerance and risqué entertainment which persists today.

Soho's main thoroughfare is **Old Compton Street**, running parallel to Shaftesbury Avenue. Continental-style pavement cafés have sprung up in recent years, though it is debatable whether London has the climate for evening *al fresco* meals. The street is the centre of the area's gay scene and has many gay bars, clubs and even a special taxi service.

One of London's distinctive characteristics is the way popular entertainment jostles for space beside historic and learned institutions. Nowhere is this more apparent than in the West End, where, only a short walk from the buzzing bars and clubs of Leicester Square, you find the magnificent halls of the **National Gallery** (pages 70-71) and **National Portrait Gallery** (pages 79-80).

The West End is also a mecca for shopaholics, with thousands of stores and boutiques lining **Regent Street**, **Oxford Street** and the many side streets leading off these main arteries. The bigger chain stores are to be found on Oxford Street, while the more exclusive department stores, such as **Liberty**, are either on or near Regent Street (see page 89).

East of Leicester Square lies **Covent Garden** (pages 72-73), a pedestrianized piazza where visitors and locals alike go to enjoy the street entertainment and visit the many interesting shops. Covent Garden is home to the **Royal Opera House**, Britain's premier venue for opera and ballet, which has recently undergone a major refurbishment.

INSIDER'S TIP

While restaurants around Leicester Square cater mainly for tourists, Londoners head for the choicer dining delights of Chinatown and Soho.

The fountains in Trafalgar Square

ADDRESS

Trafalgar Square
☎ 020-7747-2885

GETTING THERE

Charing Cross
tube station

HOURS

Mon-Sat: 10am-6pm
Wed: 10am-9pm
Sun: 10am-6pm

PRICES

Admission is free
Free guided tours:
Mon-Fri: 11.30am
and 2.30pm (also at
6.30pm on Wednesdays)
Sat: 2pm and 3.30pm.

National Gallery . . .

The National Gallery, which dominates Trafalgar Square, houses one of the world's foremost art collections.

With the majority of the gallery's 2,200 paintings on view at any one time, the best approach is to focus on what suits your taste.

The gallery was founded in 1824 after the art-loving King George IV helped persuade the government of the day to buy the small but magnificent collection of the Russian-born merchant John Julius Angerstein, including works by **Raphael**, **Rembrandt** and **Van Dyck**.

'The Arnolfini Marriage' by Van Eyck

The first section of the present building was designed by William Wilkins and opened in 1838. The gallery's first director, Sir Charles Eastlake, spent a decade scouring Italy for Renaissance masterpieces. Sir Charles's 139 purchases turned the gallery into one of the most important public collections in Europe.

Nearly all the Old Masters are represented here. In addition to those already mentioned, there are works by **da Vinci**, **Botticelli**, **Michelangelo**, **El Greco**, **Goya**, **Rubens** and **Van Eyck**.

The most prestigious individual collections include a series of **Rembrandt** paintings, nine works by **Raphael**, several by **Holbein** and a section on **Cézanne** and other Impressionists.

The **Sainsbury Wing**, opened in 1991 with a donation from a super-rich supermarket dynasty, contains the oldest paintings, including a magnificently restored altar piece, the *Wilton Diptych*. This wing contains the **Micro Gallery**, where you can create a mapped-out tour of your favourite

National Gallery from Trafalgar Square

. . . National Gallery

paintings, with touch screens allowing you to view the entire collection on the computer. There are brief but illuminating notes on each work of art.

Interior of the National Gallery

One of the most valuable collections of Italian art outside Florence can be seen here. The collection includes **Botticelli's** *Venus and Mars* and **Bellini's** *Doge Leonardo Loredan.*

British art is gathered together, and includes several works by **Thomas Gainsborough** and **Constable's** *The Hay-Wain* – perhaps the most famous British painting.

'Sunflowers' by Van Gogh

The excellent *Gallery Guide and Soundtrack*, which comprises a portable CD player and headphones, gives you a brief description of any of the 1,000 paintings on the main floor. This is available at the main entrance and Sainsbury Wing foyer and is free, though donations are invited. A highlights tour of 30 great paintings is available in six languages: English, French, Italian, Spanish, German and Japanese.

There are three excellent shops in the gallery, selling art books, CD-ROMS and videos. The Brasserie restaurant in the Sainsbury Wing has all-day table service, with a good value daily chef's choice. The Prêt à Manger café in the main building is self-service and offers hot food, salads and snacks.

'The Hay-Wain' by John Constable

For the **National Portrait Gallery**, which is just behind the National Gallery, see page 79.

DON'T MISS

The anonymous *Wilton Diptych*, **Van Eyck's** *The Arnolfini Marriage*, **Bellini's** *The Doge Leonardo Loredan*, **Botticelli's** *Venus and Mars*, **El Greco's** *Christ Driving Traders from the Temple*, **Seurat's** *Bathers at Asnières*, **Constable's** *Hay-Wain*, **Van Gogh's** *Sunflowers*, **Titian's** *Bacchus and Ariadne*, **Turner's** *Rain, Steam and Speed*.

INSIDER'S TIP

Weekday mornings are the quietest time; enter by the Sainsbury Wing to avoid the crowds at the main entrance.

Covent Garden . . .

The colourful, lively area around the old market buildings of Covent Garden is a favourite place for Londoners to socialise.

As much of the area is pedestrianised, it is ideal for strolling, browsing in quirky shops, enjoying the talents of the street entertainers or simply relaxing and watching the world go by in one of the many pavement cafés.

The name Covent Garden is derived from its former function as a convent garden. Until the 16th century, it was an area of market gardens growing produce for Westminster Abbey.

Designed by Inigo Jones in the 1630s, the square is one of the oldest in London. Initially a very up-market neighbourhood, the area became debauched in the 18th century, when there were so many brothels and gambling dens that it was dubbed the 'great Square of Venus'. Poets and dramatists such as Alexander Pope, John Dryden and Richard Sheridan used to congregate in the local coffee houses, gathering material for their savage caricatures.

In the 1830s, market buildings were constructed to replace the haphazard collection of stalls that had existed before. Designed by Charles Fowler, the new market hall was described in a contemporary London magazine as being "a structure at once perfectly fitted for its various uses; of great architectural beauty and elegance; and so expressive of the purposes for which it is erected, that it cannot by any possibility be mistaken for anything else than what it is."

The street market

The market became very popular among fashionable Londoners, who liked to mingle with the tradesmen and flower sellers. It is in Covent Garden that flower-girl Eliza Doolittle, the heroine of George Bernard Shaw's *Pygmalion*, first meets Professor Henry Higgins. The play was turned into the popular musical *My Fair Lady*.

The market hall in the centre of the piazza remained London's main fruit, vegetable and flower market until 1974, when it was transferred to Battersea. The attractive covered market buildings now house designer shops, cafés and dozens of stalls selling superior arts and crafts.

GETTING THERE

Covent Garden or Leicester Square tube stations

INSIDER'S TIP

The Covent Garden Festival, a celebration of opera and music theatre, takes place at venues around the area in late May and early June.

. . . Covent Garden

On the northern side of the square lies the **Royal Opera House**, London's most prestigious theatre, which is home to the Royal Opera and Royal Ballet. You can

visit the newly restored Floral Hall during the daytime.

To the north, and through into Neal Street, there are gimmick shops and some of London's trendiest boutiques, plus plenty of lively restaurants, bars and cafés.

Many of Britain's most innovative designers have studios around **Seven Dials**, where seven streets meet.

Covent Garden central market

On the western edge of the square is St. Paul's Church, known as the 'Actors' Church', because of the many theatres close by. Designed by Inigo Jones and completed in 1633, the interior is a simple double square, 100 feet by 50 feet.

It is filled with memorials to famous actors and actresses, including the legendary Shakespearean actress Ellen Terry, who died in 1928 and whose ashes are preserved in the south wall.

The church also has a long association with puppetry, dating back to at least 1662 when the diarist Samuel Pepys watched 'a very pretty' Italian puppet play. The tradition is upheld with a puppeteers' festival in the church on the second Sunday in May.

REFLECTIONS

'Covent Garden market, when it was market morning, was wonderful company. The great wagons of cabbages, with growers' men and boys lying asleep under them, and with sharp dogs from market garden neighbour-hoods looking after the whole, were as good as a party' – *The Uncommercial Traveller*, Charles Dickens (1861)

The Punch & Judy pub, overlooking the Piazza

The street entertainers – be they jugglers, sword-eaters, comedians or magicians – all have to audition to perform in the piazza. One of the best places from which to watch the street entertainers is the balcony of the Punch and Judy pub at the end of the market.

The balcony stretches the whole width of the building, with a shelf along the wall which is lined with dozens of pints of beer in summer! Two floors down, the Punch and Judy cellar bar opens out into a pretty, stone-flagged sunken courtyard inside the market buildings.

The **Theatre Museum** (page 78) and **London Transport Museum** (page 77) are situated off the square.

ADDRESS

London Pavilion,
Piccadilly Circus
☎ 020-7734-7203

GETTING THERE

Piccadilly Circus
tube station

Madonna

HOURS

Wed-Mon: 10am-5.30pm.
Tue: 11am-5.30pm.

PRICES

Adult £8.25
Child £6.25
Senior £7.25
Student £7.25

DISCOUNT

£1.50 off admission per
person with voucher on
page 275.

for less Rock Circus

Get close to rock and pop's biggest stars in the
musical version of Madame Tussaud's.

Michael Jackson

You wander around the
galleries with a special
head-set that plays the
greatest hits of whichever
singer you happen to be
passing. A 20-foot 'video
wall' plays archive film
footage.

More than 50 rock and pop
legends are represented,
including **Madonna**, **Eric
Clapton**, **Bono** and **Tina
Turner**. It concentrates on
the 1960s-1980s but has a
growing collection of stars from the 1990s. A model of
Lenny Kravitz, complete with tattoos and a nipple ring
donated by the singer himself, is a recent
addition. A team of 25 artists worked on the
model, which cost £25,000 to produce.

A collection of rock memorabilia, including
Eric Clapton's cowboy boots, is on display.
While he sat for his wax model, Clapton
played his hit song *Layla* for half an hour to
maintain his concentration. He even shaved
his beard off to allow the sculptor to achieve
the correct jaw-line.

The **Wall of Hands**, where the stars have left
mouldings of their hands, is interesting. You
can measure your own hands against the
imprints left by, among others, **Michael
Jackson**, **Jon Bon Jovi** and **Gloria Estefan**. **Little
Richard**'s are easily
the biggest. More
recent stars who
have contributed to
the wall include teen
band **Boyzone** and
Errol Brown (Hot
Chocolate).

Bob Geldof and Tina Turner

A 20-minute
'concert' at the end
of the 90-minute tour traces the history of rock music,
claiming that its roots date back 100 years. Rare
recordings and previously unseen archive footage are
included, as well as a new acknowledgement of the
black influence in modern music.

Other Attractions . . .

Originally a gentlemen's tennis court, the 250-year-old **Trocadero** has been, at various times, a music hall, hotel and casino. A £45 million refurbishment was completed in 1996, making it Britain's biggest hi-tech indoor entertainment complex. It also houses a selection of shops, some of which are particularly good for London-themed gift ideas. *(Piccadilly Circus,* ☎ *0891-881100. Sun-Thu: 10am-12midnight. Fri-Sat: 10am-1am. Admission is free.)*

The Trocadero

Funland, the indoor entertainment park, is the main attraction. It's geared towards families, and has a host of rides and more than 450 video games. The main rides range from traditional favourites such as dodgems and a Ghost Train to the virtual reality roller-coaster, Max Flight, and a simulated bobsleigh trip. The Carnival Zone features favourite fairground games, and there are dance stages, a pool hall and a bowling alley. There are several eateries to chose from in the six-level "park". *(*☎ *0891-881100. Sun-Thu: 10am-12midnight. Fri-Sat: 10am-1am. Admission is free, with separate prices per game or ride ranging from 20p to £3.)*

Chinatown

London's **Chinatown**, between Leicester Square and Shaftesbury Avenue, is tiny in comparison with New York's, but efforts have been made to give the area an Oriental feel. Three Chinese arches straddle the central pedestrianized avenue, Gerrard Street, and phone boxes have been turned into mini pagodas. There are plenty of Chinese arts and crafts shops and dozens of restaurants (see page 82).

Chinatown

Somerset House, a glorious example of neo-classical architecture overlooking the Thames, was completed in 1801 by Sir William Chambers. Its original purpose was to house government offices, in particular those of the Navy, and even today the Inland Revenue are still in residence. However, much of the building has recently been opened to the public for the first time.

Somerset House

The **Courtyard** of Somerset House is, by day, a peaceful respite from the bustle of London streets. In complete contrast, at night and at

. . . Other Attractions . . .

weekends it is transformed into a open-air auditorium. The **River Terrace** offers unrivalled views of the

'Dejeuner sur l'herbe' by Édouard Manet, Courtauld Institute

Thames from its elegant café and a link to Waterloo Bridge. As a reminder of the building's link with the Navy, the **King's Barge House**, the **Seamen's Waiting Hall** and the **Nelson Stair** are also accessible.

The **Courtauld Institute**, located in the North Wing of the building overlooking the Strand, boasts one of the world's greatest collections of Impressionist and Post-Impressionist works. The core of the collection was put together by industrialist Samuel Courtauld between the two World Wars, though other donations have greatly enriched it since.

Courtauld Institute

Works by **Pieter Brueghel**, **Rubens** and **Botticelli**, including the latter's *Holy Trinity with Saints John and Mary*, are the highlights of the early galleries. The more modern paintings, which tend to be better known, include some **Degas** studies of dancers and almost an entire room devoted to **Cézanne**. One of **Manet's** most popular works, *Bar at the Folies-Bergère*, is on display along with a copy of his *Déjeuner sur l'herbe*, the first Impressionist painting.

Van Gogh's famous *Self-Portrait with Bandaged Ear* is worth a visit in itself. The painter mutilated himself in a guilt-ridden frenzy after threatening fellow artist and guest **Gauguin**, whose Tahitian works are also in the Courtauld. (☎ 020-7848- 2526. Mon-Sat: 10am-6pm (last admission 5.15pm). Sun: 12noon-6pm (last admission 5.15pm). Adult £4, child free, senior £3, student free. Free entry for all on Mondays from 10am-2pm (except Bank Holidays).)

Other parts of Somerset House have recently been opened to the public for the first time. The vaults underneath the Thames-side South Terrace are now home to the spectacular **Gilbert Collection** of decorative arts. The collection was bequeathed to the nation in 1996 by Londoner Sir Arthur Gilbert, who spent the later years of his life in California amassing gold, silver and mosaics from all over the world.

Te Rerioa, *Gauguin, in the Courtauld*

The collection spans the 15th to the 19th centuries, and is estimated to be worth £75 million. The mosaic collections comprises

. . . Other Attractions . . .

examples of *pietre dure* commissioned by the 17th century Grand Dukes of Tuscany, as well as exquisite "micromosaics" made up of thousands of tiny tesserae per inch.

The gold and silver collection displays objects from several continents, and of particular interest are the examples of the 18th-century work of great English silversmiths such as Paul de Lamerie. (☎ 020-7240-5782. Mon-Sat: 10am-6pm (last admission 5.15pm). Sun: 12noon-6pm (last admission 5.15pm). Adult £4, child free, senior £3, student free. Free entry for all on Mondays from 10am-2pm (except Bank Holidays).)

19th century mosaic table top, Gilbert Collection

Other parts of Somerset House are, at the time of writing, still undergoing refurbishment. After Autumn 2000 the **Hermitage Rooms** will display items from the State Hermitage Museum of St. Petersburg.

18th century mother-of-pearl snuffbox, Gilbert Collection

Gilbert Collection

The **Photographers' Gallery**, located close to Leicester Square Tube station, showcasing work from both leading and up-and-coming snappers, often has interesting exhibitions. The gallery has a café and specialist photographic bookshop. (5 Great Newport Street, ☎ 020-7831-1772. Mon-Sat: 11am-6pm. Sun: 12noon-6pm. Admission is free.)

for less Colourful displays of trams, Tube trains, buses, maps and posters bring the story of London's transport to life, along with "hands-on" working models, bus and train simulators and touch-screen computers, at Covent Garden's **London Transport Museum**.

Photographers' Gallery

Highlights include the first ever Tube map, original horse-drawn vehicles from the 19th century and a frequently changing exhibition programme.

London Transport Museum

The museum is peopled by characters from the past 200 years, including a Victorian tunnel miner and a

. . . Other Attractions . . .

London Transport Museum

World War II bus conductress. You can sit in the driving seat of some of the old vehicles and climb on board a set of electric trams. The last tram was removed from London's streets in the early 1950s, but they are scheduled to make a comeback in the city's southern suburbs.

Fifteen giant KidZones combine fun and learning for youngsters, and there is a Funbus for children under five. A fine collection of commercial art, commissioned to adorn London's buses and tubes, is displayed in a special gallery and the museum shop sells some of the best examples in their original poster form. *(Covent Garden Piazza, ☎ 020-7379-6344. Sat-Thu: 10am-6pm. Fri: 11am-6pm. Adult £5.50, child £2.95, senior £2.95, student £2.95. 20% discount with for less card.)*

A costume workshop at the Theatre Museum

Theatre Museum

for less Next door to the London Transport museum, in Covent Garden, the **Theatre Museum** takes you behind the scenes charting the history of the British stage and its development from Shakespeare to the present.

Interactive exhibitions offer opportunities to understand and try out special effects. A range of daily activities include the chance to participate in or observe costume workshops, and theatrical make-up demonstrations showing how actors create characters. *(Russell Street, ☎ 020-7943-4700. Tue-Sun: 10am-6pm (last admission 5.30pm). Adult £4.50, child (under16) & senior free, student £2.50. 50% discount with voucher on page 275.)*

The Theatre Royal

for less Around the corner, on Catherine Street, is the famous **Theatre Royal**, the world's oldest theatre still in use. It was here that the traditions of modern theatre, as we know it, were forged in the 18th century by the brilliant actor and manager David Garrick.

The first theatre on this site was built in 1663. Kings

. . . Other Attractions . . .

George I and George III both survived assassination
attempts while attending performances. The **"Through
the Stage Door"** tours uses professional actors to
perform intriguing episodes of the theatre's history,

Cleopatra's Needle

and explore the theatre's front
of house, backstage and
understage areas. *(Theatre Royal
"Through the Stage Door" tours,
Catherine Street, ☎ 020-7240-5357.
Sun-Tue & Thu-Fri: tours at
12.30pm, 2.15pm, 4.45pm. Wed &
Sat: tours at 11am & 1pm. Adult
£7.50, child £5.50, senior £7.50,
student £7.50. £1 discount with
voucher on page 277.)*

Heading south into the main
thoroughfare of The Strand,
which links the West End with
the City, you will find several
more old theatres.

Theatre Royal

At the east end of the Strand, the road divides, with
the crescent-shaped Aldwych curving round to create
an island. At its centre stands the neo-classical **Bush
House**, the headquarters of the BBC World Service.

St Mary-le-Strand

South of Aldwych, you will find the tall narrow church
St. Mary-le-Strand marooned in the middle of the road.
Built in 1724, it has a distinctive wedding-cake
layered tower and fussily decorated exterior inspired
by Baroque churches in Rome.

Looping back towards the Thames via Lancaster Place,
there is a pleasant walk along the river, passing **Cleopatra's
Needle**. This 60-foot (18-metre) granite obelisk, carved
in 1500 BC, was presented to Britain in 1819 by the
then Turkish Viceroy of Egypt, Mohammed Ali.

Cleopatra's Needle

Opposite St. Martin-in-the-Fields,
on St. Martin's Place, is the
National Portrait Gallery, containing the
world's largest collection of portraits –
10,000 in all. The exhibition floors are
centred around a dramatic 19th-century
entrance lobby, with the earliest paintings
on the upper floors, so it's a good idea to
start at the top and work down.

Early 20th Century Galleries
at the NPG

A 23 m (75 ft) long escalator serves the
Tudor Galleries, where the oldest portrait
in the collection, that of Henry VII
painted in 1505, is carefully preserved.
The Elizabethan paintings of, among others, Elizabeth I

Other Attractions . . .

and William Shakespeare, are displayed in a magnificent Tudor-style long hall.

By the time you reach the first floor, early 20th century faces are on display, and the Balcony Gallery is devoted to icons of the late 20th century, including Paul McCartney, Harold Wilson, Joan Collins and Marianne Faithfull.

Trafalgar Square looking towards Big Ben

In addition to the paintings, there is a state-of-the-art IT Gallery, where visitors can explore the portraits in detail. There is also a Lecture Theatre and a restaurant with marvellous views across Trafalgar Square. *(St. Martin's Place, ☎ 020-7306-0055. Mon-Sun: 10am-6pm (until 9pm on Thu and Fri.) Admission is free. 10% discount on all goods at gallery shop (except books) with your for less card.)*

Trafalgar Square, officially the centre of London, is easily accessible by tube and many of London's bus routes and all night buses call at stops around the square.

The thousands of pigeons that inhabit the square will willingly eat out of your hand and perch on different parts of your body. A tub of pigeon food costs 25p from a booth on the eastern side of the square.

Unfortunately – and to the fury of many Londoners – the huge flock creates a nasty mess, which you may well skid on. The British government spends £100,000 a year removing up to a ton of pigeon droppings from Nelson's Column.

National Portrait Gallery

The square is traditionally used for political demonstrations, most famously in 1990 when a protest against the 'poll tax' turned into a mass riot.

Huge crowds gather on New Year's Eve, when barriers are erected to prevent revellers from climbing on Sir Edward Landseer's four bronze lions (1867) and from swimming in the fountains.

Trafalgar Square

St. Martin-in-the-Fields and the National Gallery from Trafalgar Square

Several fine buildings face the square, including the

. . . Other Attractions

National Gallery to the north and **Admiralty Arch** –
through which you can see the Mall and Buckingham
Palace – to the south-west.

The church of **St. Martin-in-the-Fields,** with its
distinctive tower and Corinthian columns, stands in the

Admiralty Arch

Brass rubbing

north-eastern corner of
Trafalgar Square. There is a
lively and modestly-priced
café in the crypt, entered
from the street to the south
of the church.

for less In the crypt, you will
also find the **London
Brass Rubbing Centre.** You
can create your own
souvenir from Britain's age

of chivalry by doing a 'rubbing' of one of the medieval
brasses. *(The Crypt, St. Martin-in-the-Fields, ☎ 020-7930-
9306. Mon-Sat: 10am-6pm. Sun: 12noon-6pm. 50% off any
self-made rubbings with voucher on page 277. (Average price
£5.))*

*London Brass Rubbing
Centre*

Heading towards Whitehall, the horse-and-rider statue
marooned on a traffic island just to the south of
Trafalgar Square is of Charles I. Completed in 1633, it
was removed during the English Civil War, but with the
restoration of the monarchy in 1660, it was placed on
the exact spot where the men who signed the king's
death warrant were beheaded.

Open Spaces

There are very few green spaces in the densely packed
West End and, as a result, any patch of grass tends to
be packed with sun-seeking office workers in summer.

*Victoria Embankment
Gardens*

One of the most pleasant places to relax
and have a picnic is **Victoria Embankment
Gardens**, a narrow stretch of formal
gardens alongside the Thames and close
to Embankment tube station. Statues of
famous British people line its walkways.

At the northern flank of the West End
area lies the small, but attractive, **Soho
Square**, which is surrounded by houses
once inhabited by the nobility. These days,
the buildings are mainly occupied by
entertainment businesses such as 20th
Century Fox. The mock-Tudor shed in the
square conceals an air vent for the Tube.

Soho Square

Eating and Drinking . . .

Whatever you feel like eating, be it Afro-Caribbean, Indonesian or Tex/Mex, you will find it among the thousand-plus restaurants of the West End.

Chinatown, on and around Gerrard Street, has dozens of restaurants suitable for all budgets. You can buy a four-course meal for two for as little as £14. Turn up Wardour Street and follow the smell of roast duck. **Poons** *(4 Leicester Street)* is modestly priced and serves delicious, authentic dishes. North of Chinatown is Soho, home to exotic restaurants and late-night cafés.

Gerrard Street

There are several themed restaurants in the Leicester Square/Piccadilly Circus area with menus based on burgers and steaks. These include **Planet Hollywood** (page 86), **Football, Football** *(57-60 Haymarket)*, which is stuffed with football memorabilia and the **Fashion Café** *(5-6 Coventry Street)* which has four supermodels as partners. On Aldwych you will find the **Waldorf Hotel**, famous for tea dances (page 256).

Several restaurants offer live entertainment. **Smollensky's** (page 86) has live music every night and magic shows for kids at lunchtime, while **Centre Stage** (page 84) has cabaret performers selected from the West End stage.

All Bar One

The many pubs and bars tend to be jam-packed at weekends. **All-Bar-One** *(48 Leicester Square)* is a bar/restaurant laid out like a wine cellar with huge windows allowing you to see and be seen. **De Hems** *(11 Macclesfield Street)* serves Dutch beer and has a party atmosphere most nights.

Around the corner on Greek Street is Soho's most celebrated pub, The **Coach and Horses.** It was immortalised in Keith Waterhouse's play, *Jeffrey*

Bernard is Unwell, based on the life of the heavy drinking journalist who spent much of his time here.

The listings magazine *Time Out* once nominated **The Polar Bear** *(30 Lisle Street, ☎ 020-7437-3048)* as one of the worst pubs in the West End. The pub responded by putting up a large banner declaring itself 'One of the worst pubs in the West End' and takings immediately went up by 60%. It is mainly frequented by homesick New Zealanders.

Al fresco dining in the West End

The **Lamb and Flag** *(33 Rose Street, ☎ 020-7497-9504)* has a long and chequered history and its bar has retained its old-worldliness. An inn has stood on the site for 500 years.

Si Señor

Mexican

2 St. Anne's Court
☎ 020-7494-4632

Average meal: £10-15
for less discount: 25%
AM/VS/MC

HOURS

Mon-Thu: 12noon-
12midnight
Fri-Sat: 12noon-1am
Sun: 5pm-11pm

This is the only Mexican restaurant in London owned by Mexicans. The spacious, bright décor enhances the fun and informal atmosphere. Try the taco tray or the superb range of *fajitas*.

 Steph's

Modern British

39 Dean Street
☎ 020-7734-5976

Average meal: £15-20
for less discount: 25%
AM/VS/MC/DC

HOURS

Mon-Thu: 12noon-3pm,
5.30pm-11.20pm
Fri: 12noon-3pm,
5.30pm-12midnight
Sat: 5.30pm-12midnight
Sun: closed

Steph's charming, intimate restaurant is a favourite with theatre-goers. It features an eclectic menu, with a strong, traditional British influence. Food is served in an informal, fun atmosphere by friendly, attentive staff.

 Pizza Piazza

Pizza

39 Charing Cross Road
☎ 020-7437-1686

Average meal: £5-10
for less discount: 25%
AM/VS/MC/DC

HOURS

Mon-Sun: 9.30am-
12midnight

Pizza Piazza is an up-market pizza and pasta restaurant chain. This popular restaurant has an excellent location in the heart of the West End. There are dozens of meat, fish and vegetarian pizza toppings to choose from.

HOURS

Fri-Sat: 5.30pm-1am
(show starts at 11pm)
Sun-Thu: closed

Centre Stage

Cabaret

**Mountbatten Hotel,
20 Monmouth Street
☎ 020-7836-4300**

Meal and cabaret: £43
for less discount: 25%
AM/VS/MC/DC

Centre Stage offers a two-course dinner with wine and cabaret on Fridays and Saturdays. Artistes are hand-picked from the West End stage. You must book in advance for these evenings.

Little Havana

Cuban

**1 Leicester Place
☎ 020-7287-0101**

Average meal: £15-20
for less discount: 25%
AM/VS/MC

HOURS

Mon-Fri: 4.30pm-3am
Sat: 5pm-3am

Little Havana is a fashionable restaurant with a large bar and dancefloor. It serves Cuban and Caribbean dishes with an emphasis on fish and rice. Dining here entitles you to free entry to the nightclub and bar.

Flicks Brasserie

International

**The Pastoria,
St. Martin's Street
☎ 020-7930-8641**

Average meal: £10-15
for less discount: 25%
AM/VS/MC/DC

HOURS

Mon-Sun: 7am-10pm

Just off Leicester Square, Flicks Brasserie is the ideal spot for a late-night drink, or something a little more substantial. It serves a selection of excellent international dishes.

West End · 85

 # Bella Napoli

Italian

101 Dean Street
☎ 020-7437-9440

Average meal: £10-15
for less discount: 25%
AM/VS/MC/DC

Bella Napoli is a friendly, family-run restaurant, which has been serving traditional Italian food for 25 years. The home-made pasta dishes are particularly recommended.

HOURS

Mon-Sat: 12noon-11pm
Sun: closed

 # Nusa Dua

Indonesian

11-12 Dean Street
☎ 020-7437-3559

Average meal: £10-15
for less discount: 25%
AM/VS

The extensive menu offers Indonesian, Singaporean and Malaysian dishes. Customers include businessmen at lunchtime and theatre-goers at night. Use the set menu to sample a wide range of dishes at an excellent price.

HOURS

Mon-Fri: 12noon-2.30pm,
6.30pm-11.30pm
Sat: 6.30pm-12midnight
Sun: 6.30pm-10.30pm

 # Donuts and Company

Doughnuts

3 Glasshouse Street
☎ 020-7287-2129

Average meal: £1-5
for less discount: 25%
(present voucher on page 285)

Choose from a huge range of flavoured doughnuts at Donuts and Company. Over 50 flavours include strawberry, chocolate, apricot and toffee apple. Sandwiches and beverages are also available.

HOURS

Mon-Sat: 7am-
12midnight
Sun: 8am-12midnight

HOURS

Mon-Sat: 12noon-1am
Sun: 12noon-12midnight

Planet Hollywood

American

13 Coventry Street
☎ 020-7287-1000

Average meal: £15-20
for less discount: 25%
(present voucher on page 285)
AM/VS/MC

Planet Hollywood is a fun-filled theme restaurant. The walls are covered with film and Hollywood memorabilia, and the menu features American favourites such as burgers and ribs.

HOURS

Mon-Sat: 11am-11pm
Sun: 12noon-10.30pm

Old Orleans

American / Cajun

29-31 Wellington Street
☎ 020-7497-2433

Average meal: £10-15
for less discount: 25%
AM/VS/MC/DC

Old Orleans re-creates the ambience of the Deep South, in the heart of Covent Garden. The menu is an assortment of Cajun and Creole specialities, plus steaks, burgers, barbecue ribs and various Mexican dishes.

HOURS

Mon-Wed: 12noon-
12midnight
Thu-Sat: 12noon-12.30am
Sun: 12noon-5.30pm,
6.30pm-10.30pm

Smollensky's

American

105 The Strand
☎ 020-7497-2101

Average meal: £15-20
for less discount: 25%
AM/VS/MC/DC

Smollensky's serves modern and traditional American food. Its full and varied menu caters for every taste, including vegetarians. The atmosphere is young, relaxed and fun, with live music every night.

Dial Restaurant & Bar

Modern British

**Mountbatten Hotel,
20 Monmouth Street
☎ 020-7848-8607**

Average meal: £20-25
for less discount: 25%
AM/VS/MC/DC

HOURS

Mon-Fri: 12.30pm-
2.30pm, 5.30pm-11pm
Sat: 5.30pm-11pm
Sun: 6pm-10pm

Recently opened in the core of Covent Garden, Dial Restaurant & Bar is a cool contemporary setting for your social lunch or business dinner. Feast your eyes and your taste buds.

Ed's Easy Diner

American

**Pepsi Trocadero
Piccadilly Circus
☎ 020-7287-1951**

Average meal: £5-10
for less discount: 25%
AM/VS/MC

HOURS

Mon-Sun:
11.30am-12midnight

Ed's is an authentic 1950s-style American diner. As well as serving the finest burgers, it is famous for its thick milkshakes. Rock and roll from mini-jukeboxes accompanies your meal.

La Crêperie Bretonne

Pancake House

**26 New Row
Covent Garden
☎ 020-7240-3603**

Average meal: £5-10
for less discount: 25%
AM/VS/MC/DC

HOURS

Mon-Thu: 12.30pm-11pm
Fri-Sat: 12.30pm-
12midnight
Sun: 12.30pm-10.30pm

La Crêperie Bretonne boasts a choice of sixty-five crêpes, and there is a wide selection of wines and beers to complement your meal. You can dine outside or in the air-conditioned restaurant.

HOURS

Mon-Sat: 12.30pm-
2.30pm, 6pm-11pm
Sun: 12.30pm-2.30pm,
6pm-10pm

HOURS

Mon-Sat: 12noon-2.15pm,
6pm-11.15pm
Sun: 5pm-10.15pm

HOURS

Mon-Thu: 10am-11.30pm.
Fri-Sat: 10am-
12midnight.

Apex *for less*

Modern British

Hampshire Hotel
31 Leicester Square
☎ 020-7666-0902

Average meal: £15-20
for less discount: 25%
AM/VS/MC/DC

Located in the centre of Leicester Square, the Apex restaurant is ideal for entertaining friends, or for pre-theatre dinners. The restaurant's style is a fusion of contemporary and classical designs, giving a luxurious and elegant feel

New Jakarta *for less*

Indonesian

150 Shaftesbury Avenue
☎ 020-7836-2644

Average meal: £5-10
for less discount: 25%
AM/VS/MC

New Jakarta offers good Indonesian food at reasonable prices. For two or more, the *rijsttaffel* is highly recommended. For lunch, the set menu is extremely good value.

Bella Pasta *for less*

Italian

22 Leicester Square
☎ 020-7321-0016

Average meal: £5-10
for less discount: 25%
(present voucher on page 285)
AM/VS/MC

This chain of Italian restaurants offers excellent value. They are great places to go for a quick lunch or a relaxed dinner. The discount also applies at 61 Shaftesbury Avenue and 25 Argyll Street.

Shopping . . .

Oxford Street is London's main shopping artery. Stretching from Marble Arch to Tottenham Court Road, it contains almost two miles of chain stores, a number of 'megastores' such as the **Virgin** and **HMV** music shops, and numerous small boutiques.

Only buses and taxis are allowed along Oxford Street, but the traffic is still bumper to bumper. It is not much better on the wide pavements, which are flooded with shoppers when the shops are open.

Selfridges department store

Selfridges *(400 Oxford Street, ☎ 020-7629-1234)* is an enormous department store with a very long and grand façade of neo-classical columns. Above the main entrance sits a statue of the Queen of Time, riding the Ship of Commerce. London's up-market answer to Macy's, Selfridges was founded in 1909 by Chicago millionaire Gordon Selfridge. It sells almost everything, but specializes in popular designer fashion.

Two other, much better value department stores are **John Lewis** *(278 Oxford Street, ☎ 020-7629-7711)* and two large branches of **Marks & Spencer** *(173 Oxford Street, ☎ 020-7437-7722 and 458 Oxford Street, ☎ 020-7935-7954)*, renowned for its reliable clothing, particularly underwear.

Selfridges

For those looking for cheap fashion, branches of H&M *(261-271 Regent Street, ☎020-7493-4004)*, Top Shop *(214 Oxford Street, ☎0207-636-7700)* and Miss Selfridge *(40 Duke Street, ☎020-7318-3833)*, are all close by.

Bond Street contains exclusive fashion stores, including special outlets of **Donna Karan** *(19 New Bond Street, ☎ 020-7495-3100)* and **Calvin Klein**.

Liberty

Liberty department store

A short distance along the elegantly curved **Regent Street** is **Liberty** *(210 Regent Street, ☎ 020-7734-1234)*, probably London's most charming department store. Behind the striking black and white mock-Tudor façade is a labyrinth of rooms and alcoves selling tasteful gifts, clothes, scarves and exotic goods. It is most famous for its gorgeous fabrics.

Close to Liberty is the toy emporium **Hamley's** *(188 Regent Street, ☎ 020-7494-2000)*, which has several floors overflowing with everything from traditional toys

REFLECTIONS

'London is *hot*...right across the board in London now there is daring and finesse'. – Karl Lagerfeld (1997)

. . . Shopping

to the latest computer games – many of which can be played with by children before they are bought. You

Regent Street

could save a lot of money, however, by buying the same toy from a department store such as John Lewis which has a policy of being 'never knowingly undersold'.

Running parallel with Regent Street is the youth fashion showcase of **Carnaby Street**. Shops here sell leather jackets, jeans, nightclub wear and all manner of gimmicks. Carnaby Street still encapsulates the Swinging Sixties for middle-aged British people, though it has re-invented itself for each generation of teenagers.

Carnaby Street

Further to the east is **Berwick Street Market**, a street market packed with stalls selling cheap fresh fruit and vegetables. Alongside the colourfully stacked stalls are several specialist popular music shops.

Book lovers will be in seventh heaven on **Charing Cross Road**. There are dozens of specialist bookstores such as **Silver Moon** for feminist writing *(64 Charing Cross Road, ☎ 020-7836-7906)*, **Zwemmer's** for art *(24 Litchfield Street, ☎ 020-7240-4158)*, and **Forbidden Planet** for sci-fi *(71 New Oxford Street, ☎ 020-7836-4179)*. Although it is very old-fashioned, **Foyles** *(Charing Cross Road, ☎ 020-7437-5660)* is one of the largest general bookshops.

Foyles

Tottenham Court Road, which runs on from Charing Cross Road at the top of Oxford Street, has many shops selling electronic equipment and computers. It's convenient for shopping around for the best

Neal's Yard

prices. If it's Hi-Fi equipment you're after, try **Hi-Fi Experience** *(227 Tottenham Court Road, ☎ 020-7580-3535)*. For special offers on electronic equipment and computers, visit

Gultronics *(52 Tottenham Court Road, ☎ 20-7637-1619)*.

Neal Street

A host of specialist and cult shops, ranging from a store selling hundreds of types of tea to one devoted to the cartoon character Tintin, are to be found on and around **Neal Street**, near Covent Garden. If you want to buy a kite, try **The Kite Store** *(69 Neal Street, ☎ 020-7836-1666)*. If it is beads you need, step into **The Bead Shop** *(43 Neal Street, ☎ 020-7240-0931)*. If your skateboard is seizing up, **Slam City Skates** *(16 Neal's Yard, ☎ 020-7240-0928)* will sort you out.

Neal's Yard, tucked away off Neal Street, is a mecca for vegetarians and healthfood fanatics. Mock-rustic shops specialize in cheeses, herbal remedies and other wholesome goods.

For fashion victims, **Floral Street** has major outlets of the top designers **Paul Smith** *(40-44 Floral Street, ☎ 020-7379-7133)* and **Nicole Farhi** *(11 Floral Street, ☎ 020-7497-8713)*. On the parallel street, **Long Acre**, is **Stanford's**, the world's oldest and largest map and travel guide shop *(12-14 Long Acre, ☎ 020-7836-1321)*.

HOURS

Mon-Sat: 9am-6pm
Sun: 10am-4pm

Saks

Women's Fashion

1 Oxford Street
☎ **020-7437-4542**

for less discount: 20%
AM/VS/MC/DC

Saks is a popular women's fashion store located close to Tottenham Court Road. A wide selection of women's wear in different styles is sold. Souvenir London T-shirts can also be purchased.

HOURS

Mon-Sat: 10am-7pm
Sun: 12noon-6pm

Back Packer

Outdoor & Camping Goods

136 Charing Cross Road
☎ **020-7836-1160**

for less discount: 20%
AM/VS/MC

Back Packer has everything you need for outdoor activities, from a penknife to a tent, plus a wide range of sleeping bags and travelling accessories. It stocks major brands such as Karrimor, Vango and Dr. Marten's.

HOURS

Mon-Sat: 10.30am-
6.30pm
Sun: closed

HOURS

Mon-Wed & Fri-Sat:
10.30am-7pm
Thu: 10.30am-8pm
Sun: 11am-6pm

Marmalade

Men's Clothes

85 Oxford Street
☎ 020-7439-1675

for less discount: 20%
AM/VS/MC

Marmalade specializes in high-fashion men's clothes, both casual and formal. The designer clothes are notable for their unique styles. It is a great place to buy unusual up-to-the-minute men's designer wear.

HOURS

Mon-Fri: 10am-6.30pm
Sat: 9.30am-6.30pm
Sun: closed

Sherry's

Men's Fashion

24 Ganton Street
☎ 020-7734-5868

for less discount: 20%
VS/MC

If you like Mod clothes, you will love this shop. Sherry's specializes in 1960s-style clothing, and you will find names such as John Smedley and Fred Perry on the shelves.

HOURS

Mon-Fri: 10am-6pm
Sat: 12noon-5pm
Sun: 1pm-5pm

The Face

Men's Fashion

38 Beak Street
☎ 020-7437-3491

for less discount: 20%
VS/MC

The Face offers a full range of 1960s-style clothing. Ben Sherman button-down shirts are among the more popular items. For high quality woollen wear, try the John Smedley range.

Woollen Centre

Men's Tailored Suits

149 Regent Street
☎ 020-7437-7077

for less discount: 20%
VS/MC

At the Woollen Centre, you can have a suit hand-tailored for you in one week. Choose a cloth and a style to suit your personal taste. The suit will then be made to your exact size and requirements.

HOURS

Mon-Sat: 9.30am-6.30pm
Sun: 12noon-5.30pm

Old Time Photographers

Photographic Portrait Shop

**Trocadero Centre,
Piccadilly Circus**
☎ 020-7734-8709

for less discount: 20%
AM/VS/MC/DC

Old Time Photographers offers you a unique souvenir photo service. First, choose the historical period in which you want to be photographed. Then, put on the relevant costume and have your portrait taken.

HOURS

Sun-Fri: 12noon-9pm
Sat: 11am-12midnight

Piccadilly Souvenirs

Gifts

217 Piccadilly
☎ 020-7734-2175

for less discount: 20%
AM/VS/MC/DC

Packed with souvenirs and woollen goods, this store is designed for visitors. Located in Piccadilly Circus, it is a convenient place to purchase gifts. Items sold range from T-shirts to shortbread biscuits.

HOURS

Mon-Sat: 11am-9pm
Sun: 12noon-9pm

HOURS

Mon-Sat: 10.30am-7pm
Sun: closed

Violet

Candles & Gifts

23a Beak Street
☎ **020-7734-3754**

for less discount: 20%
VS/MC

This fascinating shop sells candles of every shape, colour and scent. Some can be made to your personal specification while you wait. It is a great place to purchase a novelty gift or an unusual souvenir of London.

Estridge *for less*

Woollen & Cashmere Clothing

60-62 Regent Street
☎ **020-7734-0195**

for less discount: 20%
AM/VS/MC/DC

HOURS

Mon-Sat: 9am-6pm
Sun: 10am-4pm

Situated at the bottom of Regent Street close to Piccadilly Circus, Estridge specializes in cashmere, cotton and woollen knitwear for men and women. Many famous British clothing brands are sold here.

Supreme *for less*

Woollen & Cashmere Clothing

31 Carnaby Street
☎ **020-7437-0768**

for less discount: 20%
AM/VS/MC/DC

HOURS

Mon-Sat: 9am-6pm
Sun: 10am-4pm

Carnaby Street was famous in the 1960s as the home of London fashion. Supreme specializes in top brand lambswool and cashmere products, as well as accessories from famous English clothing companies.

Mayfair and St. James

Introduction . . .

Built to accommodate royal courtiers 300 years ago, Mayfair and St. James's remain the playground of the aristocracy and the seriously rich.

These areas boast the highest concentration of exclusive shops, luxury hotels and expensive art

galleries. There are few attractions or sites open to the public in Mayfair and St. James's, the notable exception being the **Royal Academy of Arts** (page 98) with its world famous Summer Exhibition.

Luxury service at a Mayfair hotel

Bordered by three royal parks – Hyde Park, Green Park and St. James's Park – Mayfair and St. James's are the most up-market of London's areas. It is no coincidence that the most expensive properties in the British version of the boardgame Monopoly are all here or close by, with Mayfair and Park Lane the most likely to bankrupt unlucky players.

Mayfair takes its name from the 15-day fair that was held in the area every May for almost 100 years until 1764, when wealthy residents protested about the noise and succeeded in closing it down.

INSIDER'S TIP

For a taste of Mayfair as it was two hundred years ago, stroll down Chesterfield Street, the area's best preserved Georgian terrace, which runs between Curzon Street and Charles Street.

Unlike Covent Garden and Soho, which were once fashionable with the aristocracy before going into decline, Mayfair has managed to retain its social cachet. Few aristocrats now live here, but hundreds of extremely wealthy foreign nationals have made their London homes in Mayfair in recent years.

Hard Rock Café, Old Park Lane

Of the six great estates established in the 18th century, the Grosvenor estate was by far the largest, and remains intact in the hands of a direct descendant, the Duke of Westminster. The original street pattern survives, punctuated by four very grand squares: Grosvenor, Hanover, Berkeley and St. James's. Many of the Georgian houses have had stucco facings and new porticos added, but most of the structure underneath is original.

. . . Introduction

The area first attracted aristocrats when **St. James's Palace** (page 99), originally one of Henry VIII's hunting lodges, became the official royal London palace after fire had destroyed Whitehall Palace in 1698.

The high concentration of the *haut monde* meant hundreds of fine craftsmen and purveyors of luxury

The Saudi Arabian embassy

goods set up shop locally. Many of these businesses are still open today, clustered on Jermyn Street and Bond Street, and you will find that far more shops in Mayfair and St. James's display the coveted Royal Warrant (denoting a supplier to the Royal family) than in any other area of London (see pages 104-108).

REFLECTIONS

'He had strayed simply enough into Bond Street, where his imagination... caused him now and then to stop before a window in which objects massive and lumpish, in silver and gold...were as tumbled together as if in the insolence of the Empire, they had been loot of far-off victories.'
– *The Golden Bowl*, Henry James (1904)

St. James's has long been known as 'Clubland', because of the large number of gentlemen's clubs in the area. Several can be found along **Pall Mall** (page 99), one of London's grandest streets, which was laid out in 1661 with extravagant mansions built for dukes and earls. The street began to acquire its present commercial character in the Victorian period, though two of Queen Victoria's grand-daughters, Princess Helena Victoria and Princess Marie Louise, lived here until 1947.

Large sections of Mayfair and St. James's have, in the last 50 years, been taken over by service industries seeking prestigious addresses for their headquarters. Banks, advertising agencies and luxury car showrooms now occupy the buildings around **Berkeley Square**.

Claridges

Many of London's most famous hotels are to be found in Mayfair. Several, such as **Claridges** on Brook Street, have illustrious histories stretching back into the 19th century. The **Ritz Hotel** on Piccadilly is perhaps the most famous of Mayfair's exclusive hotels. A sister of the Paris Ritz, it opened in 1906 and still serves its legendary afternoon teas in the exotic Palm Court.

Royal Academy of Arts

The Royal Academy **Summer Exhibition** is one of London's cultural highlights, showcasing the work of both established and up-and-coming artists and sculptors.

The Royal Academy of Arts

The painter Sir Joshua Reynolds was the first president of the Academy, which was founded as Britain's first formal art school in 1768, with George III as patron. It has occupied its present home, Burlington House – one of the few aristocratic mansions left on Piccadilly – since 1837.

ADDRESS

Burlington House, Piccadilly
☎ 020-7439-7438

GETTING THERE

Piccadilly Circus tube station

The Academy is approached through a courtyard, sadly used as a car park, around which are housed several other learned societies, including the Geological Society and the Royal Astronomical Society.

Interior of the Royal Academy

The Academy's permanent collection includes at least one work from every member in its history (one of the traditions of membership is that you must contribute a piece of your work). The artists Turner and Constable were members. Living members include artists David Hockney and Sir Hugh Casson, and architects Richard Rogers and Sir Norman Foster. Royal Academicians may put 'RA' after their name.

The prize exhibit is the *Taddei Tondo*, a sculpted disc of the Madonna and Child by Michelangelo. It is found at the top of the glass staircase, inside the astounding light-filled Arthur Sackler Galleries which were designed by Norman Foster and opened in 1991.

HOURS

Mon-Sun: 10am-6pm (Fri: until 8.30pm)
The Summer Exhibition is held Jun 1-Aug 10.

Several special exhibitions, for which there is an entry fee, are staged annually.

The Academy shop has an enormous selection of art books, prints, postcards and paraphernalia, which are ideal as tasteful gifts to take back home.

'Taddei Tondo' by Michelangelo

PRICES

Prices vary between £4-6 depending on exhibition.

There is a good restaurant serving excellent, reasonably priced food. It is open every day from 10am to 5.30pm (8.30pm on Fridays).

Other Attractions . . .

Wandering through the streets of Mayfair will afford a glimpse into the rarefied world of the people who live in the area. Whether it be a gorgeous crystal chandelier spied through a window, or gentlemen in dinner suits accompanied by ladies in gowns making their way to evening functions, you will get a taste of the lavish lifestyle enjoyed here for more than 300 years.

Pall Mall

Pall Mall, lined with gentlemen's clubs and elite societies, was the first gas-lit street in London. It was illuminated to celebrate George III's birthday on June 4, 1807. Royal hangers-on have traditionally lived here, including Charles II's mistress, Nell Gwyn, at No. 79. Charles's dying words

Pall Mall

were 'Let not poor Nelly starve'.

Filled with privately educated, rich males, the Pall Mall clubs foster Britain's peculiar 'old boys network'. The clubs offer sports facilities for younger members and libraries where the older ones can snooze in plush leather armchairs behind a copy of *The Times*. **The Athenaeum** *(107 Pall Mall)*, flanking Waterloo Place, counts many aristocrats, top politicians and several bishops among its members. Traditionally, women have been banned from joining most of these clubs, but the **Oxford and Cambridge University Club** *(71 Pall Mall)* recently voted to admit women as full members.

St James's Palace

Guarding St. James's Palace

St. James's Palace stands on the site of an 11th-century hospital for women lepers dedicated to St. James, hence the palace's name. A single sentry stands outside the Tudor brick building. Built by Henry VIII in 1532 as a hunting lodge, only the original octagonal towered Gatehouse and Chapel Royal remain.

Clarence House

The palace became the main royal residence until

. . . Other Attractions . . .

Spencer House

Queen Victoria moved into Buckingham Palace in 1837. Foreign ambassadors are still described as being attached to the 'Court of St. James' and they are accredited here before riding to Buckingham Palace in the Glass Coach. *(Corner of Pall Mall and St. James's Street).*

Beside St. James's Palace is **Clarence House**, built by John Nash in 1825 for the Duke of Clarence, who became William IV. It is the home of the Queen Mother, who is undoubtedly Britain's best-loved royal. She greets well-wishers at the gates on her birthday, August 4, but there is no public entry to the house.

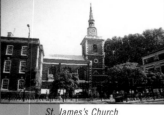
St. James's Church

There are several other mansions in the immediate area that were built for dukes and duchesses, including **Marlborough House**, built in 1709 by Sir Christopher Wren and the 1820 **Lancaster House**, venue for the 1978 conference that ended white rule in Rhodesia (now Zimbabwe).

Spencer House is a magnificent mid-18th century Palladian mansion with eight finely decorated rooms open to the public. Its beautiful parquet floors, ornate plaster ceilings and classical murals were designed for the first Earl of Spencer, an ancestor of the late Diana, Princess of Wales. Look out for the ostentatious gilded palm tree columns in Lord Spencer's Room. *(27 St. James's Place, ☎ 020-7499-8620. Sun only: 10.30am-4.45pm. Aug & Jan closed. Adult £6, child £5, senior £5, student £5. Children under 10 not admitted.)*

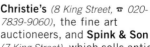
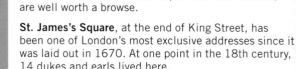
Michael Faraday

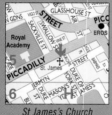
St James's Church

Christie's *(8 King Street, ☎ 020-7839-9060)*, the fine art auctioneers, and **Spink & Son** *(7 King Street)*, which sells antique coins and medals, are well worth a browse.

Museum of Mankind

St. James's Square, at the end of King Street, has been one of London's most exclusive addresses since it was laid out in 1670. At one point in the 18th century, 14 dukes and earls lived here.

. . . Other Attractions

St. James's Church, completed in 1684, was the last of the many London churches built by Wren and was his personal favourite. It was destroyed in the Second World War bombing of London, but has since been restored. There is a craft market in the courtyard. *(197 Piccadilly, usually open Mon-Sun: 8am-7pm)*

Shepherd Market

A few streets to the west stands the grand façade of the **Royal Institution**, a scientific body founded in 1799. Several famous inventors were members, including Michael Faraday, the man who discovered the electromagnetic force. His old laboratory has been preserved and turned into the small **Faraday Museum**. *(21 Albemarle Street, ☎ 020-7409-2992 (visits must be booked in advance). Mon-Fri: 9am-6pm. Sat-Sun: closed. Adults £1, child £1, senior £1, student £1.)*

Faraday Museum

Hidden between Piccadilly and Curzon Street is an attractive enclave of shops and cafés known as **Shepherd Market** (page 102). It is a popular lunchtime and evening meeting place for Londoners, who come here to this residential haven to escape from the traffic.

Open Spaces

The largest open space in the area is **Green Park** (page 198), at the western end of Piccadilly. There are hundreds of well-maintained wrought iron benches lining the long, leafy avenues that criss-cross the park, and deckchairs can be hired.

Berkeley Square

Grosvenor Square, at the northern end of Mayfair near Oxford Street, is the second largest square in London (only Lincoln's Inn Fields is bigger). It was the grandest address in London in the 18th and 19th centuries, when elegant terraces occupied all four sides and more than half the occupants had aristocratic titles. The west side was removed in the late 1950s to make way for the curiously ugly US embassy.

Berkeley Square

In the heart of Mayfair is **Berkeley Square**, where a group of tall plane trees provides leafy shade. This is a key address for upper class offspring, for whom the annual Berkeley Square Ball is *the* place to be seen. Annabel's, London's top night-club for the rich and famous, is also here.

Eating and Drinking

Most of the restaurants in Mayfair and St. James's serve the upper end of the market. They include the celebrity-packed **Le Caprice** (Arlington Street, ☎ 020-7629-2239) and Michel Roux Jnr's **Le Gavroche** (Upper Brook Street, ☎ 020-7499-1826). **Quaglino's** (16 Bury Street, ☎ 020-7930-6767), established in 1929 and remodelled in the 1990s by Sir Terence Conran, is especially glamorous.

Le Caprice

Many restaurants are tucked away in **Shepherd Market**, which is a warren of alleyways and passages leading off a square. In the 18th century, this area was a notorious den of gambling and prostitution. It still retains some of its old colour, but is, in addition, a charming, traffic-free location for a drink or meal. Several pubs and cafés here have tables on the pavement during the summer. One of the best places for an evening meal is **Sofra** (18 Shepherd Market, ☎ 020-7493-3300), which serves delicious Turkish specialities.

Hard Rock Café, Old Park Lane

Shepherd Market

Most of the better hotels have restaurants open to people who are not staying at the hotel. **Chez Nico** (90 Park Lane, ☎ 020-7409-1290), at the Grosvenor House Hotel on Park Lane, serves classic French cuisine. The restaurant at **The Chesterfield** (see opposite) has won several awards.

If you arrange to meet someone in the Red Lion pub, make sure you know which one you are heading for, because there are two in this area and 22 more across London.

The **Red Lion** (☎ 020-7930-4141) of St. James's is a tiny 400-year-old pub hidden in a narrow alley known as Crown Passage, which runs between Pall Mall and King Street. The **Red Lion** (☎ 020-7499-1307) of Mayfair, on Waverton Street, has a blazing fire in winter and a forecourt for the summer.

Chez Nico at 90 Park Lane

A typically British afternoon tea at the **Ritz** (150 Piccadilly, ☎ 020-7493-8181) is an English traditional that shouldn't be missed if you're feeling rich and well-dressed. The mid-afternoon spread of sandwiches, scones, cakes and tea is served between 2pm and 6pm and must be booked at least month in advance, and smart dress is required.

Bullochs

International

116 Piccadilly
☎ 020-7470-3333

Average meal: £20-25
for less discount: 25%
AM/VS/MC/DC

HOURS

Mon-Fri: 12.30pm-
2.30pm, 6pm-11pm
Sat: 6pm-11pm
Sun: 7pm-11pm

Bullochs serves high quality food in an exclusive atmosphere. It offers a modern and romantic setting in which to have a pleasant meal. The extensive menu changes with the seasons.

 # The Chesterfield

Modern British

35 Charles Street
☎ 020-7491-2622

Average meal: £15-20
for less discount: 25%
AM/VS/MC/DC

HOURS

Mon-Fri: 12noon-2.30pm,
5.30pm-11pm. Sat:
5.30pm-9.30pm. Sun:
12noon-2pm, 6pm-10pm

This elegant hotel restaurant, located in the heart of fashionable Mayfair, has won numerous awards for the quality of its dining experience. The superb menu offers an exciting choice of speciality dishes.

 # Bella Pasta

Italian

64 Duke Street
☎ 020-7495-1110

Average meal: £5-10
for less discount: 25%
(present voucher on page 285)
AM/VS/MC

HOURS

Mon-Sun: 11am-12.30am

Bella Pasta serves good-value Italian food from restaurants all over London. Best known for its pasta dishes, it also serves pizzas. It is a great place for a reasonably priced dinner.

Shopping . . .

Many of the exclusive stores in Mayfair and St. James's proudly announce that they supply to members of the royal family, with the title 'By appointment to...' and the appropriate coat of arms for the person in question. There are currently around 800 Royal Warrant holders, supplying the occupants of Buckingham Palace and their extended family with anything from shirts and toiletries to silverware and jewellery, and the honour is a prestigious one which needs to be renewed every ten years.

Bond Street

H.M. Queen Elizabeth II

Brace yourself for the very expensive price tags on the luxury goods sold in this neighbourhood, even in those shops without a Royal Warrant. Many people just come to window shop at the exquisitely displayed stores.

Bond Street is the main north-south shopping artery. Silver, paintings and antiques are found in the southern section, while to the north are designer-label clothing and shoe shops. The shops are more upmarket the farther from Oxford Street you go.

Savile Row

Burlington Arcade

Gucci *(33 Old Bond Street, ☎ 020-7629-2716)*, **DKNY** *(27 Old Bond Street, ☎ 020-7499-8089)* and, most recently, **Calvin Klein** *(41 New Bond Street, ☎ 020-7491-9696)*, all have major outlets on Bond Street.

Asprey & Co. *(165-169 New Bond Street, ☎ 020-7493-6767)*, the prestigious jewellers serving the royal family, marks the junction of **Old Bond Street** (laid out in 1686) and **New Bond Street** (1721). This is where Prince Charles bought the late Diana's engagement ring.

Fenwicks, on the corner of Brook Street, is a department store selling Bond Street quality goods at more affordable prices.

Running parallel with Bond Street is **Saville Row**, a byword for fine gentlemen's tailoring. Many of the bespoke tailors have moved with the times to provide a

Burlington Arcade

. . . Shopping

modern look for today's gentleman; cutting-edge designer **Oswald Boateng** *(9 Vigo Street, ☎ 020-7734-6868)* has his shop nearby.

Burlington Arcade, beside the Royal Academy, is one of London's oldest shopping arcades, dating from 1819. The mahogany-fronted shops sell English fancy goods and finery. Rules of propriety, including an ancient ban on whistling, singing and running, are enforced by Beadles, top-hatted ex-soldiers who are happy to give advice and directions.

A traditional hat shop

Piccadilly has several traditional English shops. The most prestigious store is **Fortnum & Mason** *(181 Piccadilly, ☎ 020-7734-8040)*, London's top grocer, which supplies delicacies like turtle soup and exotic teas to the Royal Household. It's a good place to find delicious, edible souvenirs to take home, and there are fashion, homewares and toy departments too, as well as three restaurants and a champagne bar.

Jermyn Street

Jermyn Street is famous for selling all the accessories required by a young lord. Several of the shops are patronised by the royal family.

Bates the Hatter *(21 A Jermyn Street, ☎ 020-734-2722)*

Berry Brothers & Rudd, wine merchants

sells deerstalkers, top hats and other high society head gear; **Floris** *(89 Jermyn Street, ☎ 020-7930-2885)* supplies perfumes to the Queen; **Paxton & Whitfield** *(93 Jermyn Street, ☎ 020-7930-0259)*, founded in 1740, sells the world's finest cheeses; and **Prestat** *(14 Princes Arcade, ☎ 020-7629-4838)* supplies chocolates to the Queen.

Fortnum and Mason

St. James's Street has several very fine shops, notably **Berry Brothers & Rudd** Wine Merchants *(3 St. James's)* and **Lock & Co.** *(6 St. James's)*.

Mon-Sat: 9.30am-6pm
Sun: 11am-5.30pm

Mackenzie's *for less*

English & Scottish Wear

169 Piccadilly
☎ 020-7495-5514

for less discount: 20%
AM/VS/MC/DC

Mackenzie's, located between The Ritz Hotel and Fortnum & Mason's, is a perfect place to buy traditional English clothing, such as wax jackets. A 20% discount is also available at Forbes menswear at 166 Piccadilly.

HOURS

Mon-Wed: 10am-6pm
Thu-Fri: 10am-8pm
Sat: 9.15am-5.30pm
Sun: closed

Cobella *for less*

Hair & Beauty

52 Shepherd Market
☎ 020-7409-0606

for less discount: 20%
VS/MC

Cobella is one of London's outstanding hair and beauty salons. It has won many awards including 'London Stylists of the Year'. A full range of hair and beauty treatments is available.

HOURS

Mon-Fri: 10am-5.30pm
Sat: 10am-4pm
Sun: closed

Bucci *for less*

Leather Goods

16 Prince's Arcade
☎ 020-7734-1846

for less discount: 20%
AM/VS/MC/DC

Situated in Prince's Arcade, Bucci sells the finest quality leather accessories. Exclusive handbags, belts, wallets and executive cases, many hand-crafted and hand-finished, are stocked.

Taylor

Gift Shop

74 Jermyn Street
☎ 020-7930-5544

for less discount: 20%
AM/VS/MC/DC

HOURS

Mon-Sat: 8.30am-6pm
Sun: closed

Established in 1854, Taylor is run by the great-grandson of the founder. It sells a superb range of gentlemen's accessories and grooming products. The exclusive shop is renowned for its quality of service.

House of Cashmere

Menswear & Cashmere

471 Oxford Street
☎ 020-7493-3493

for less discount: 20%
AM/VS/MC

HOURS

Mon-Sat: 9.30am-6.30pm
Sun: 11am-5pm

House of Cashmere, situated close to Selfridges, stocks menswear, cashmere knitwear and textiles. A wide range of items, including well-known brands such as Daks, can be purchased.

 # Benson and Clegg

Gentlemen's Accessories

9 Piccadilly Arcade
☎ 020-7409-2053

for less discount: 20%
AM/VS/MC/DC

HOURS

Mon-Fri: 8.30am-5.30pm
Sat: 8.30am-5pm
Sun: closed

Benson & Clegg stocks a fine selection of gentlemen's accessories. Of particular note are the cuff-links and ties, but it also specializes in blazer buttons and engraving. Special orders can be taken.

HOURS

Mon-Sat: 9am-6pm (until 7pm Thu)
Sun: closed

HOURS

Mon-Sat: 10am-7pm
Sun: closed

HOURS

Mon-Sat: 9.30am-6.30pm
Sun: 12noon-5pm

John Bray *for less*

Men's Suits

78-79 Jermyn Street
☎ **020-7839-6375**

for less discount: 20%
AM/VS/MC/DC

Well-dressed gentlemen of all ages shop for clothes on Jermyn Street. John Bray specializes in modern-style designer suits from famous designers like Versace and Corneliani.

Bellini *for less*

Men's Clothes

77 New Bond Street
☎ **020-7409-3005**

for less discount: 20%
AM/VS/MC

Bellini sells designer-label suits at reduced prices, including Hom, Fendi, Versace and Valentino items. It is located in Bond Street, the heart of elegant West End shopping.

London House *for less*

Classic English Clothes

231 Regent Street
☎ **020-7355-3293**

for less discount: 20%
AM/VS/MC/DC

London House specializes in classic English clothing. The range includes cashmere goods, woollens and rainwear. Blazers, sweaters, cardigans, shirts, ties, hats and scarves are all stocked.

South Kensington and Chelsea

Introduction . . .

London's upper crust inhabits the elegant streets of South Kensington and Chelsea, which have hundreds of fine shops, great restaurants and several historic institutions. All of these combine to make this perhaps the capital's most complete area.

For the visitor, South Ken (as it is known to locals) is

Kensington Palace

Museumland. Several of the world's finest museums – the **Victoria & Albert** (pages 112-113), the **Science** (page 114) and the **Natural History** (page 115) – are located in this area.

South Ken is flanked to the north by the vast green expanse of **Kensington Gardens** and **Hyde Park** (page 120).

Chelsea, to the south, includes one of the most attractive stretches of the **River Thames**.

South Ken acquired its fine museums during the Victorian period, when Prince Albert decided to channel the profits from the **Great Exhibition** (page 26) into lasting cultural institutions.

North of the museums lie a number of colleges and the **Royal Albert Hall** (page 117), where the Promenade Concerts (better known as the 'Proms') take place from July to September. Across the road from the Hall, on the edge of Kensington Gardens, is the enormous **Albert Memorial** (page 117), which has recently undergone a lengthy restoration. A ten-minute walk into the park brings you to **Kensington Palace** (page 194).

With its fine museums and seats of learning like Imperial College, the area became highly fashionable in the last century, resulting in a network of streets lined with impressive Italianate terraced houses. Today, these are inhabited by wealthy Londoners and foreign nationals from every country.

London is one of the world's most cosmopolitan cities and nowhere is this more manifest than in South Ken. Several embassies are located here and many foreign diplomats live in the area. It has French, German and Islamic institutes, a French Lycée, dozens of language schools and hundreds of foreign restaurants, cafés and delicatessens.

REFLECTIONS

'It seems as if only magic could have gathered this mass of wealth from all the ends of the earth - as if none but supernatural hands could have arranged it thus, with such a blaze and contrast of colours.' – Charlotte Brontë on visiting the Great Exhibition in Hyde Park (1851)

. . . Introduction

Knightsbridge, the exclusive shopping street, boasts Britain's grandest department store, **Harrods** (page 116).

Chelsea has an even older pedigree than South Ken. It

became fashionable in the early 16th century when statesmen like Sir Thomas More lived here. During the latter half of the last century, Chelsea was a haven for artists, writers and intellectuals, including Thomas Carlyle and Oscar Wilde. The area's artistic character has mutated over time, with 1960s flower-power people and, later, the mods and punks of the 1970s claiming a special affinity with the **King's Road**.

Royal College of Organists

INSIDER'S TIP

Ignore signs at South Kensington tube station for the underpass to the museums – the route above ground is more interesting and almost as quick.

This famous road is so-named because, until the 18th century, it was a private royal highway running down to the palaces at Hampton Court and Kew. Today, the King's Road stretches for more than a mile through the heart of Chelsea. Since the 1960s, it has been one of London's trendiest shopping streets. Wacky fashion designer Vivienne Westwood has a shop at No. 430. There are also hundreds of cafés, bars, fine antiques shops and clothes stores. On Saturday, the 'beautiful people' arrive to parade up and down the street in their latest outfits.

The oldest part of Chelsea is by the river, close to Battersea Bridge. To the left of the bridge is **Chelsea Old Church**, the south chapel of which was built in

1528 for Sir Thomas More's own use. The church contains a monument to More and, outside, there is a colourful statue of him in his Lord Chancellor's robes.

Royal Albert Hall

The road running alongside the river is the famous **Cheyne Walk**, which has been one of the city's most fashionable addresses since the 18th century. George Eliot, Henry James and Dante Gabriel Rossetti are among the famous writers and artists who have lived here.

ADDRESS

Cromwell Road
☎ 020-7942-2000
www.vam.ac.uk

GETTING THERE

South Kensington
tube station

 # Victoria & Albert Museum . . .

This vast museum is a treasure trove of art drawn from the world's great cultures. Thousands of exquisite, decorative objects are displayed in an imposing Victorian building.

Founded in 1852, the V&A (as it is usually known) houses priceless collections of sculpture, jewellery, glass, silver, furniture, ironwork, ceramics, photographs and costumes. The idea for the museum originated after the Great Exhibition of 1851, when Prince Albert declared that there should be a permanent collection of the best commercial art, crafts, designs and industrial products in the world.

It began life as part of the Museum of Manufactures alongside what is now the Science Museum (page 114). When the two factions split, the V&A was then known as the Museum of Ornamental Art. The present building was inaugurated by Queen Victoria in 1899, a ceremony which was to be one of her last public appearances.

If you only have a couple of hours, the best way to see the V&A is simply to browse through a few galleries, dwelling on objects that appeal. There is also a varied programme of temporary exhibitions and exciting events.

Victoria & Albert Museum

Don't miss the two cast rooms, which include an astonishing actual-size replica of **Trajan's Column**, which was so tall it had to be cut in two. Ironically, this copy contains more detail than the original in Rome, which has been eroded by 20th-century pollution. Michelangelo's *David* is also reproduced here.

Look out, too, for **Tippoo's Tiger**, an Indian sultan's 18th- century life-size wooden model of a tiger mauling a British soldier – complete with wind-up sound effects of roars and screams. Other highlights include the **Gloucester Candlestick**, **Ardabil Carpet**, **Eltenburg Reliquary** and **Chinese Jade Geese Box**. The **Great Bed of Ware**, which dates from 1590 and has been referred to in works by Shakespeare and Jonson, shouldn't be missed.

The V&A also boasts the largest collection of Italian

HOURS

Mon-Sun: 10am-5.45pm
(Wed Late View: 6.30pm-
9.30pm)

. . . Victoria & Albert Museum

Renaissance sculpture outside Italy, a priceless selection of paintings and drawings by **John Constable**, the superb **Dress Gallery**, covering over four hundred years of fashion, and the **Canon Photography Gallery**. The museum was the first to hold a photography exhibition, as early as 1858.

The Cast Room

The spectacular glass collection, comprising 7,000 objects dating from 2,000 BC to the present day, has recently been re-displayed in the high-tech **Glass Gallery** after an absence of fifty years.

Other redesigned galleries include the T.T. Tsui **Gallery of Chinese Art**, with its exotic jade and rhino horn carvings, and the Toshiba **Gallery of Japanese Art**, with its elaborate Samurai armour.

The **Silver Galleries** and the **Raphael Gallery** were re-opened at the end of 1996 after major refurbishment. The latter displays the Raphael Cartoons, huge designs for tapestries intended for the Sistine Chapel.

The second phase of the re-display of the Silver Galleries opened in February 2000. **Silver 1800-2000** showcases spectacular objects from the National Collection of Silver, celebrating two centuries of experimentation and inventiveness in this precious metal.

Other improvements are still ongoing. The **British Galleries** project will tell the story of British design from 1500 to 1900, and is scheduled to open in 2001.

Galleries at the V & A

The innovative **Spiral** extension, which will house temporary exhibitions, will be completed in 2005. The unusual design, by Daniel Libeskind and Cecil Balmond, has been criticised by some for its space-age incongruity, but is nevertheless a most dramatic improvement to the facade.

PRICES

Adult £5
Child (under 18) free
Senior free
Student free

DISCOUNT

20% off with *for less* card (not valid for Wed Late View, special exhibitions or in conjunction with any other offer)

INSIDER'S TIP

For major exhibitions book in advance.
Information:
☎ 0870-442-0809

ADDRESS

Exhibition Road
☎ 020-7942-4000

GETTING THERE

South Kensington tube

HOURS

Mon-Sun: 10am-6pm

PRICES

Adult £8.50
Child (under 16) free
Senior free
Student £5.50
Additional charges apply
to IMAX cinema and
secondary charged
exhibitions.

DISCOUNT

20% off with voucher on
page 277

for less Science Museum

Mankind's greatest inventions, including dozens of planes, trains and automobiles, as well as imaginative demonstrations of scientific discoveries and principles, are on display at the Science Museum.

Making science fun is the emphasis throughout and, of all London's museums, the Science Museum has made the greatest effort to meet the hands-on demands of today's visitors. The museum's seven floors contain more than 10,000 exhibits, so – unless you're planning to spend all day here – it is best to head for a few highlights.

Making the Modern World is a stunning new gallery on the ground floor. It charts the history of science and technology from 1750 to the modern day using iconic objects such as Stephenson's Rocket and the real Apollo 10 command module.

More than 20 aircraft are on display in the third floor **Flight Gallery**. These include a copy of the Wright brothers' 1903 *Flyer*, Amy Johnson's *Gipsy Moth* and a group of fighter planes from the two world wars. Next

The new Wellcome Wing at the Science Museum

door is the **Flight Lab**, with hands-on demonstrations of flight principles, including a hot-air balloon and a pedal plane. There is an admission charge for the popular flight simulator.

The Basement is entirely dedicated to children. The newly refurbished **Launch Pad** is a superb attraction for young children with dozens of giant toys which demonstrate scientific principles. For younger children **The Garden** and **Things** are perfect –let your kids learn through play as they splash around in the water area or move the giant mechanical head. For the even younger, **Pattern Pod** (on the ground floor) is the place to be, designed for children 3 months and upwards it allows the child and adult to learn together. All areas are staffed by the friendly green-shirted ' explainers' who are on hand to help and demonstrate.

Newly opened in July 2000, the **Wellcome Wing** is a breathtaking theatre of contemporary science. It houses 6 cutting-edge exhibitions, a 450 seat 3D IMAX cinema and simulator. For the first time, visitors will be able to discover for themselves what is happening in the world of science and join the debate on the key ideas and issues of the day.

Natural History Museum

What was once a lifeless collection of specimens in glass cases has recently been transformed with the help of exciting virtual reality displays. The museum occupies a fine neo-Gothic building, with a glorious 675-foot (200-metre) pink and gold terracotta façade. It is not just a major attraction, but also an important research institution, with a staff of 800 maintaining and studying the 68 million objects in its collection.

Natural History Museum

The museum is divided into two main sections: the **Life Galleries** and the spectacular new £12 million **Earth Galleries.** The Life section starts with a hall dominated by an 85 foot plaster cast of a **Diplodocus** skeleton. Around it are displayed some of the wonders of the natural world, including a model of a sabre-tooth tiger.

The new **Dinosaur Gallery** features three robotic life-size Deinonychi ripping apart a Tenontosaurus. There are also 14 complete dinosaur skeletons. The **Ecology Gallery** has a reconstructed patch of rain forest in a rather politically correct exhibition on green issues.

An unparalleled collection of stuffed birds and animals, some dating back to the 18th century, can be found in the **Bird Gallery**. The museum's most famous exhibit is the full-size model of a blue whale, stretching the length of the **Whale Hall**.

The Earth Galleries, the first of which opened in 1996, are still being completed. They start with an audiovisual **Story of the Earth**, which includes simulated erupting volcanoes. The **gemstones** collection contains a dazzling display of Siberian diamonds, indigo-blue lapis lazuli from Afghanistan and many more precious stones.

One of the most visually-stunning galleries is **The Power Within**, which includes a reconstruction of Japan's Kobe earthquake, complete with moving floors and shaking walls. In another gallery, one of the world's highest escalators carries you through a massive revolving metal globe 35 feet (10 metres) in diameter.

ADDRESS

Cromwell Road
☎ 020-7938-9123

GETTING THERE

South Kensington
tube station

HOURS

Mon-Sat: 10am-5.50pm
Sun: 11am-5.50pm

PRICES

Adult £7.50
Child (under 17) £3
Senior £4.50
Student £4.50
Family £16
Free Mon-Fri: after
4.30pm, Sat-Sun:
after 5pm

DON'T MISS

Earth Galleries, Dinosaur
Gallery, Blue Whale, slice
of Giant Sequoia.

The Earth Galleries

ADDRESS

Knightsbridge
☎ 020-7730-1234

GETTING THERE

Knightsbridge
tube station

HOURS

Mon-Tue and Sat:
10am-6pm
Wed-Fri: 10am-7pm

Harrods

The green and gold doormat at the entrance to the world's most famous department store bears the slogan "Enter a Different World".

Harrods is neither the world's biggest nor the oldest department store, but it is without doubt the classiest, and thousands enter its doors every day just to browse. There are 300 departments on seven floors, selling everything from pets to polo mallets.

Harrods at night

The store's history dates back to 1849, when a wholesale tea merchant, Henry Charles Harrod, took over a small grocer's shop in what was then the village of Knightsbridge. His son, Charles Digby Harrod, took control in 1861 and within 20 years had branched out into perfumes, stationery and patented medicines, employing 100 assistants.

In December 1883, the store was destroyed by fire, but Harrod still managed to dispatch all his Christmas orders. Customers were so impressed that, when rebuilding work finished a year later, turnover doubled.

The huge **Food Halls** on the ground floor are a must for any visitor. The lavish displays of exotic foods include 350 cheeses and 151 varieties of tea. Other memorable sections include the **Egyptian Hall**, the elegant **Georgian Restaurant** and the **Fine Jewellery Room**.

Harrods' Food Halls

Unfortunately, Harrods' prestige made it an attractive target for IRA bombers, who struck twice at the store, in 1983 and 1993. Though five people were killed in the first bomb, Harrods continued undaunted and in 1985 was bought by the Al Fayed brothers for £615 million.

Throughout the year, the store's façade is beautifully illuminated at night by 12,500 light bulbs. Sales are held in January and July, the first days of which attract upwards of 300,000 people.

INSIDER'S TIP

A dress code has been introduced banning shorts, vest T-shirts and backpacks.

Other Attractions . . .

The **Royal Albert Hall**, overlooking Kensington
Gardens, is the grandest concert hall in London.
Modelled on Roman amphitheatres, the round building
was originally to be called the Hall of Arts and
Science, but Queen Victoria changed the name to the
Royal Albert Hall in memory of her husband. The high
frieze around the top of the red-brick building is the
work of various artists and depicts 'The Triumph of the
Arts and Sciences'.

Royal Albert Hall

The hall's former notorious echo was discovered during
prayers at the opening ceremony in 1871, when the
'Amen' reverberated around the
building. The acoustics improved
after saucer-like shapes were
suspended from the ceiling in 1968.
The popular 'Proms' series of
classical concerts (page 202) take
place at the hall from July to
September.

Refurbishment to improve facilities
for both performers and visitors are
underway at the time of writing, and
are due to be finished in 2003. *(Kensington Gore, ☎ 020-
589-3203.)*

Royal Albert Hall

Opposite the Royal Albert Hall is the 180-foot (54-
metre) **Albert Memorial**. Queen Victoria took a close
interest in Sir George Gilbert Scott's design for this
national memorial to Prince Albert. The Gothic canopy
is inlaid with polished stone, enamels and mosaics. The
base has 169 life-size figures carved in white marble,
and seven tiers of statuary rise above the base. The
memorial's iron frame had rusted badly by the time it
was placed under wraps in 1990 for a decade-long
restoration programme.

Royal College of Organists

The most bizarrely decorated building in the area is
the **Royal College of Organists**. The ornate cream and
maroon plasterwork is capped by a frieze depicting
youths and maidens playing musical instruments.
(Behind the Royal Albert Hall.)

The neo-Gothic **Royal College of Music** building
contains a collection of 600 musical instruments,
some dating from the 15th century. Instruments
played by George Handel, Franz Haydn and other great
composers are on display. *(Prince Consort Road, ☎ 020-
589-3643. Wed only: 2pm-4.30pm. Adult £1.20, child £1,
senior £1, student £1.)*

Royal College of Music

The 280-foot (84-metre) **Queen's Tower**, on Imperial
College Road, is all that remains of the huge Imperial

. . . Other Attractions . . .

Institute built in the 1880s. The rest of it has been demolished to make way for the office blocks of Imperial College.

Queen's Tower

South Kensington has hundreds of Italianate terraces and mansions with colonnaded entrances and uniformly whitewashed façades. The finest are to be found in Onslow Square and along Queen's Gate.

Brompton Oratory

Queen Victoria is one of the historical figures you can hear talking at the **National Sound Archive**. Order what you want to hear in advance. *(29 Exhibition Road, ☎ 020-7412-7418. Mon: 10am-6pm. Tue-Wed: 9.30am-8pm. Thu: 9.30am-6pm. Fri-Sat: 9.30am-5pm. Admission is free.)*

The Italian baroque **Brompton Oratory**, next to the V&A on Brompton Road, is London's grandest Catholic church. It was built in 1880-1884 and is based on the church of Chiesa Nuova in Rome. The main features of interest are the striking, white stone façade, the magnificent Italian altar-piece and the stunning 200-foot (60-metre) high dome. The Oratory, famous for its acoustics, is a renowned concert venue. *(Thurloe Place, Brompton Road, ☎ 020 7808-0900. Mon-Sun: 7am-8pm)*

Brompton Oratory

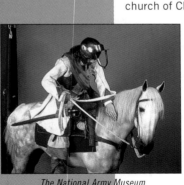

The National Army Museum

Chelsea Physic Garden, overlooking the Thames on Chelsea Embankment, contains a collection of rare trees, herbs and plants. This small but fascinating garden was founded by the Apothecaries' Company in 1676. It boasts the world's first rock garden and a statue of Sir Hans Sloane, the 18th-century physician who bequeathed his antiquities to found the British Museum. *(66 Royal Hospital Road, Swan Walk, ☎ 020-7352-5646. Apr-Oct: Wed: 12noon-5pm. Sun: 2pm-6pm. Admission £4, child £2, senior £2, student £2.)*

Chelsea Physic Garden

A short walk from the garden, along Royal Hospital Road, is the **National Army Museum**. It is mainly of interest to the military-minded. The skeleton of Marengo, Napoleon's charger, and a 420-square-foot model of the Battle of Waterloo with 70,000 model

. . . Other Attractions

oldiers, are two of the most popular exhibits. A new
ermanent exhibition, *The Rise of the Redcoat*,
ells the story of the British Army from
gincourt to the American Revolution. *(Royal
ospital Road, ☎ 020-7730-0717. Mon-Sun: 10am-
.30pm. Admission is free.)*

he **Commonwealth Institute** was founded in the
960s as a celebration of the various cultures
hat make up the British Commonwealth. It stages
emporary exhibitions devoted to the countries.
*Kensington High Street, ☎ 020-7603-4535. Tue-Sun:
0am-5pm. Mon: closed. Admission free.)*

Commonwealth Institute

short distance from the Galleries, tucked
way on Holland Park Road, is **Leighton House**, home
f one of Queen Victoria's favourite artists, Frederic
eighton. There are paintings by Leighton and his
ontemporaries, including works by all the leading Pre-
aphaelites. Evening concerts are held in Leighton's
ast studio. *(Holland Park Road, ☎ 020-7602-3316. Wed-
lon: 11am-5.30pm (last admission 5pm). Tue: closed.
dmission is free).*

eighton House was once part of a Victorian artists'
olony around Holland Park. Holman Hunt, who
ainted the *Light of the World* which hangs in St.
aul's Cathedral (page 134-135), lived at No.18
lelbury Road, while sculptor George Frederick Watts,
hose equestrian figure *Physical Energy* stands in
ensington Gardens, lived at No.6.

National Army Museum

lore Victorian art and decoration is on display at
**inley Sambourne
louse**. The house
stensibly celebrates
e work of
ambourne, the
amous 19th-century
unch magazine
artoonist, but is in
ct a superbly
reserved example of
te Victorian taste,
omplete with William
lorris wallpaper. *(18
tafford Terrace, ☎ 020-
742-3438. Mar-Oct:
led: 10am-4pm. Sun:
pen for guided tours
nly at 2.15pm, 3.15pm
nd 4.15pm. Adult £3,
hild (under 16) £1.50, senior £2.50, student £3.)*

Leighton House

Commonwealth Institute

Open Spaces

There is a hidden green space behind Brompton Oratory surrounded by pretty pastel-painted cottages. It is small, but ideal for picnics as the trees offer some shade.

Holland Park

For longer walks, **Hyde Park** (page 192) and **Kensington Gardens** (page 194) can easily be reached from most parts of South Kensington and Chelsea. These two linked parks combine to make central London's largest green expanse, stretching from the West End to Kensington Palace. Dozens of paths criss-cross the parks through open and wooded areas, making it ideal for either walking or playing ball games. On fine days, you will find thousands of Londoners relaxing in the sunshine.

Holland Park, which contains central London's largest area of woodland, lies at the western end of Kensington High Street. The remains of Holland House, a 17th-century stately home, stand in the centre of the park. Among the formal areas are the Kyoto Japanese Garden and the Dutch Garden. The latter contains a statue by the English sculptor Eric Gill. In summer, open-air plays and concerts are held in the Court Theatre. There is an inexpensive café at the top of the main field, with tables set under the trees.

Ranelagh Gardens

The largest open space in Chelsea is **Ranelagh Gardens**, where the famous Chelsea Flower Show is held in the third week of May. The gardens alongside the River Thames afford excellent views of Sir Christopher Wren's **Royal Hospital**, completed in 1686 and now known as the Chelsea Hospital. It was founded by Charles II as a home for veteran soldiers and it is still used for this purpose. The 'Chelsea Pensioners', as the residents are known, are easy to identify by their distinctive winter blue and summer scarlet uniforms.

Holland Park

Just across the river, reached by either Chelsea Bridge or Albert Bridge, is **Battersea Park**. The **London Peace Pagoda**, built in 1985 beside the river, is the park's distinctive landmark. A children's zoo, a deer park and a boating lake are among the other amenities.

Eating and Drinking

South Kensington and Chelsea both have a huge range of international restaurants, partly because of the cultural diversity of many of their residents, and many interesting pubs for a more traditionally British experience. The several embassies and their foreign diplomats located in the area demand a top-class selection of eateries.

The main thoroughfares, including Old Brompton Road, Fulham Road, King's Road and Kensington High Street, all have dozens of good places to eat and drink.

In Knightsbridge, **Walton Street** has a number of classy restaurants, including **Turner's** *(87-89 Walton Street)* and **San Martino** *(103 Walton Street)*. Harvey Nichol's expensive restaurant, **The Fifth Floor** *(Knightsbridge, ☎ 020-7235-5250)*, is a trendy place to be seen, and the relatively new **Isola** *(145 Knightsbridge, ☎ 020-7838-1044)* offers fine Italian fare.

Walton Street

Brompton Cross, where the Fulham and Brompton Roads meet, has several trendy cafés. **Joe's Café** *(126 Draycott Avenue, ☎ 020-7225-2217)* attracts the 'fashion crowd'. For Japanese food with a modern twist, try the conveyor-belt *sushi* at **Tsu** *(118 Draycott Avenue, ☎ 020-758-5522)*.

One of the most glamorous of the South Kensington restaurants is one of Sir Terence Conran's masterpieces, **Bibendum** *(81 Fulham Road, ☎ 020-7581-5817)*. The setting is half the attraction, as the restaurant and affiliated Oyster Bar

The Fifth Floor

Punks on the King's Road

are located in the 1911 Art Nouveau **Michelin House**.

Within a stone's throw of South Kensington tube station is an eclectic mix of venues. Try **Cactus Blue** *(86 Fulham Road, ☎ 020-7823-7858)* for Californian and Mexican specialities or the authentically Polish **Wodka** (page 126).

Vegetarians will be delighted with **Veg** *(8 Egerton Garden Mews, ☎ 020-7584-7007)*, a Chinese restaurant which offers all the popular favourites meat-free. You can choose anything from crispy "duck" to chilli "beef"

Bibendum

and keep a clear conscience – the recipes use tofu and soya for delicious, authentic tastes.

Chelsea's King's Road swarms with pubs, cafés and restaurants and is good for any budget. The **Chelsea Kitchen** (No. 98, ☎ 020-7589-1330) offers cut-price, wholesome food for under £5. **Henry J. Bean's** (No. 195, ☎ 020-7352-9255) is a bar and restaurant specialising in American favourites.

At the other end of the scale, there's another taste of Terence Conran luxury, **Bluebird** (No. 350, ☎ 020-7559-1000).

The **Phene Arms**, slightly off the beaten track at 9 Phene Street (☎ 020-7352-3294), is a Chelsea pub-goers favourite. There's also an attractive terrace for summer drinking.

Cactus Blue

HOURS

Mon-Sat: 12noon-11.30pm
Sun: 12noon-11pm

Nachos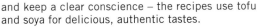

Mexican

212 Fulham Road
☎ **020-7351-7561**

Average meal: £15-20
for less discount: 25%
VS/MC

Nachos offers a variety of Mexican dishes in vibrant surroundings. The restaurant is lively and relaxed, with great music. The discount is also available at the branch at 147 Notting Hill Gate.

Made in Italy

Italian

249 King's Road
☎ **020-7352-1880**

Average meal: £15-20
for less discount: 25%
VS/MC

HOURS

Mon-Fri: 12noon-3pm, 6pm-11.30pm
Sat: 1pm-11.30pm
Sun: 1pm-10.30pm

Good-value Italian food is offered at this popular restaurant, where the dining areas, on three levels, have a rustic Italian charm. It is best known for its large reasonably priced pizzas.

for less South West 7

Modern British

**Gloucester Hotel,
Courtfield Road**
☎ 020-7411-4212

Average meal: £15-20
for less discount: 25%
AM/VS/MC/DC

HOURS

Mon-Sat: 5.30pm-10pm
Sun: closed

This sophisticated restaurant serves contemporary British food in a spacious and relaxed atmosphere. Try the grilled sea bream with leek compote and saffron risotto.

for less Borshtch 'n' Tears

Russian

46 Beauchamp Place
☎ 020-7589-5003

Average meal: £10-15
for less discount: 25%
AM

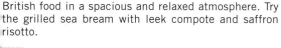

HOURS

Mon-Sun: 6pm-1am

Borshtch 'n' Tears has been offering fine Russian food since 1965. The portions are generous and the atmosphere is always lively. Every evening the informal ambience is enhanced by live Russian music.

for less Memories of India

Indian/Tandoori

18 Gloucester Road
☎ 020-7581-3734

Average meal: £10-15
for less discount: 25%
AM/VS/MC

HOURS

Mon-Sun: 12noon-11pm

This stylish Indian restaurant is close to the Royal Albert Hall. The menu reflects the various tastes of India. Try the house specialities, chicken *tikka massala* and lamb *passanda*.

Khan's of Kensington

Indian

3 Harrington Road
☎ 020-7581-2900

Average meal: £10-15
for less discount: 25%
AM/VS/MC/DC

Mon-Sat: 12noon-2.30pm,
5.30pm-11.30pm
Sun: 1pm-11pm

Khan's is the perfect place to enjoy a relaxed lunch. House specialities include *murgh makhni* and *Karachi gosth*. The wine bar is a good place to meet friends for a drink.

Spago 2

Italian

45 Kensington High Street
☎ 020-7937-6471

Average meal: £5-10
for less discount: 25%
VS/MC

HOURS

Mon-Sun:
12noon-12midnight

Spago 2 is a great place to take a break from shopping. You could pop in for a cup of coffee or settle down for a proper meal. It specializes in pizza and pasta dishes. Try the spaghetti *vongole veraci*.

Bella Pasta

Italian

60 Old Brompton Road
☎ 020-7584-4028

Average meal: £5-10
for less discount: 25%
(present voucher on page 285)
AM/VS/MC

HOURS

Sun-Thu:
10.30am-11.30pm
Fri-Sat:
10.30am-12midnight

Bella Pasta serves unpretentious Italian food. It is best known for its home-made pizza and pasta dishes. The discount also applies at Bella Pasta restaurants located at 155 Earls Court Road and 313 Fulham Road.

Rotisserie Jules

French

338 King's Road
☎ 020-7351-0041

Average meal: £5-10
for less discount: 25%
AM/VS/MC

Open long hours, Rotisserie Jules is popular with visitors and residents alike. The menu offers a good range of exciting chicken dishes. It is ideal either for an afternoon snack or a reasonably priced meal.

68-86 Bar & Restaurant

Modern British

Vanderbilt Hotel
86 Cromwell Road
☎ 020-7666-1891

Average meal: £10-15
for less discount: 25%
AM/VS/MC/DC

Serving modern British cuisine with an Australian twist, this restaurant has a modern classical feel - with wooden floors, unusual art objects, and a striking cracked glass bar as the central feature.

Café Lazeez

Indian

93-95 Old Brompton Road
☎ 020-7581-9993

Average meal: £10-15
for less discount: 25%
AM/VS/MC/DC

Winner of several awards, including "Best Indian Restaurant", Café Lazeez is regarded as one of the top Indian restaurants in Europe. There are three dining environments: *al fresco*, café/bar and formal.

HOURS

Tue-Fri: 5pm-11.30pm
Sat: 12noon-11.30pm
Sun: 12noon-10.30pm
Mon: closed

HOURS

Mon-Sat: 12.30pm-2.30pm, 5.30pm-10pm
Sun: 12.30pm-2.30pm, 6.30pm-10pm

HOURS

Mon-Sat: 11am-1am
Sun: 11am-10.30pm

HOURS

Mon-Fri: 12.30pm-
2.30pm, 7pm-11pm
Sat: 7pm-11pm
Sun: 7pm-10.30pm

Wodka

Polish

12 St. Alban's Grove
☎ 020-7937-6513

Average meal: £15-20
for less discount: 25%
AM/VS/MC/DC

Wodka is the best-known Polish restaurant in London.
The décor is modern and the food, which offers great
variety, is classic Polish cuisine. To finish, try one of the
frozen vodkas.

Trattoo

Italian

2 Abingdon Road
☎ 020-7937-4448

Average meal: £10-15
for less discount: 25%
AM/VS/MC

HOURS

Mon-Sat: 12noon-3pm,
6pm-11pm
Sun: 6.30pm-10.30pm

Trattoo is best known for its romantic garden setting and
delicious food. It is a perfect place to have lunch or
dinner on warm summer days. A speciality is home-made
gnocchi verdi pasta and seafood salad.

Bugis Street Brasserie

Asian

Gloucester Hotel
Ashburn Place
☎ 020-7411-4234

Average meal: £10-15
for less discount: 25%
AM/VS/MC

HOURS

Mon-Sun: 12noon-
10.30pm

Bugis Street Brasserie serves inexpensive multicultural
dishes from Asia. The décor is contemporary and the
atmosphere lively. Try the chef's special seafood *ho fun*
or the *laksa*.

Shopping

Harrods (page 116) is a must for tourists and is often as high on the list of things to see as any of the major attractions in the city. The presence of this, the most famous department store in the world, has made **Knightsbridge** one of London's most exclusive shopping areas, especially for high fashion.

The other major department store in Knightsbridge, **Harvey Nichols** *(Knightsbridge, ☎ 020-7235-5000)*, is now largely devoted to expensive women's clothes, although it also has stylish food halls with a range of exotic delicacies. It can also boast the finest window displays in the whole of London, and a superb restaurant on the fifth floor (page 121).

Harvey Nichols

There are several expensive designer fashion shops on Sloane Street, Walton Street and Beauchamp (pronounced 'beecham') Place, which are all nearby. They include **Armani** at 37 Sloane Street *(☎ 020-7235-6232)*, **Dior** at number 31 *(☎ 020-7235-1357)* and **Dolce and Gabbana** at number 175 *(☎ 020-7659-9000)*.

Liveried doormen at Harrod's

Caroline Charles' shop is at 56 Beauchamp Place *(☎ 020-7589-5850)*.

Brompton Cross, at the eastern end of the Fulham Road, has several 'design' shops, the most famous of which is the **Conran Shop** *(81 Fulham Road, ☎ 020-7589-7401)*. It occupies the tiled Michelin House, an exuberant example of early 20th-century architecture which was designed to promote the French tyre manufacturer.

Conran Shop

The Conran Shop specializes in classic designer furniture, such as Kandinsky chrome and hide chairs and Travieso steel bedframes.

King's Road has long been synonymous with trendy, way-out fashion. **Vivienne Westwood**'s eclectic garments can still be found at no. 430 *(☎ 020-7352-6551)*, and newer arrivals include **Joanna's Tent** *(no. 289b, ☎ 020-7352-1151)*. For vintage and second-hand gear, visit **Steinberg and Tolkein**, a retro fashion-lover's paradise.

King's Road is also good for furniture and housewares. **Habitat** *(no. 208, ☎ 020-73511211)* and **Heals** *(no. 234, ☎ 020-7349-8411)* are well-known names for contemporary items, and department store **Peter**

Kensington High Street

Jones (*Sloane Square, ☎ 020-7730-3434*) has a faithful following.

Kensington High Street (known locally as 'High Street Ken') is a smaller, and more up-market, version of Oxford Street, with larger stores at the eastern end and specialist shops further west.

Barkers of Kensington (*63 High South Kensington Street, ☎ 020-7937-5432*), close to High Street Kensington tube station, is an art deco-style department store, recommended for its men's fashion. You can buy a pair of Church's brogues, Calvin Klein jeans or a Pour Homme shirt.

Branching off the High Street, leading up to Notting Hill Gate, is **Kensington Church Street**, where you will find many up-market antique shops.

Kensington High Street

Gallops *for less*

Men's Clothing

16 Old Brompton Road
☎ 020-7589-1734

for less discount: 20%
AM/VS/MC

HOURS

Mon-Sat: 8.30am-6.30pm
Sun: closed

Gallops has been selling luggage to Londoners since the turn of the century. It carries a wide selection of travel and leather goods, and also operates a 24-hour repair service if your luggage has been damaged.

Createx *for less*

Children's Clothing

25-27 Harrington Road
☎ 020-7589-8306

for less discount: 20%
AM/VS/MC/DC

HOURS

Mon-Fri: 10am-6pm
Sat: 10am-6pm
Sun: closed

Createx sells high quality, stylish French and Italian designer children's clothes. It provides a "top-to-toe" service that includes accessories such as hats, with each item complementing the outfit.

Paul and Shark

Men's Clothing

24 Brompton Arcade
☎ 020-7581-0846

for less discount: 20%
AM/VS/MC/DC

HOURS

Mon-Sat: 10am-6.30pm
Sun: closed

Paul and Shark sells classic Italian designed clothes. A complete range of men's clothes is available. All items are made from natural materials such as cotton, wool, cashmere or silk.

 Cashmere Stop

Cashmere & Silk Clothing

4a Sloane Street
☎ 020-7259-6055

for less discount: 20%
AM/VS/MC/DC

HOURS

Mon-Sat: 10am-6.30pm
Sun: 11am-5.30pm

In this classic shop, all goods are either cashmere (pure or mix) or silk. An extensive collection of top brand sweaters is stocked. Cardigans, jackets, overcoats, capes and accessories are also available.

Hari's

Hair & Beauty

305 Brompton Road
☎ 020-7581-5212

for less discount: 20%
AM/VS/MC

HOURS

Mon-Sat: 10am-6.30pm
Sun: closed

On the lower floors is Hari's hairdressing salon, while the top two floors offer a comprehensive beauty facility. The service is friendly and attentive, with all customers being offered tea or coffee.

HOURS

Mon-Fri: 10am-4pm
Sat-Sun: closed

Make-up Centre

Make-up

26 Bute Street
☎ 020-7381-0213

for less discount: 20%
AM/VS/MC/DC

This shop is an Aladdin's cave of professional make-up brands. It is ideal for ladies who want to buy the cosmetics used by the experts. You can even pay for a make-up lesson from a make-up artist.

Leather Classics

Leather Garments

113 King's Road
☎ 020-7352-2480

for less discount: 20%
AM/VS/MC/DC

HOURS

Mon-Sat: 10am-7pm
Sun: 12noon-6pm

This fashionable King's Road store sells a wide range of stylish leather jackets. Motorcycle racing jackets and a wide range of leather clothing are stocked. Among the brands available are Avirex and Red Skins.

Cashmere Gallery

Woollen & Cashmere Clothing

25 Brompton Road
☎ 020-7838-0048

for less discount: 20%
AM/VS/MC/DC

HOURS

Mon-Sat: 9am-6.30pm
Sun: 10am-4pm

Cashmere Gallery specializes in wool, cotton and cashmere products. All of the top brands are stocked in a range of colours and sizes. It also sells men's and women's clothing accessories.

Introduction . . .

The compact area known as **'the City'**, spelled with a capital 'C', is not to be confused with the wider city of London.

The Barbican Centre

The City is Europe's financial centre, where the world's leading banks and financial services companies are located. Also known as the 'Square Mile' (for that is the area it covers) the City is a rabbit warren of narrow streets and tall office blocks.

Paradoxically, this is at once the most ancient and most modern part of London. Its boundaries are still roughly equivalent to those of the old Roman walled city, but its skyline is now dominated by high-rise buildings, many built during the 1980s commercial property boom. The great exception, of course, is the magnificent domed **St. Paul's Cathedral** (pages 134-135).

INSIDER'S TIP

The tube journey to the City can be crowded during morning and evening rush hours. For a scenic ride to St. Paul's catch a bus on the Strand.

Visit on a weekday if you want to find restaurants, pubs and shops open, or at the weekend to avoid the crowds.

The narrow, winding, medieval street pattern remains, and there are clues to the City's long history in many of the street names, such as Bread Lane, Milk Street and Poultry. Cheapside, now full of banks and company headquarters, was once London's main shopping street.

Tower Bridge

Other than a few medieval churches and the **Tower of London** (pages 136-137), the City's oldest surviving buildings mainly date from the reconstruction that followed the **Great Fire** of 1666, which ravaged two-thirds of the area. This destroyed old St. Paul's Cathedral along with the City's medieval slums (where over 75,000 people had died the previous year in the **Great Plague**). More recently, many beautiful buildings were razed to the ground during the Second World War bombing 'Blitz' of 1940-41.

Lloyd's of London building

As a result of all the necessary building and rebuilding through the ages, the City is a confusing maze of streets and a hotchpotch of architectural styles.

Some of the City's modern office architecture is impressive, notably the space-age **Lloyd's of London**

. . . Introduction

building (page 144) and the huge **Broadgate** development (page 146) around Liverpool Street Station, with its open-air ice rink and plentiful modern sculptures.

City skyline from St. Paul's

Only 8,000 people actually live in the City. It is a ghost town in the evenings and at weekends, when offices are closed. However, more than 300,000 commuters flood into the City's offices each weekday morning.

Do not, however, expect warm greetings from City workers going about their business; as the poet T.S. Eliot put it: "A crowd flowed over London Bridge...each man fixed his eyes before his feet".

Commuters on London Bridge

The City still enjoys the semi-autonomous status conferred upon it by William the Conqueror. It is controlled by 'The Corporation of London', a select, somewhat mysterious and very powerful group. A range of feudal titles – Beadle, Alderman, Sheriff and the Lord Mayor – are conferred each year on members of the Corporation. Genuine democracy has yet to invade this anachronistic old boys' club, which draws its electors from the City's 90 **Livery Companies** (page 145). In the City, the Lord Mayor ranks above all, except the Sovereign. He (there has only ever been one woman) is invested on the second Saturday in November with a grand pageant, known as the **Lord Mayor's Show** (page 247).

REFLECTIONS

'There are not more useful members in a common-wealth than merchants. They knit mankind together in a mutual intercourse of good offices, distribute the gifts of nature, find work for the poor, add wealth to the rich, and magnificence to the great.' – Joseph Addison, writing about The Royal Exchange (1711)

While most visitors to the City come just to see St. Paul's or the Tower of London, there is a wealth of smaller churches and museums tucked away, which are well worth seeking out. **Dr. Johnson's House** (page 142) celebrates the life of one of England's greatest men of letters and has many 18th-century

Lord Mayor's Show

artefacts, including first editions of Johnson's great dictionary. Sir Christopher Wren's **St. Bride's Church** (page 141) has one of the most beautiful steeples ever built and interesting Roman mosaics in the crypt.

 ## St. Paul's Cathedral . . .

Sir Christopher Wren's masterpiece is London's greatest architectural treasure.

St. Paul's is a majestic building with the second largest cathedral dome in the world (after St. Peter's in Rome). It is venerated by the British as a place of public triumph and is where, instead of the more traditional Westminster Abbey, Prince Charles chose to marry Lady Diana Spencer in 1981.

The modern St. Paul's is the fourth cathedral dedicated to London's patron saint to be built on the site – the first was a wooden building founded by King Ethelbert in the 7th century.

Wren began planning the present cathedral only days after the Great Fire of London destroyed old St. Paul's in 1666. The only monument to survive the fire was that of **John Donne**, the poet and Dean of St. Paul's. It can still be seen in the south choir aisle.

St. Paul's Cathedral

Wren had a furious row with the Church authorities over his original plan, which they considered too "modern". The architect himself oversaw the 33 years of construction. In 1697, Parliament became frustrated with the slow progress of the project and halved Wren's £200 salary. But Wren, though approaching 70, remained in close control of the building work and was regularly hoisted 300 feet (90 metres) up into the great stone lantern that sits above the dome. It was his son, however, who laid the final stone.

Wren is buried in the crypt, where his simple tomb is easy to miss. However, immediately under the dome is the inscription: "Reader, if you seek his monument, look around you."

St. Paul's in fact has two domes: the smaller dome seen from the inside and a larger, outer shell rising 60 feet (18 metres) above it. In between the two domes is a brick cone, a clever architectural device to support the great weight of the lantern. Sir James Thornhill's frescoes on the inner dome depict scenes from the life of St. Paul.

ADDRESS

Top of Ludgate Hill
☎ 020-7236-4128

GETTING THERE

St. Paul's tube station

HOURS

Mon-Sat: 8.30am-4pm
(galleries open 9.30am)
Sun: closed to sightseers

PRICES

Adult £5
Child £2.50
Senior £4
Student £4

DISCOUNT

20% off admission prices
with *for less* card

. . . St. Paul's Cathedral

Relatively few monuments or paintings adorn St. Paul's, though Holman Hunt's copy of his own **The**

'The Light of the World' by Holman Hunt

Light of the World, one of the finest Pre-Raphaelite paintings, is in the south aisle (the original is in Keble College, Oxford).

The 530 steps to the **Golden Gallery** are gruelling, but are divided into three stages, with a viewing point at each.

The first leg, much the easiest, takes you up to the **Whispering Gallery** where the extraordinary acoustics allow you to hear words whispered into the wall at the other side of the dome, 107 feet away. This was a favourite place for lovers in the Victorian period, who would whisper secret messages to each other.

The next flight of steeper, spiralled stairs leads to the **Stone Gallery**, with grand views and benches on which to rest.

Even more magnificent is the view across London from the **Golden Gallery**, though for this pleasure you will have to climb another 160 fire-escape type steps. On the way up, don't miss the small spy window through which you can view the monochrome marble floor a dizzying drop below.

Interior of St. Paul's

You can see many famous landmarks from the viewing galleries, including the Houses of Parliament to the west and Tower Bridge to the east. On a clear day, the galleries offer views stretching across to the distant hills that surround London.

For a less energetic experience, the **Crypt** contains the tombs of some of Britain's greatest war heroes, including those of Nelson and Wellington. More recent memorials commemorate the hundreds of men who died in the Falklands and Gulf Wars. The **Treasury** at the west end of the crypt displays ancient chalices and gorgeously embroidered robes used for state occasions.

DON'T MISS

Whispering Gallery, John Donne's memorial, *The Light of the World.*

INSIDER'S TIP

St. Paul's is very popular, so try to go before 11am if you want to appreciate the peaceful holiness of the Cathedral.

ADDRESS

Tower Hill
☎ 020-7709-0765

GETTING THERE

Tower Hill tube station

HOURS

Mar-Oct:
Mon-Sat: 9am-5pm
Sun: 10am-5pm

Nov-Feb:
Sun-Mon: 10am-4pm
Tue-Sat: 9am-4pm

 # Tower of London . . .

The **Crown Jewels** might be the most famous exhibit, but every inch of this ancient palace-fortress is steeped in history.

The Tower has served many functions in its nine centuries: it was the fortress of William the Conqueror, the palace of medieval kings, the prison of Sir Thomas More, Anne Boleyn, Sir Walter Raleigh and, most recently, Rudolph Hess. It has also housed the Royal Mint,

Tower of London

making the nation's money, and is now the stronghold for the priceless Crown Jewels.

The Tower is guarded by 40 Yeoman Warders, popularly known as **Beefeaters**. They are all ex-servicemen and wear elaborate red and dark blue Tudor tunics with large, round hats.

The Beefeaters' guided tours, free with the entrance price, are superb, with just the right mix of history and humour. They tell you about the kings and queens who were murdered or executed in the Tower, but also point out where Errol Flynn was filmed holding up a three-ton portcullis in *Robin Hood*.

The Ravenmaster

The **Bloody Tower** is so named because of the many dastardly crimes committed inside, including the murders of the boy-king Edward V and his ten-year-old brother in 1483. Shakespeare famously blamed the murders on Richard of Gloucester, young Edward's protector. This theory is attractive from a theatrical perspective as the hunchbacked villain of Shakespeare's history plays benefits from his crime by becoming Richard III. However, many historians have since sought to redeem Richard's reputation.

The oldest part of the fortress is the **White Tower**, built by William the Conqueror in the 11th century. The Tower's Chapel of St. John is ringed by graceful columns which have been restored to their original appearance.

The **Instruments of Torture** gallery in the White Tower contains the execution block used for the last public

. . . Tower of London

beheading on Tower Hill, which took place in 1747. The grooves cut by the falling axe can still be seen.

Most of the **Royal Armouries'** enormous collection of weapons and suits of armour has been moved to a special museum in Leeds. However, there is still a small collection of royal armour in the Tower.

St. Thomas's Tower, built in the 13th century, has been restored to show how it would have looked during the reign of Edward I.

Imperial State Crown

Queuing at the **Jewel House**, which was refurbished in 1994, is made relatively painless as the line is filtered through three rooms. Each of the rooms has a large video screen telling the history of the Crown Jewels.

The Jewels themselves are viewed from a conveyor belt, which glides you past glass cases, inches from the crowns and sceptres.

The Queen Mother's crown contains the legendary **Koh-i-noor** diamond. Charles II's sceptre is fitted with the 530-carat **Star of Africa** – the world's largest cut diamond.

A Yeoman of the Watch

Security is so tight at the Jewel House that the gift shop feels confident enough to sell a board game in which the aim is to steal the Crown Jewels.

Traitors' Gate, which connects with the River Thames, is where prisoners would arrive by boat. Elizabeth I entered the Tower through this gate in 1554 when her sister, Queen Mary, briefly imprisoned her on suspicion of treason.

Tower Green, which is lined with benches, is an ideal place to have a picnic lunch. Look out for the huge ravens that live within the Tower and have been protected by Royal Decree since the reign of Charles II. Legend has it that, should they desert the Tower, the kingdom will fall. Just to be safe, they have their wings clipped.

Medieval actor guides

PRICES

Adult £11
Child £7.30
Senior £8.30
Student £8.30

DISCOUNT

10% off admission per person with voucher on page 277.

INSIDER'S TIP

Get there for opening time to avoid the hordes (especially in summer) and bring a snack, as there's no café in the Tower (although there is a new Prêt á Manger just outside)

DON'T MISS

Crown Jewels, Chapel of St. John, Royal Armouries, Henry VIII's codpiece.

ADDRESS

River Thames
☎ 020-7378-1928

GETTING THERE

London Bridge / Tower Hill
tube station

HOURS

Apr-Oct: Mon-Sun:
10am-6.30pm
Nov-Mar: Mon-Sun:
9.30am-6pm

 # Tower Bridge Experience . . .

One of London's most famous landmarks, Tower Bridge is a triumph of Victorian engineering. It is the only London bridge which opens to allow the passage of ships along the Thames.

Thoughtfully designed by Horace Jones and John Wolfe Barry to complement the nearby Tower of London, the building of the spectacular bridge began in 1886.

Tower Bridge

The exuberant, Gothic-style towers were described by Jones himself as 'steel skeletons clothed with stone', and since its ceremonial inauguration on 30 June 1894, the bridge has become an instantly recognisable symbol of London.

Ten men died during the eight-year construction of the bridge, the main frame of which contains 12,000 tons of steel to support the great weight of the two arms (known as bascules).

Each bascule weighs an incredible 1,000 tons. In spite of this, the lifting of the bridge only takes about 90 seconds. Before the bridge was built, pedestrians and trams relied on the Tower Subway, constructed in 1869, to cross the Thames.

Several daredevil pilots have flown through the 200-foot (60-metre) wide and 100-foot (30-metre) high gap between the towers – the first was Frank McLean in 1912. At least one later attempt proved fatal.

The engine room

In 1952, a red double-decker bus (No. 78), passing through traffic lights stuck on green, jumped a three-foot gap as the bridge was opening.

More recently, in 1986, a crane on a boat crashed into the gantry as it attempted to pass underneath. Such a mishap could be blamed on the changing tide of the Thames.

. . . Tower Bridge Experience

An historical tour retraces the origins of the bridge, from its conception through to the present day, using an animatronic worker called 'Harry' as a guide.

The high-level walkways connecting the twin towers have incredible views both up and down the Thames. For many years the walkways proved a popular spot from which suicides would launch themselves into the river.

The problem was overcome by first closing them completely in 1910 and, before reopening them many decades later, enclosing them in glass. This does not, however, detract from the spectacular views.

The unique panorama of London is the highlight of the tour, and interactive video displays introduce the sights along the Thames.

The mechanically-minded will be fascinated by the displays on the design and operation of the bridge, which culminate in the **Engine Room** containing the massive steam-driven pumps used to raise the two arms.

The operation has been run by electricity since 1976, but the old pumps are still in perfect condition.

If you are lucky, you will witness the bridge being

Tower Bridge is stunning when illuminated at night

raised to allow a ship to pass through. When the bridge first began operating, this used to happen 6,000 times a year, hence the high-level walkways allowing pedestrians to continue crossing the bridge.

Declining traffic on the Thames means the bridge is now only lifted around 500 times annually. In summer, however, it can be raised up to ten times a day.

It is sometimes lifted for purely ceremonial reasons. In 1967, it was raised to welcome Sir Francis Chichester home from his solitary journey around the world in Gypsy Moth IV. Richard Branson was similarly honoured in 1986, when he had completed his Atlantic crossing by balloon.

If you call ☎ 020-7378-7700, a recorded message will give the times when the bridge will be lifted the following week.

PRICES

Adult £6.25
Child £4.25
Senior £4.25
Student £4.25

DISCOUNT

20% off admission with *for less* card

Other Attractions . . .

The area on the western edge of the City is the centre of legal London, which includes the labyrinthine **Royal Courts of Justice** on the Strand and the beautiful **Inns of Court**, where Britain's top barristers practise.

Lincoln's Inn

Lincoln's Inn is the best-preserved of the four Inns of

Barristers at the Inns of Court

Court (the others are Gray's Inn, Middle Temple and Inner Temple). Famous alumni include Sir Thomas More and Oliver Cromwell. Some of the buildings (including the Chancery Lane Gatehouse) date from the 15th century and are best appreciated by taking a stroll around the gardens. The chapel was remodelled by Inigo Jones in 1620. *(Chancery Lane, ☎ 020-7405-1393. Mon-Fri: call for times of tours. Admission is free.)*

Sir John Soane's Museum

On the north side of Lincoln's Inn stands the exquisite **Sir John Soane's Museum**. Because it is off the beaten track, most visitors to London miss this treasure-trove of lovely, and often peculiar, works of art collected in the early 19th century by Bank of England architect Sir John Soane. The collection is housed on several floors of three linked Georgian houses, artfully redesigned by Sir John with domes, skylights and mirrors that play tricks with space and light.

Hogarth's famous morality tale, *The Rake's Progress*, hangs in a picture gallery with false walls that open to reveal yet more pictures. The vast sarcophagus of Seti I stands in a colonnaded atrium, surrounded by classical statues.

There is an excellent free lecture tour on Saturdays at 2.30pm and a special tour (£3; free to students) takes place on the first Tuesday of every month from 6pm-9pm. *(13 Lincoln's Inn Fields, ☎ 020-7405-2107. Tue-Sat: 10am-5pm. Sun-Mon: closed. Admission is free.)*

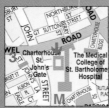

Order of St John's Museum

Just outside the City boundary is the ancient district of **Clerkenwell**, which in medieval times was a hamlet with abundant springs that supplied water to local monasteries. Remnants of two of the monasteries survive. The **Order of St. John's Museum** is housed in a 16th century gatehouse on the south side of Clerkenwell Road. *(St. John's Gate, Clerkenwell Road, ☎ 020-7253-6644. Mon-Fri: 10am-5pm. Sat: 10am-4pm. Sun:*

. . . Other Attractions . . .

closed. Guided tours Tue and Fri: 11am and 2.30pm; Sat: 2.30pm. Admission is free.)

Charterhouse, founded by the Carthusians in 1371, but rebuilt in the Tudor period, is tucked away off St. John Street. *(☎ 020-7253-3260. Apr-Aug: guided tour Wed only: 2.15pm. Adult, child, senior, student £3.)*

House of Detention

Clerkenwell became a fashionable spa in the 18th century, but a huge influx of people meant the area was a slum by the Victorian period. Despite redevelopment, some of the old street pattern and atmosphere remain, with traditional artisans like lockmakers and printers still plying their trade.

The House of Detention

for less The **House of Detention** allows visitors to experience the horrific conditions of Victorian prison life. The site, used as a prison from 1616 to 1890, has a history as deep and dark as the network of underground tunnels that lead visitors back through time.

Learn of Jack Sheppard's escape and execution, the Gordon Riots of 1780, the floating hulks which sailed prisoners to Australia and America and the sinister practises of the Victorian Age of Reform. Visitors can walk through the warden's room, the washhouse and the kitchen, and see many of the cramped, airless prison cells. *(Clerkenwell Close, ☎ 020-7253-9494. Mon-Sun: 10am-5.15pm. Adult £4, child £2.50, senior £3, student £3. 50% off admission with voucher on page 277.)*

St Bride's Church

The main thoroughfare linking the City with the West End has a series of different names: the **Strand** becomes **Fleet Street** at a point just past the Royal Courts. Fleet Street was once the headquarters of nearly all the national newspapers and its name is still used as a sobriquet for the British press. The last paper moved out several years ago, but some of the stylish buildings remain, including the *Daily Telegraph's* Art Deco edifice.

At the eastern end of Fleet Street stands **St. Bride's**, adopted by journalists and printers as their mother church. Of special interest is the graceful multi-tiered steeple, the tallest ever designed by Sir Christopher Wren, which inspired a local baker to create the first multi-layered wedding cake. The crypt contains Roman mosaics, which only

Fleet Street sign

. . . Other Attractions . . .

Dr. Johnson's House

came to light when the church was hit during the Blitz, and a small museum that catalogues Fleet Street's newspaper history. *(Fleet Street, ☎ 020-7353-1301. Mon-Fri: 8am-4.45pm. Sat: 9.30am-4.30pm. Sun services: 9.30am, 12noon, 5.30pm-7.30pm. Free admission.)*

for less Hidden in a cul-de-sac north of Fleet Street is **Dr. Johnson's House**. This is one of the best of the capital's string of writers' museums created inside the former homes of famous literary Londoners. A host of memorabilia includes first editions of Dr. Johnson's great dictionary, which was put together in the attic and first published in 1755. The house was rescued from demolition by Lord Harmsworth in 1911 and opened to the nation. Today, it is one of the City's few surviving residential houses of its age. *(Gough Square, ☎ 020-7353-3745. May-Sep: Mon-Sat: 11am-4.45pm. Sun: closed. Oct-Apr: Mon-Sat: 11am-5pm. Sun: closed. Adult £4, child £3, senior £3, student £3. 50% discount with voucher on page 277.)*

Dr Johnson's House

The **Central Criminal Court,** nicknamed **The Old Bailey** after the street on which it stands, is Britain's most famous criminal court and is where many of the highest profile cases are heard. Visitors can watch trials from the public galleries.

The dome of the huge courthouse is topped by the gold statue of Justice, holding sword and scales in outstretched arms. The notorious **Newgate Prison**, whose inmates included Daniel Defoe, Ben Jonson and Casanova, stood on this site until 1902. *(Old Bailey, ☎ 020-7248-3277. Public admitted when court is in session: Mon-Fri: 10.30am-1pm and 2pm-4.30pm. Free admission. No admission to children under 14. Strict entry regulations: no cameras, food, large bags or mobile phones.)*

Old Bailey

'Justice' on top of the Old Bailey

North of Newgate Street lie the sprawling ancient and modern buildings of **St. Bartholomew's Hospital**, London's oldest hospital. It was founded in 1123 by Henry I's court jester, who said he was acting on the orders of St. Bartholomew, which had been delivered in

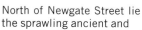

. . . Other Attractions . . .

visionary experience in Italy. The painter William Hogarth was made a governor in 1734 and two of his most famous paintings, *The Good Samaritan* and *The Pool of Bethesda*, now hang on the main staircase. *(West Smithfield, ☎ 020-7377-7000.)*

Smithfield Market

The long, low Victorian buildings of **Smithfield Market**, modernized in the early 1990s, accommodate London's main meat market. *(West Smithfield, best views are from Grand Avenue).* The legendary Bartholomew Fair was held here from 1123 until its suppression for debauchery in 1855. Several pubs in the area, including the Fox and Anchor (page 147), open at 7am to serve huge cooked breakfasts to market traders and other early risers.

Smithfield Market

The **Museum of London** traces more than 2,000 years of London's social history – from the tiny Roman town to the sprawling modern metropolis. There is a wealth of information on London, but you would need to have a strong interest in the city's history to want to spend the recommended minimum of two hours.

Roman lamp in the shape of a human foot

Each of the museum's galleries, arranged in chronological order, covers a different era. The Roman gallery has recently been revamped to reflect new discoveries, but by far the best gallery chronicles the life of the 'Imperial Capital', from the Victorian to the Edwardian periods. The Suffragettes' collection includes the chains women used to lock themselves to the railings outside the Prime Minister's house in Downing Street.

Museum of London

The 'London Now' gallery brings the museum up-to-date with artefacts relating to London's recent history – from a Ford Cortina to punk fashion. The tour of the museum ends with the magnificent gold Lord Mayor's State Coach. *(London Wall, ☎ 020-7600-3699. Mon-Sat: 10am-5.50pm. Sun: 12noon-5.50pm. Adult £5, child (under 15) free, senior £3, student £3, family £9.50. Free admission Tue-Sat after 4.30pm.)*

The Museum of London

. . . Other Attractions . . .

Royal Exchange

St. Stephen Walbrook is the Lord Mayor's parish church. Built by Sir Christopher Wren in 1672-1679, it has an ornate dome and intricately carved pulpit canopy. The central polished stone altar is by Henry Moore. *(39 Walbrook.)*

Some of the City's most splendid buildings, such as the **Mansion House** (built in 1753 as the Lord Mayor's

The Royal Exchange

residence) and the **Royal Exchange** (originally founded in 1565 as a centre for commerce, but rebuilt in 1844) are, sadly, not open to the public. The colonnaded facades of these buildings, however, are well-known City landmarks.

Mansion House

Beside the Royal Exchange is the **Bank of England**, known as Old Lady of Threadneedle Street. Established by William III in 1694 to raise money for his war against France, the Bank now regulates the banking industry and issues bank notes. The Bank's **museum**, entered from Bartholomew Lane, displays gold bars and historical bank notes. *(Bartholomew Lane, ☎ 020-7601-5545. Museum: Mon-Fri: 10am-5pm. Sat-Sun: closed. Admission free.)*

Leadenhall Market is a beautiful Victorian arcade nestling amid the office blocks of the financial district. Meat, poultry and fish have been sold here since the 14th century. In addition to an old-style fishmonger and other traditional shops, the arcade now houses pubs and restaurants popular with City workers.

Leadenhall Market

(Gracechurch Street. Mon-Fri: 10am-6pm. Sat-Sun: closed.)

Leadenhall Market

At the back of Leadenhall Market is the astonishing **Lloyd's of London** building *(Lime Street, ☎ 020-7623-7100)* – an enormous, complicated steel structure designed by modernist architect Richard Rogers (famous for creating the Pompidou Centre in Paris, another 'innards on the outside' building). It houses the world's biggest insurance market and is best seen by night, when blue fluorescent lights make it look like a spaceship.

. . . Other Attractions

The 202-ft (62-m) column north of London Bridge is known simply as **'Monument'**. Designed by Wren, it commemorates the Great Fire of London in 1666 and is said to be 202 feet west of where the fire started in Pudding Lane. You can climb the 311-step spiral staircase to the viewing platform. *(Monument Street, ☎ 020-7626-2717. Apr-Sep: Mon-Sun: 10am-5.40pm. Oct-Mar: Mon-Sat: 9am-3.30pm. Sun: closed. Adult £1.50, child 50p, senior £1.50, student £1.50.)*

Lloyd's of London

Lloyd's of London

The City's **Livery Companies** hark back to the medieval craftsmen's guilds, though modern members may have little or no connection with the trade from which they take their name. The livery companies occupy halls dotted around the City, including Fishmongers' Hall, Merchant Taylor's Hall and Apothecaries' Hall. These and others can be viewed either free of charge or for a small fee, though advance booking is usually necessary. *(Tickets available from the City of London Tourist Information Centre, ☎ 020-7332-1456.)*

Monument

Monument

On the north-eastern fringe of the City is an area known as **Spitalfields**. The area's most striking piece of architecture is **Christ Church**, with its 205-ft (62-m) spire. The finest view of Nicholas Hawksmoor's church, completed in 1729, is from the western end of Brushfield Street.

The church lay derelict for much of this century, but reopened after restoration in 1987. It hosts classical concerts and the Spitalfields Festival in June. *(Commercial Street, ☎ 020-7247-7202. Mon-Fri: 12noon-2.30pm. Sunday service: 10.30am.)*

Spitalfields

Petticoat Lane is one of London's most famous street markets, trading every Sunday for more than 200 years. The Huguenots sold petticoats here and the market still specializes in clothing. *(Centred on Middlesex Street. Sun: 9am-2pm. Mon-Sat: closed.)*

Petticoat Lane Market

Open Spaces

Lincoln's Inn Fields

Broadgate Arena

Broadgate Arena

There are no parks and few gardens in the City, where all available open spaces and benches tend to be filled by office workers taking a break.

Lincoln's Inn Fields, a 17th-century square between Kingsway and Chancery Lane, is shaded by tall plane trees. It also has tennis courts and a café frequented by lunching lawyers. At the other end of the social spectrum, homeless people tend to sleep in the bushes.

The **Broadgate** complex, around and above Liverpool Street Station, is an impressive 1980s office development with plenty of piazzas and a liberal scattering of outdoor sculpture. Among the most striking of the office blocks is Exchange House, suspended over the railway line by means of huge supporting steel arches. **Broadgate Arena** doubles as an ice-rink and a performance space.

St. Paul's Churchyard, the tiny garden at the rear of St. Paul's Cathedral, was the centre of London's book trade from 1500 until it was obliterated in the Second World War by the Blitz.

St Paul's Churchyard

North of Moorgate, off City Road, lies **Bunhill Fields**, a peaceful old cemetery shaded by great plane trees and with lots of benches. The cemetery, last used for a burial in 1854, dates from the mid-17th century. The Corporation of London created a burial ground here for use in the Great Plague. In fact, few plague victims were buried at Bunhill, and it was mainly used for burying dissenters.

Bowls in Lincoln's Inn Fields

The grim-looking spiked gate at the north-east corner was erected to deter body-snatchers. Most of the cemetery is fenced off, but you can see the monuments to John Bunyan (1628-1688), Daniel Defoe (1660-1731) and William Blake (1757-1827). In the adjoining Quaker graveyard lies George Fox (1624-1691), who founded the Society of Friends.

Eating and Drinking

There are plenty of restaurants and pubs serving City office-workers, but most close early in the evening once the commuters have gone home.

There are several good restaurants near Bank tube station and in the Broadgate complex. Many visitors, however, join busy City folk in opting for traditional pub grub.

The Old Bell

Smithfield, to the north of the City, was once renowned for the pubs that served hearty breakfasts to the blood-splattered meat porters from the meat market. **The Fox and Anchor** *(115 Charterhouse Street)* still serves English breakfast with pints of ale from 7am to 3pm, but the porters are now outnumbered by men in suits on the way to their offices. North of Smithfield Market is **Vic Naylor's** (page 148), a lively bar and restaurant which stays open late.

Ye Olde Cheshire Cheese *(15 Fleet Street)* is probably the City's most famous pub. Once patronized by Dr. Samuel Johnson and Charles Dickens, this restored old tavern has six cosy bars and three restaurants. The ground-floor bar has a faded sign above the door that reads 'Gentlemen Only', but this is not to be taken seriously.

The Fox and Anchor

The Fox and Anchor

The Old Bell *(95 Fleet Street)* was built by Christopher Wren and was initially used by the workers who were building St. Bride's church nearby. It serves a good selection of traditional food.

St. Paul's Wine Vaults *(Knightrider Street)* is handy for a £10 set lunch after visiting St. Paul's Cathedral. Built in 1665, this was the Horn Tavern mentioned by Dickens in *Pickwick Papers*. Mr Pickwick, incarcerated in Fleet Prison, asked the pub to send him two bottles of good wine.

Ye Olde Cheshire Cheese

The Lamb Tavern *(Leadenhall Market)* is a favourite place for pin-striped City gents to come at lunchtime and in the early evening, though the pub gets much quieter after 9pm. The best of the four pub floors are the cavernous smoking bar in the basement and the top bar, with its tall windows and fine views of the market's intricate cast-ironwork. Food is available on all the levels.

The Lamb Tavern

HOURS

Mon-Sun: banquet begins
7.45pm.

The Beefeater

Themed traditional English

Ivory House,
St. Katharine's Dock
☎ 020-7480-5353

Dinner/Show: £39.50
for less discount: 25%
AM/VS/MC

'Merrie England' is the theme at the Beefeater. The five-course traditional banquet is accompanied by a live show, where court jesters and minstrels whisk you back to the Middle Ages.

HOURS

Mon-Fri: 12noon-3pm,
6pm-11pm
Sat-Sun: closed

Terrazza Est

Italian

109 Fleet Street
☎ 020-7353-2680

Average meal: £10-15
for less discount: 25%
AM/VS/MC/DC

Terrazza Est is unique: every weekday evening, from 7.30pm-11pm, opera is performed in the restaurant. Located close to St. Paul's, it serves excellent Italian food.

HOURS

Mon-Sat: 12noon-
12midnight
Sun: closed

Vic Naylor's

Traditional English

38-40 St. John Street
☎ 020-7608-2181

Average meal: £15-20
for less discount: 25%
AM/VS/MC

This large, fashionable restaurant has the feel of a New York bar. The daily specials are fresh from London markets. Busiest at lunchtime, it stays open until late in the evening.

South of the River

Introduction . . .

Long neglected, the south bank of the Thames has enjoyed a remarkable renaissance in recent years. New theatres and galleries have been opened, old pubs restored and decaying dock buildings transformed into elegant shopping arcades.

The river is now lined by an attractive walkway, from which there are stunning views across to London's more salubrious north bank. The walk from Lambeth Bridge to Tower Bridge, a little over two miles, takes you past many of London's most famous landmarks. There are several museums *en route* and a couple of good riverside pubs serving lunch.

View of Westminster from the river's south bank

INSIDER'S TIP

Take the footbridge beside Embankment tube station for a fast and scenic route to the South Bank Centre.

The area between Blackfriars Bridge and Tower Bridge, known as **Southwark**, has a long and chequered history. With most forms of entertainment banned in the City in the 16th and 17th centuries, Southwark was home to dozens of theatres, bear gardens, brothels and taverns.

Shakespeare's **Globe Theatre**, now reconstructed, and the **Rose** were two of the best known theatres which attracted City dwellers across London Bridge.

The character of the area changed in the 18th and 19th centuries, with docks and warehouses built along the Thames. Some of these buildings have since been demolished to make way for offices. Others, like **Hay's Galleria** (page 164), have been imaginatively restored and put to new use.

The construction of the railways in the 19th century cut great swathes through Southwark and, to the west, Lambeth. Two of London's biggest train stations, Waterloo (from where the Channel Tunnel trains depart) and London Bridge, are located in the vicinity. Avoid the ugly road junctions

Hay's Galleria

around Waterloo Station, which are awkward to negotiate on foot, although the huge new **BFI London IMAX Cinema** (page 159) is worth a visit on a rainy day.

. . . Introduction

Londoners living north of the Thames sometimes sneer at Southwark and Lambeth. While the dreary residential area beyond the riverside has little to attract the visitor, the south bank of the Thames is packed with curiosities and cultural attractions. Stylish new riverside restaurants, like the one at the **Oxo Tower** (page 164) with its fantastic views, now attract London's 'beautiful people' across the river.

Bankside Power Station, now the Tate Modern

There are museums to suit all tastes dotted along the south bank, including the **Design Museum** (page 162) for the style-conscious, the **London Dungeon** (pages 152-153) for the bloodthirsty and **Bankside Gallery** (page 159) for watercolour enthusiasts. The former Greater London Council building, County Hall, is now home to the **London Aquarium** (pages 154-155).

South Bank Centre

The **South Bank Centre** beside Waterloo Bridge, is London's premier arts complex. Inspired by the 1951 Festival of Britain, the centre is housed in a mass of concrete, which people either love or hate. The **Royal Festival Hall**, now almost 50 years old and still one of London's top classical concert venues, was the first part of the centre to be built.

Several other leading arts institutions were later established here, including the **Royal National Theatre** (page 201), with its three stages, and the **Hayward Gallery**. The **National Film Theatre** and the **Museum of the Moving Image** (page 159) have added film to the list of art forms celebrated at the centre.

Several major developments have heralded the beginning of the 21st century and helped bring more visitors across the river. A new footbridge connects St. Paul's Cathedral with the **Tate Modern** (page 156), and the **BA London Eye** (page 157) takes passengers on "flights" to see an unrivalled view of the whole city.

REFLECTIONS

'When I whom sullen care, / Through discontent of my long fruitless stay … Walked forth to ease my pain / Along the shore of silver streaming Thames.' – *Prothalamion*, Edmund Spenser (1594)

The Hayward Gallery

ADDRESS

Tooley Street
☎ 020-7403-7221

GETTING THERE

London Bridge
tube station

HOURS

Mon-Sun: 10am-6.30pm
(until 8pm in peak season)
Last admission 5.30pm

 # London Dungeon . . .

Every grisly form of torture and death is featured in this nightmarish tour, which uses moving models and actors to recreate the goriest episodes of history.

More than 2,000 years of the grim and bloody past are revealed in the London Dungeon, made all the more blood-curdling by the knowledge that every event displayed really did happen!

The idea for the museum came from housewife Annabel Geddes. Her children, much like those today, were enthralled by all things gory and disappointed at the lack of 'blood and thunder' in the Tower of London. Mrs Geddes' idea for an exhibition devoted to the more chilling moments of history is enough to satisfy the bloodthirsty of any age.

A few people you'll meet at the Dungeon

The Dungeon's location under Victorian railway arches makes for a suitably cavernous and gloomy atmosphere. Even the trains rumbling overhead seem to add to the atmosphere.

Bloodcurdling screams echo around the halls as you pass barbaric scenes of execution, with lifelike effigies being hanged, boiled, garrotted, guillotined, crushed and even stretched on a rack.

Even the guides enter the chilling spirit of the show, dressed as historical characters

Jack the Ripper

such as plague victims and prostitutes.

In **Great Fire of London**, take a horrific trip back in time to discover the devastation of 1666 when an inferno raged for days wiping out large parts of the capital. Discover Pudding Lane, where it

Just one of the Dungeon's gruesome characters

started, before running the gauntlet of flames to escape the fire ravaged streets.

. . . London Dungeon

In another of the special shows, **Jack the Ripper**, a guide takes you on a walk through the re-created slums of smog-filled Victorian London where the notorious serial killer terrorized the population by chopping out the vital organs of prostitutes.

The gallows

The horrific events of 1888 occurred in Whitechapel, just a mile from the London Dungeon, and are all the more spine-chilling to those aware that the identity of the Ripper has never been discovered.

Other displays, which are made all the more lifelike with models, sound-effects and props, involve the seiging of a medieval town by ruthless invaders. Innocent townspeople are subjected to terrible retribution from the moment the enemy breaks through the gates.

Almost every era is covered. Witness the awful demise of Bubonic Plague sufferers, unlucky victims of the

The death sentence

most feared epidemics in history. More than 75,000 lives were lost in the most horrible manner in 1665.

Other tableaux depict the beheading of Anne Boleyn, the martyrdom of St. George and famous public hangings.

With **Judgement Day**, the London Dungeon has taken its gruesome theme one stage further by actually turning the visitor into the victim. This attraction reconstructs the grim final journey prisoners took to the Bloody Tower before execution.

PRICES

Adult £9.95
Child £6.50
Senior £6.50
Student £8.50

DISCOUNT

£2 off admission prices with *for less* card

You face a sombre judge as he dons the dreaded black cap to pronounce a sentence of death on you and your fellow prisoners. You are then herded on board a barge to travel along a specially constructed waterway through a mock-up of Traitors' Gate at the Tower of London. From there you are taken to meet your fate!

Judgement Day

The Dungeon is not recommended for very young children or those of a nervous disposition.

ADDRESS

County Hall
Riverside Building
Westminster Bridge Road
☎ 020-7967-8000

GETTING THERE

Westminster
tube station

HOURS

Mon-Sun: 10am-6pm
Last admission 5pm

 # London Aquarium . . .

The London Aquarium, newly opened in March 1997, is one of Europe's largest and most impressive exhibits of marine life.

The £25 million attraction is housed within the magnificent Edwardian County Hall, a Grade Two listed building, overlooking the Thames and the Houses of Parliament.

Piranha fish

The Aquarium covers 170,000 square feet of floor space, and the two main tanks, devoted to Atlantic and Pacific life, together hold nearly 2 million litres of water.

The three levels of exhibits are centred around the vast tanks, allowing uninterrupted views of the exciting species of marine life as visitors make their descent into the exhibition levels.

The **Atlantic Tank** features stingray, conger eels, bream, bass and other dwellers of the dark depths of this huge ocean.

The **Pacific Tank** is primarily the home of sharks, with species from all corners of the ocean. Watch sand, tiger and brown sharks gliding through the water in this thoughtfully constructed, authentic habitat.

The Touch Pool

In addition to these two main exhibits there are thirty-nine other dramatic displays devoted to marine life from many parts of the world.

The **Indian Ocean** display features poisonous lionfish, carpet sharks and stunning anemones. The **Barrier Reef** and **Living Corals** hold dazzling creatures such as seahorses, angelfish and clown fish in beautiful, natural settings.

The **Tropical Freshwater** tank is home to lethal piranhas and a 300 million year-old species, the lung-fish, while the clever archer fish resides in the dense **Mangrove** swamp.

The **Temperate Waters**, based around a picturesque

. . . London Aquarium

fishing harbour, feature octopuses and cuttlefish. In addition there is a film show about the giant squid and the venomous box jellyfish. Other displays are devoted to the **Mediterranean**, **European Freshwater** life and **Rivers and Ponds**.

As well as being visually stunning in their thoughtful presentation of near-natural habitats, the displays are enhanced by special sound, light and even aromatic effects. Descent into the **Deep Sea Zone** is accompanied by atmospheric sound and lighting.

The **Rainforest**, featuring exotic creatures from South America, Asia and Africa, is made all the more realistic by its misty, tropical atmosphere and cascading waterfalls.

Rainforest

At the **Beach Pier** visitors can stroke the rays which swim into the shallows. This zone is enhanced by the seaside aromas which waft onto the man-made shore.

A particular favourite for children is the **Touch Pool**. Accompanied by qualified Aquarium staff, visitors of all ages can handle crabs, starfish and mussels.

Among the thousands of specimens represented at the Aquarium, there are several which have never been seen in this country before. They include the Snake Pipefish, the Emperor Angel Fish, Blue Gourami and the Dog Faced Puffer Fish.

The Aquarium runs an active rescue and breeding programme, as well as a rehabilitation scheme for hobbyist's fish.

It also presents daily sessions devoted to various aspects of marine life, where visitors can learn more about the underwater environment. The themed tanks are carefully planned to provide the species with authentic habitats, and a team of professionals are on hand to monitor their health.

A diver braving the depths

PRICES

Adult £8.50
Child (3-14) £5
Senior £6.50
Student £6.50

DISCOUNT

20% discount with
for less card

DON'T MISS

Daily descents into the Pacific and Atlantic tanks are made by qualified divers who swim with the creatures who live there

Tate Modern

ADDRESS

25 Sumner Street
☎ 020-7887-8000

GETTING THERE

Blackfriars or Southwark
tube station

HOURS

Mon-Thu & Sun: 10am-
6pm. Fri-Sat: 10am-10pm

PRICES

Admission is free

The former Bankside Power Station has been thoughtfully transformed to maximize space and light and provide an ultra-modern, flexible exhibition space for the contemporary art collections of the Tate Modern. The gallery opened in May 2000, and has since taken its prestigious place among the modern arts museums of the world.

Tate Modern

The seven levels of exhibition rooms are centred around the vast former turbine hall, now glass-roofed. Many of the spaces enjoy natural light, and some have unrivalled views of the Thames and St. Paul's. One unique gallery is 39ft (12m) high.

Composition with red, yellow and blue, *Mondrian*

The gallery chooses to display the huge collection of modern art, of which about 60% is on view at any one time, in an innovative manner. Rather than chronologically tracing the progress of the genre, the exhibitions are arranged according to themes, such as landscape, the body and still life. This allows visitors to choose a certain area of interest and see works spanning a range of genres and eras.

The artists represented by their paintings, sculptures and installations are too numerous to mention here, but better-known names include Bacon, Picasso, Bonnard, Warhol, Matisse, Monet, Rothko, Spencer, Gilbert and George, Cézanne, Dali and Beckmann. Within the themed areas, Fauvism, Cubism, Surrealism, Performance Art and various movements such as de Stijl and Bauhaus are all covered.

The End of the Twentieth Century, *Joseph Beuys*

The turbine hall houses specially commissioned installations which change every year, and level four has gallery space for temporary exhibitions. The Tate Modern has two restaurants, one of which enjoys marvellous views of the river, and shops selling gifts and books.

Other Attractions . . .

The **British Airways London Eye** is the largest observation wheel in the world, three times the height of Tower Bridge.

The slow-moving, 30-minute "flight" in 32 glass pods affords views as far as Windsor and Guildford on a clear day. *(Jubilee Gardens, ☎ 0870-5000-600. Apr-Oct: Mon-Sun: 9am-10pm. Adult £7.45, child (under 16) £4.95, senior £5.95, student £7.45. Booking advisable.)*

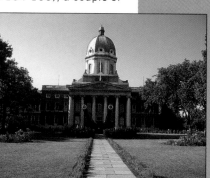
BA London Eye

The former County Hall, behind the wheel, houses the London Aquarium (pages 154-155), a couple of restaurants, a hotel, the London Eye ticket office and the **FA Premier League Hall of Fame**. This celebration of Britain's favourite game features wax models of football stars, videos, photographs and an interactive display about what football will be like in the middle of the 21st century. *(County Hall, ☎ 0870-848-8484. Mon-Sun: 10am-6pm. Adult £9.95, child £6.50, senior £7.50, student £9.95.)*

Imperial War Museum

for less Some of the world's most lethal inventions are on display in the **Imperial War Museum,** housed in what was once the infamous Bedlam mental hospital.

Sopwith Camel

The imposing 47-ft (14-m) V2 rocket stands in the main exhibition hall, among an array of tanks, fighter planes, heavy artillery and an atomic bomb (minus warhead). Hitler's deadliest weapon, the V2, delivered a ton of explosive unseen and unheard by its victims.

There are two 'experiences' which portray the horror of war – **Trench** and **Blitz**. As you wander through a First World War trench, passing soldiers huddled in dugouts and manning the walls, the sound of machine gun fire rattles overhead.

The Blitz experience begins in an air raid shelter,

Imperial War Museum

Other Attractions . . .

where the seats vibrate with the impact of bombs.

Florence Nightingale Museum

Then you emerge into a devastated street, where the only motion is the rotating wheel of an upturned pram.

The **Holocaust Exhibition** tells the story of the Nazis' persecution of the Jews and other groups both before and after the Second World War.

The museum keeps abreast of recent conflicts and has regular temporary exhibitions. *(Lambeth Road, ☎ 020-7416-5320. Mon-Sun: 10am-6pm. Adult £5.50, child free, senior free, student £4.50. 20% off admission with for less card.)*

Florence Nightingale Museum

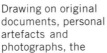 The **Florence Nightingale Museum** tells the remarkable story of the 'Lady of the Lamp', who nursed the wounded soldiers of the Crimean War (1853-1856) and four years later founded the first school of nursing at St. Thomas's Hospital.

Lambeth Palace

Drawing on original documents, personal artefacts and photographs, the museum commemorates Florence Nightingale's unique contribution to medical care and hospital standards. The exhibition includes the lamp which she carried and which was to become her symbol. There is also a dramatic representation of her with the war-wounded at Scutari. *(2 Lambeth Palace Road, ☎ 020-7620-0374. Mon-Fri: 10am-4pm. Sat-Sun: 11am-4pm. Adult £4.80, child £3.60, senior £3.60, student £3.60. 50% off admission with voucher on page 279.)*

The Old Vic

The **Museum of Garden History** lies in and around the 14th-century tower of St. Mary's Church on Lambeth Palace Road. Charles I's royal gardeners are buried here and the museum includes a 17th-century-style garden. *(Lambeth Palace Road, ☎ 020-7261-1891. Mon-Fri and Sun: 10.30am-5pm. Sat: closed. Admission is free.)*

Lambeth Palace *(Lambeth Palace Road)*, overlooking the Museum of Garden History, has been the London residence of the

. . . Other Attractions . . .

Archbishop of Canterbury, the head of the English
Church, since 1207. It is closed to the public, but
there is an impressive twin-towered redbrick Tudor
gatehouse.

Old Vic

The **Old Vic** is one of London's finest theatres. Opened
in 1816, it became a celebrated venue for Victorian
'music hall' entertainment before turning to more
serious Shakespearean drama in the early 20th
century. It was beautifully restored in 1983. *(Waterloo
Road, ☎ 020-7928-2651.)*

The UK's biggest cinema screen can be found on a
roundabout near Waterloo Station. The **BFI London
IMAX Cinema** has a screen taller than five double-
decker buses and 85ft (26m) wide, and shows both 2D
and 3D films. Digital surround-sound adds to the
experience. *(1 Charlie Chaplin Walk, Waterloo, ☎ 020-7902-
1234. Mon-Sun: screenings: 12noon, 1.15pm, 2.30pm,
3.45pm, 5pm, 6.15pm, 7.30pm, 8.45pm (also 10pm on Fri
& Sat.) Adult £6.50, child £4.50, senior £5.50, student
£6.50.)*

BFI London IMAX Cinema

The fun-filled **Museum of the Moving Image** (MOMI)
takes you for a hands-on tour from the earliest magic
lanterns to the latest movie special effects. At the
time of writing, it is closed until at least 2003 for
refurbishments. *(Southbank, Waterloo, ☎ 020-7401-2636.
Call for reopening information.)*

Museum of ...

The unusually named **"Museum of . . ."** is located in the
Oxo Tower Building, a former warehouse converted to
shops, galleries, restaurants and apartments. This
innovative exhibition has no permanent theme, instead
featuring temporary "museums" running for 16 weeks
each and covering a wacky and eclectic range of topics.
It opened in 1999 with the Museum of Collectors, which
was followed by the Museum of Me
and the Museum of the Unknown.
*(The Bargehouse, Oxo Tower Wharf,
Bargehouse Street, ☎ 020-7928-1255.
Call for exhibition information. Wed-
Sun: 12noon-6pm. Mon-Tue: closed.
Admission is free.)*

Bankside Gallery

for less **Bankside Gallery** holds
regular art exhibitions at its
attractive Thames-facing
location, midway between
Blackfriars Bridge and Southwark
Bridge. It is the headquarters of the Royal Watercolour
Society and Royal Society of Painter-Printmakers.
Many of the works on view are for sale. *(48 Hopton
Street, ☎ 020-7928-7521. Tue-Fri: 10am-5pm (until 8pm*

. . . Other Attractions . . .

Tue). Sun: 1pm-5pm. Sat and Mon: closed. Adult £3.50, child free, senior £2, student £2. 2 admissions for the price of 1 with voucher on page 279.)

The exterior of the Globe

Sir Norman Foster's **Millennium Bridge** opened in June 2000 and links the Tate Modern (page 156) to St. Paul's Cathedral on the other side of the river. It is the first bridge to be built across the Thames since the completion of Tower Bridge in 1894 *(tollbridge).*

Standing a short distance from the site of the original, the meticulous reproduction of Shakespeare's original

Shakespeare's Globe Theatre

Globe Theatre – constructed using Elizabethan building techniques – offers authentic performances and guided tours. The wooden, thatched theatre, which has an open-air stage, specializes in plays by Shakespeare and his contemporaries. *(New Globe Walk, ☎ 020-7401-9919. Exhibition: May-Sep: Mon-Sun: 9am-2noon. Oct-Apr: Mon-Sun: 10am-5pm. Adult £7.50, child £5, senior £6, student £6. Call for information about performances.)*

The Clink Prison Museum

Vinopolis, the "City of Wine", is a paradise for lovers of the tipple, not least of all because of the several wine-tastings on offer as you make your way around the interactive exhibits. Vineyards of the world and wine-making techniques are explored, and there are tips how to choose the best wine for any occasion. The Wine Odyssey is a virtual journey through the world's wine cultures. Vinopolis also has four restaurants, a food shop and a massive off-licence, but the admission charges to the exhibitions are rather steep. *(1 Bank End, ☎ 020-7645-3700. Mon-Sun: 10am-5.30pm (last admission 4.30pm). Adult £11.50, child £5, senior £10.50, student £11.50.)*

Vinopolis

for less The **Clink Exhibition** stands on the site of the old Clink Prison, a dungeon attached to the Bishop of Winchester's House, where dissenting clerics were sent for punishment. In medieval times, this was London's red-light district and the museum re-creates the brothels in lurid detail. *(1 Clink Street, ☎ 020-7403-6515. Mon-Sun: 10am-6pm. Adult £4, child £3, senior & student £3, family £8. 50% discount on admission with voucher on page 279.)*

Clink Exhibition

Equally gory is the **Old Operating Theatre, Museum and**

. . . Other Attractions . . .

Herb Garret. This church attic was the operating theatre of St. Thomas' hospital until 1862, in the days when hygiene was dubious and anaesthetic was undiscovered. Surgical instruments, preserved body parts and displays about herbal medicines make for an interesting, if stomach-churning, visit. *(9a St. Thomas Street, ☎ 020-7955-4791. Mon-Sun: 10am-5.30pm. Adult £3.25, child £1.60, senior £2.25, student £2.25.)*

Southwark Cathedral

Just west of London Bridge lies **Southwark Cathedral**, a fine medieval church, parts of which date from the 12th century. The early 15th-century tomb of poet John Gower, a contemporary of Geoffrey Chaucer, is in the north aisle. A memorial to Shakespeare stands in the south aisle. John Harvard, who founded Harvard University, was baptized here in 1607. Refurbishments to improve visitor facilities are underway at the time of writing, but the cathedral is still accessible. *(Montague Close, ☎ 020-7367-6700. Mon-Sun: 9am-6pm. Suggested donation £2.)*

The Golden Hinde

The **Golden Hinde**, moored at St. Mary Overie Dock near London Bridge, is a full-scale reconstruction of Sir Francis Drake's famous galleon in which he circumnavigated the globe in the 16th century. *(St. Mary Overie Dock, Cathedral Street, ☎ 020-7403-0123. Mon-Sun: 10am-6pm. Adult £2.50, child (4-13) £1.75, senior £2.10, student £2.10.)*

for less The **Britain at War Experience**, on Tooley Street next to the London Dungeon, celebrates the famous British 'stiff upper lip' when the country stood alone against Hitler in the Second World War. It begins with an air raid simulation: you wait in a bombed out department store and then walk through the charred remains of a cinema, pub and houses.

Southwark Cathedral

Golden Hinde

Britain at War Experience

Britain at War

. . . Other Attractions

HMS Belfast

Original newsreels and radio broadcasts give an authentic 1940s flavour. Artefacts include a child's 'Mickey Mouse' gas mask. *(64-66 Tooley Street, ☎ 020-7403-3171. Apr-Sep: Mon-Sun: 10am-5.30pm. Oct-Mar: Mon-Sun: 10am-4.30pm. Adult £5.95, child £2.95, senior £3.95, student £3.95. 50% off admission per person with voucher on page 279.)*

HMS *Belfast*, a floating naval museum since 1971, was the Royal Navy's largest Second World War battle cruiser. Its six torpedoes and 14-mile range guns helped it sink the German cruiser

HMS Belfast

Scharnhorst in 1943. The network of cabins, which is open to the public, accommodated a crew of 800. The tour includes the heavily armoured Shell Rooms and Magazines, the Mess Decks, Officers' Cabins and Sick Bay. You can see inside the gun turrets and operate the light anti-aircraft guns. *(Morgan's Lane, Tooley Street, ☎ 020-7940-6328. Mar-Oct: Mon-Sun: 10am-6pm (last admission 5.15pm). Nov-Feb: Mon-Sun: 10am-5pm (last admission 5.15pm). Adult £5, child (under 16) free, senior £3.80, student £3.80.)*

Design Museum

Classic designs of mass-produced items – including collections of bizarre hairdryers and modish TV sets – are on display at the **Design Museum**. Housed in an uninspiring tier of white blocks, it faces the Thames east of Tower Bridge. *(Butler's Wharf, Shad Thames, ☎ 020-7403-6933. Mon-Fri: 11.30am-6pm. Sat-Sun: 10.30am-6pm. Adult £5.50, child £4, senior £4, student £4.50.)*

Bramah Tea and Coffee Museum

for less Close by, at Butler's Wharf, is the **Bramah Museum of Tea and Coffee**. The 350-year history of the tea and coffee trade is told in a lively exhibition that includes a collection of 1,000 coffee–makers and

Bramah Museum of Tea and Coffee

teapots. The museum was founded in 1992 by Edward Bramah, a former tea planter and taster who is an acknowledged world expert on the traditional British tea-drinking habit. Butler's Wharf is an appropriate place for the museum, for it was used for three centuries to unload millions of chests of tea and coffee. The museum includes a café and shop selling 'slow-infusing' Bramah teas. *(The Clove Building, Maguire Street, ☎ 020-7378-0222. Mon-Sun: 10am-6pm. Adult £4, child £3, senior £3, student £3. 50% off admission with voucher on page 279.)*

Open Spaces

The three-mile riverside footpath, on the south bank of the Thames from Lambeth Bridge to Tower Bridge, is one of the finest walks in London.

Well removed from traffic, the footpath is partly tree-lined and has lots of benches that make excellent picnic spots.

There are astounding views across the river incorporating many of London's finest buildings and landmarks, such as the Houses of Parliament, St. Paul's Cathedral, the Tower of London and Tower Bridge. You will also see some of London's more interesting modern structures, including Charing Cross Station and the controversial South Bank Centre.

Tower Bridge from the South Bank

On the way, there are several fascinating sites, including the reconstructed Shakespeare's Globe Theatre (page 160), Southwark Cathedral (page 161) and HMS *Belfast* (page 162).

A few hundred yards east of the South Bank Centre is **Gabriel's Wharf**, a charming collection of craft shops, cafés and bars surrounding a pretty piazza.

There are few decent-sized open spaces in the area immediately south of the Thames. **Jubilee Gardens,** running alongside the Thames, is sandwiched between the South Bank Centre and County Hall (formerly the home of the defunct Greater London Council and now containing an hotel, a conference centre and the London Aquarium (pages 154-155)).

The only sizeable public park in the area is the **Geraldine Mary Harmsworth Park,** beside Lambeth Road. Dominated by the Imperial War Museum, it occupies the central block of what was the Bethlehem Royal Hospital, or 'Bedlam' for short. This notorious mental asylum had been a tourist attraction in the 17th and 18th centuries, with visitors coming to gape at the patients who were chained in their cells and regularly whipped. Hence the English word 'bedlam', meaning madhouse. Recreational visitors were banned in 1770, when it was decided that they 'tended to disturb the tranquillity of the patients' by 'making sport and diversion of the miserable inhabitants'. The hospital closed in 1930.

Riverside Walk

Gabriel's Wharf

Jubilee Gardens

Geraldine Mary Harmsworth Park

Eating and Drinking

Most of the more interesting pubs and restaurants overlook the River Thames on Bankside and near the **South Bank Centre**.

The roof top Harvey Nichols's Restaurant, Bar and Brasserie, at **Oxo Tower** *(Barge House Street)* has wonderful views up and down the Thames. The newly refurbished tower is one of London's riverside landmarks.

Oxo Tower

Sir Terence Conran has a row of Thameside restaurants with spectacular views of Tower Bridge. **Le Pont de la Tour** *(36D Shad Thames)* is the grandest, serving expensive modern French cuisine. Less pricey is Conran's Italian restaurant, **Cantina del Ponte** *(36E Shad Thames)*. Booking is essential for these restaurants, especially for the tables outside on the river terrace.

Hay's Galleria *(Tooley Street)*, a soaring atrium full of cafés and shops, is the most visually striking of the wharf developments south of the river. The weird fountain sculpture in the centre of the arcade is very ugly, but children love it. At the end of the Galleria is **Horniman's**, a spacious pub which serves lunch and dinner on weekdays.

Dining South of the River

For a grand view across the river of St. Paul's Cathedral, the big riverside terrace of **The Founders Arms** *(52 Hopton Street)* near to Blackfriars Bridge would be hard to beat. Indeed it has a sign by the door boasting of 'The finest view in London'. The restaurant serves lunch and dinner.

Hay's Galleria

The Anchor *(34 Park Street)* is a charming 18th-century restored riverside pub. Sam Wanamaker used to eat here while overseeing the development of the new Globe Theatre (page 160).

The George Inn, Southwark

George Inn

The **George Inn** *(77 Borough High Street)* is London's only surviving traditional galleried coaching inn. Owned by the National Trust, it is both a bar and a restaurant with live entertainment in summer in the cobbled yard

Bloomsbury and Marylebone

Introduction . . .

Over the last 100 years, **Bloomsbury** has become a byword for intellectual and literary endeavour. The Bloomsbury Group, a subversive and brilliant circle of writers that included Virginia Woolf and Lytton Strachey, lived and worked in the area in the early decades of the last century.

The presence of the **British Museum** (page 168-169) and University College, plus a number of other learned institutions and several hospitals, confirm the intellectual pedigree of the area. It is home to thousands of students and a long-established publishing industry. The spirit of the Bloomsbury Group, who believed in the 'pleasures of human intercourse and the enjoyment of beautiful objects', is still apparent.

Hotel Russell

There are several fine Georgian squares, the largest of which is **Russel Square** behind the British Museum. Much of the distinctive architecture was built under successive Dukes of Bedford in the 18th and early 19th centuries.

North of Bloomsbury are three major train stations serving the north of England and Scotland: Euston, St Pancras and King's Cross. St. Pancras, with its newly restored curved red brick façade and clock tower, is one of London's greatest Victorian Gothic buildings.

Fitzrovia is the area immediately to the west of Tottenham Court Road. Writers such as Dylan Thomas named the neighbourhood after the pub they drank in: the Fitzroy Tavern. Most of the area's cafés and restaurants, are to be found along Charlotte Street. The 580-foot (174-metre) **BT Tower** dominates Fitzrovia. Built in 1965, this cylindrical jumble of transmitters and radio masts once had a revolving restaurant at the top, but it is now closed to the public.

For a while, it was London's tallest building, but it was superseded by the NatWest Tower (which in turn has been gazumped by Canary Wharf in Docklands).

Wigmore Street is a pleasant, up-market shopping street, much quieter and more civilized than Oxford Street, which runs parallel

REFLECTIONS

'I came home from the Elgin Marbles melancholy. I almost wish the French had them; we do not deserve such productions. There they lie, covered with dust and dripping with damp, adored by the artists, admired by the people, neglected by the Government...and reverenced and envied by foreigners because they do not possess them.' – Benjamin Haydon (1815)

A Lewis Chessman (British Museum)

. . . Introduction

ınd to the south. Renowned chocolate manufacturer Bendick's, at No.53, was founded soon after the First World War by Captain Benson and Mr Dickson.

Christopher's Place, an alleyway running south off Wigmore Street near the James Street junction, is where London's upper crust comes to shop.

Grand Georgian architecture covers much of **Marylebone**. Edward Harley, the 2nd Earl of Oxford, bought the land in 1713 and developed it to accommodate the rapid westward expansion of London.

A typical Bloomsbury house The area became highly ashionable from the 1760s, when George II's daughter, Amelia, lived at No.16 Cavendish Square.

INSIDER'S TIP

The prettiest part of Bloomsbury lies north of the British Museum between Coram's Fields and Tavistock Square. Woburn Walk, with its bow-fronted buildings dating from 1822, is particularly beautiful.

'here is a maze of smart streets, some with chic little hops, running off Marylebone High Street. Among the nany exclusive addresses in the area is **Harley Street**, synonymous with the prestigious private nedical practices that have been here since the .840s.

'here are dozens of imposing mansions in Marylebone. The finest, built by the architect Robert Adam in the 1770s, include Chandos House on Chandos Street and Home House on Portman Square. Adams's 125-foot (37-metre) vide **Portland Place** is London's grandest 18th-entury street. Appropriately, it is the home of he Royal Institute of British Architects (No.66).

Madame Tussaud's

'he smart, cream-coloured stucco terraces and illas around **Regent's Park** were built by John Nash for high society families in the early 19th entury. The buildings were intended to circle he park in two continuous rings, but the evelopers ran out of money.

'he grandest section is the 800-foot (240-metre) açade of Cumberland Terrace, where Wallis Simpson ved at No.16 in the early days of her relationship with King Edward VIII.

Many visitors come to Marylebone simply to visit **Madame Tussaud's** (pages 170-171), but close by is n enchanting and often overlooked museum: the **Wallace Collection** (page 173) has fabulous paintings, rmour and porcelain on display.

ADDRESS

Great Russell Street
☎ 020-7636-1555

GETTING THERE

Russell Square or
Tottenham Court Road
tube stations

HOURS

Open:
Mon-Sat: 10am-5pm
Sun: 12noon-6pm

Guided Tours of museum:
Mon-Sat: 11.15am and
2.15pm
Sun: 3pm and 3.30pm

PRICES

Admission is free.

Guided tours of the
museum: £6

British Museum . . .

The two and a half miles of galleries in the British
Museum contain fragments of the seven wonders of

British Museum

the ancient
world, amid
countless other
treasures from
the very early
histories of
Greece, Rome,
Egypt, China
and other great
cultures.

Six million
people a year
visit the British Museum, making it the most popular
attraction in London. Surprisingly, you are allowed to
take photos in the museum.

Probably the best-known exhibit is the **Elgin Marbles**,
the Parthenon sculptures taken from Athens by Lord
Elgin in 1801. The 2,500-year-old marble friezes are
the subject of a long and bitter campaign by Greece to
persuade Britain to return them home.

The **Rosetta Stone** – initially discovered by Napoleon's
soldiers in the Nile delta – was acquired during the
same period. Its importance derives from the
inscriptions in three
languages, which enabled
scholars to unlock the
mystery of Egyptian
hieroglyphs. In 1997 the
Egyptian government
dropped its demand for
the return of the Rosetta
Stone.

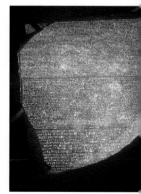

The wizened remains of
Lindow Man, slaughtered
by druids and dumped in a
peat bog 2,000 years
ago, offer the peculiar
experience of staring into
the only face to survive
from prehistoric Britain.

Rosetta Stone

Many of the galleries and rooms are worth visiting
simply for their stunning visual impact. The **Mexican
Collection** – laid out inside a re-created temple – is
the museum's commendable first attempt to display
objects in their native context.

. . . British Museum

The **HSBC Money Gallery** opened in January 1997. Devoted to the history of money over the last 4,000 years, it traces changing forms of payment, starting with the grain, metal and shells used in ancient Mesopotamia, Egypt and China. The **Celtic Europe Gallery** displays Celtic coins and Roman jewellery recently unearthed in Alton, Hampshire.

The two-acre space at the centre of the museum is currently being transformed and is due to open in Autumn 2000. The **Great Court** scheme has been designed by architect Sir Norman Foster, and includes new mezzanine floors, a restaurant and a glass and steel canopy covering the whole area. It will provide a dramatic new public space, with new galleries, late-opening cafés and shops, and will improve access to existing parts of the museum.

Egyptian Sculpture Gallery

The vast, copper-domed **Reading Room** is astounding, and has been fully restored as a centrepiece of the development since it lost its collection to the new British Library at St. Pancras. Karl Marx wrote *Das Kapital* here and, in 1902, Lenin also came here to study. The 19th-century American writer Washington Irving described the Reading Room as being filled with great cases of venerable books and odd personages at long tables pouring intently over dusty volumes, rummaging among mouldy manuscripts and making copious notes'.

Now, the Reading Room contains a public reference library, where visitors have electronic access to the museum's collections.

In addition to the new developments, the British Museum has regained its **Ethnographic** collection, which was formerly displayed as the

Portland Vase

Museum of Mankind in Burlington House, Piccadilly, due to lack of space. These works of art, crafts and artefacts from non-industrialised cultures are now housed in the new Sainsbury African Galleries.

INSIDER'S TIP

Visit early in the morning or after 3pm on weekdays to avoid large school parties

DON'T MISS

Elgin Marbles, the Mausoleum at Halikarnassos, the Rosetta Stone, Lindow Man, the Lewis Chessmen, Portland Vase

ADDRESS

Marylebone Road
☎ 020-7935-6861

GETTING THERE

Baker Street tube station

HOURS

Mon-Fri: 9am-5.30pm
Sat-Sun: 9.30am-5.30pm
Closed Christmas Day

 Madame Tussaud's . . .

The chance to be photographed shoulder-to-shoulder with your favourite movie star, world leader or member of the British royal family makes Madame Tussaud's collection of more than 400 wax figures London's most popular (paid for) visitor attraction.

It is also one of the oldest, for Madame Tussaud opened her first exhibition around the corner on Baker Street in 1835. Her skill as a wax artist helped save her from the guillotine in revolutionary France – she was only freed on the condition that she sculpt the severed heads of aristocrats. Tussaud's own models of Benjamin Franklin and Voltaire are still on display.

Naomi Campbell

The first room, known as the **Garden Party** and laid out as an English country garden, contains contemporary figures such as Oprah Winfrey, Mel Gibson, Liz Taylor, Arnold Schwarzenegger and Brad Pitt. This is one of the best places to take pictures.

Supermodels past and present are represented by Jerry Hall and the recently-added Naomi Campbell. Hall's 1990 sitting is re-created in a special exhibition, which demonstrates the technology behind the model-making.

The **Hollywood** section is split into two – **Legends**, which features the likes of Marilyn Monroe, and **Superstars**, which includes Sylvester Stallone and Pierce Brosnan. Some of the most entertaining exhibits re-create famous movie scenes, such as the 'rolling boulder' episode in Indiana Jones and the Temple of Doom.

James Bond

Royalty and world leaders are displayed downstairs in the **Grand Hall**. Here you can see Henry VIII and his six wives – brought together in wax as they never were in life. Several American presidents line up together, with Bill Clinton on the podium for a second

. . . Madame Tussaud's

term. The wax artists have had to add a few pounds to Helmut Kohl, who has grown steadily fatter since he first joined the cast at Madame Tussaud's. One of the most uncannily lifelike portraits is of French President Jacques Chirac.

The British royal family is grouped at the end of the room. The previous model of Princess Diana was improved recently, after she agreed to a new sitting at Kensington Palace in 1996, the first since before she was married. The model is amazingly lifelike and captures the princess as she will always be remembered.

The Chamber of Horrors

The most popular section, the **Chamber of Horrors**, was refurbished in 1996. It contains displays of infamous killers, like Vlad the Impaler, and working execution models. A few genuine historical artefacts are on display, including the actual guillotine blade that beheaded Marie Antoinette. Among the infamous British murderers featured is John Christie, hanged in 1953 for murdering his wife and strangling five other women. His execution is re-created in gruesome detail, with a clock counting down, a lever being pushed and a trapdoor opening. The lights black out as Christie takes 'the drop'. The accompanying sound effects send shivers down the spine.

This is not, however, the most disturbing part of the Chamber. Visitors who are even remotely squeamish should avoid the end of Jack the Ripper alley, where lies a chillingly-real disembowelled victim. At the entrance to the Chamber, there is an 'escape route' for those wanting to bypass the Horrors.

The exhibition ends with the **Spirit of London** – a ride though the history of the capital in a vehicle resembling a London black cab. Unlike in the rest of the museum, the figures in this section move and speak thanks to sophisticated computer and robotic technology.

PRICES

Adult £11
Child £7.50
Senior £8.50
Student £11
50p higher in peak season

DISCOUNT

£1.50 off admission per person with voucher on page 279.

Diana, Princess of Wales

for less
London Planetarium

A breathtaking 3-D trip through the solar system in the huge domed auditorium is the centrepiece of the London Planetarium, which adjoins Madame Tussaud's.

Space Zone

Built on the site of a cinema destroyed in the Second World War Blitz, the Planetarium opened in 1958. Its great green copper dome has become a familiar London landmark. When the model of Saturn was fixed to the top of the dome, it acquired the nickname 'Sputnik' after the first spacecraft launched the year before the building opened.

The main show uses the world's most advanced star projector, the £1 million Digistar Mark 2, which is capable of displaying more than 9,000 stars. Entitled **Planetary Quest**, the 30-minute narrated show invites you to imagine you are a space traveller and uses 3-D images to challenge how you look at the universe. Highlights include a trip across the canyons of Mars, an exploding supernova, Neptune's hurricane storms and a close-up view of the rings and moons of Saturn. Perhaps the most spectacular sequence is the Big Bang, when the projector simulates the beginning of the universe. You will also be sent zooming through central London.

You can prepare for your journey into space at the three exhibition areas outside the auditorium – **Launch Zone**, **Planet Zone** and **Space Zone** – which have interactive demonstrations, including a gravity well.

Wax portraits of famous astronomers and astronauts help give a human dimension when explaining often

ADDRESS

Marylebone Road
☎ 020-7935-6861

GETTING THERE

Baker Street tube station

HOURS

Mon-Sun: 9.40am-5pm
Shows every 40 minutes

PRICES

Combined ticket with
Madame Tussaud's
Adult £13.45
Child £9
Senior £10.30
Student £13.45
50p higher in peak season

DISCOUNT

£2 off the combined ticket to Madame Tussaud's with voucher on page 281.

Inside the dome of the Planetarium

difficult concepts about space and time. Interactive video screens are available for those who want to find out more. A figure of theoretical physicist and motor neurone sufferer Stephen Hawking can be heard discussing the mystery of black holes. He explains his theories on time travel, but adds a word of caution: "The best evidence we have that time travel is not possible, and never will be, is that we have not been invaded by hordes of tourists from the future."

Wallace Collection

After fighting through the masses at the British Museum and the National Gallery, the tranquil corridors and rooms of this elegant town house offer a gentle respite for art lovers.

The Wallace Collection

Bequeathed to the nation in 1897 by the widow of art collector Sir Richard Wallace, the sumptuous collection of paintings, armour, porcelain and furniture is displayed in the perfectly proportioned Hertford House. Overlooking one of London's most charming residential squares, the house dates back to the 18th century, when it was built by the Duke of Manchester as a lodge for the good duck shooting nearby.

The Wallace Collection was mostly put together by Sir Richard, his father and his grandfather. Their eclectic interests included Oriental armour, 18th-century French paintings and Limoges enamels. Sir Richard, a philanthropist, was knighted for helping British people trapped by the Franco-Prussian war. The conditions of Lady Wallace's bequest were that nothing be added or taken away, and this is reflected in the museum's graceful old-world atmosphere.

The most famous painting in the collection is **Frans Hals**' *The Laughing Cavalier*, famous for the swaggering self-confidence expressed in the subject's face and the gorgeous detail of his coat. However, there are hundreds of delightful, lesser-known exhibits, such as a collection of gold snuff boxes and carved furniture inlaid with tortoiseshell.

The galleries fill two floors. Fine paintings by **Jean Fragonard** hang on the opulent white marble staircase. The iron and bronze balustrade flanking the staircase was originally in Louis XV's Palais Mazarin, but was torn down and later bought by Sir Richard and shipped to London. One upper room is filled with the world's foremost private collection of French 18th-century paintings and furniture.

The gallery's central courtyard has recently been the centre of a major refurbishment, during which a glass roof was added to make an all-weather sculpture garden. There's also a café, a drop-in library, a lecture theatre and extra gallery space.

ADDRESS

Hertford House, Manchester Square
☎ 020-7935-0687

GETTING THERE

Bond Street or Baker Street tube stations

HOURS

Mon-Sat: 10am-5pm
Sun: 2pm-5pm

PRICES

Admission is free

'The Laughing Cavalier' by Franz Hals

DON'T MISS

Velazquez's *Lady with a Fan*, Titian's *Perseus and Andromeda*, Hals' *Laughing Cavalier*, views of Venice by Canaletto, Arms and Armour.

ADDRESS

48 Doughty Street
☎ 020-7405-2127

GETTING THERE

Russell Square
tube station

HOURS

Mon-Sat: 10am-5pm
Sun: closed

PRICES

Adult £4
Child £2
Senior £3
Student £3

DISCOUNT

2 admissions for the price
of 1 with voucher on page
281.

The Drawing Room

🖼 Dickens House

The great Victorian novelist Charles Dickens (1812-70) lived in this house from March 1837 to December 1839. It is the only one of his many London homes to survive.

His years here were among his most creative. It was in this house that he wrote *Oliver Twist* and *Nicholas Nickleby*, and also finished *The Pickwick Papers*. The

latter was so popular in America that readers gathered at the dock to meet the ship carrying each new instalment.

The exterior of Dickens House

The museum contains a wealth of Dickens memorabilia, including letters, manuscripts, furniture, pictures, first editions of his novels and personal possessions. The earliest known portrait of Dickens, painted by his aunt when he was 18, hangs in one of the rooms (which have been reconstructed to their 1830s appearance).

The author's brother-in-law, Henry Burnett, recalled an evening spent in the house when Dickens excused himself and went to a corner of the living room to work on *Oliver Twist*. He encouraged everyone to go on talking and sometimes himself chipped in with a remark, 'the feather of his pen still moving rapidly from side to side'.

Dickens's first two daughters were born in this house and his wife's 17-year-old sister died here. He was still happily married at this stage and it wasn't until 20 years later, at the height of his fame, that he deserted his wife for the 18-year-old actress Ellen Ternan.

The house was bought by the Dickens Fellowship in 1924 and opened the following year as a museum. It is run by an independent charitable trust.

By the end of 1839, Dickens had moved into No.1 Devonshire Terrace, beside Regent's Park. Unfortunately, this building was demolished in 1960 to make way for an office block.

Other Attractions . . .

The **Percival David Foundation of Chinese Art** has an important collection of Chinese porcelain dating from

the 10th to the 18th centuries. The 1,500 items were given to London University by the scholar and collector Sir Percival David in 1951. *(53 Gordon Square, ☎ 020-7387-3909. Mon-Fri: 10.30am-5pm. Sat-Sun: closed. Admission is free.)*

St Pancras Station

The **Petrie Museum of Egyptian Archaeology** displays the Egyptian artefacts bequeathed to University College London in the 1930s. Sir Flinders Petrie was one of the most tireless of the early 20th

St. Pancras Station

century Egyptologists, bringing back clothing, utensils and mummies from his many excavations. *(University College London, Malet Place, ☎ 020-7504-2884. Tue-Fri: 1pm-5pm. Sat: 10am-1pm. Sun-Mon: closed. Admission is free.)*

The **British Cartoon Centre** is a gallery devoted to the art of cartoonists and caricaturists. It stages temporary exhibitions on such themes as political cartoons in newspapers and the history of comics. *(Brunswick Centre, Bernard Street, ☎ 020-7278-7172. Mon-Fri: 12noon-6pm. Admission is free.)*

The British Library

St. Pancras Station, on Euston Road, is one of London's grandest Victorian Gothic buildings. Its fairy-tale turrets soar into the sky, making it look more like Dracula's castle than a railway station.

It was built in 1874, the ornate facade housing the Grand Midland Hotel and providing a grand screen for the workings of the station behind it. George Gilbert Scott, the designer of the red telephone box and countless London architectural landmarks, was aptly responsible for this gem on the skyline.

Next door, to the west, is the new **British Library**, described by Prince Charles as 'a dim collection of brick sheds groping for some symbolic significance'! Many Londoners were up in arms when the ancient collection of the national library was moved from the

British Library

Pollock's Toy Museum

. . . Other Attractions . . .

lovely Reading Room in the British Museum to this modern sprawl, but there is far more space here, and better facilities.

As well as containing the precious 65,000-volume library of George III and one copy of every British publication, the library has several permanent exhibitions which are open to the public, and also stages temporary displays and events.

The **John Riblatt Gallery** spans hundreds of years with its display of historic documents, first editions and written manuscripts, from the Lindisfarne Gospels (c.700 AD) and the Magna Carta (1215) to the diary of Captain Scott. The **Workshops of Words, Sound and Images** examines the history of book production and the printing process.

The **Pearson Gallery of Living Words** charts the story of

writing, book illustration, children's books and scientific writing. At the time of writing it is also hosting an exhibition on the 1000-year history of English Literature, **Chapter and Verse**, alongside related events and workshops featuring well-known authors. *(96 Euston Road, ☎ 020-7412-7332. Mon-Sat: 9.30am-6pm (Tue: until 8pm). Admission to the library and permanent exhibitions is free; admission charge to temporary exhibitions.)*

Pollock's Toy Museum

for less **Pollock's Toy Museum** contains a captivating collection of historical toys from around the world. Toy maker Benjamin Pollock's famous Victorian paper theatres, complete with puppets, are displayed in one room. He kept the art going until his death in 1937, whereafter the tradition was sustained by some of his customers.

The six child-sized rooms, connected by narrow winding staircases, are filled with toy treasures. These include a collection of 19th-century dolls houses, hand-painted model soldiers and vintage teddy bears. *(1 Scala Street, entrance to museum at 41 Whitfield Street ☎ 020-7636-3452. Mon-Sat: 10am-5pm. Sun: closed. Adult £3, child £1.50, senior £3, student £3. 50% discount on admission with voucher on page 281.)*

All Souls, Langham Place

All Souls, Langham Place, built in 1824, is architect John Nash's only London church. Best seen from Regent Street, the church has a distinctive round

. . . Other Attractions

frontage and slender spire. BBC lunchtime and evening classical concerts are frequently recorded here.

All Souls and Broadcasting House

(Langham Place, ☎ 020-7580-3522. Mon-Fri: 9.30am-6pm. Sun: 9am-9pm with services at 9am, 11am and 6.30pm. Sat: closed.)

The curving, Portland stone building behind the church is **Broadcasting House**, constructed in 1931 to function as the headquarters of the newly formed BBC. Both the company and the Art Deco building have become national institutions, though much of the BBC's programming has been moved to newer studios in Shepherd's Bush.

Broadcasting House

The **BBC Experience**, a guided tour behind the scenes, takes place in the basement. Visitors can watch excerpts of popular and historic BBC programmes, learn about early wireless broadcasting and even try being a television presenter. Booking for the tours is advisable. *(Broadcasting House, Portland Place, ☎ 0870-603-0340. Tours: Mon: 11am-6pm (last tour 4.30pm). Tue-Sun: 10am-6pm (last tour 4.30pm). Adult £6.95, child £4.95, senior and student £5.95.)*

The **Sherlock Holmes Museum** claims to be at 221b Baker Street, the famous fictional address of Sir Arthur Conan Doyle's sleuth. The museum is actually located at Nos. 237-239. The rooms are in the Victorian style, but there is little of interest to the Holmes fan and the expensive entrance price is hardly justified by what you see. *(237-239 Baker Street, ☎ 020-7935-8866. Mon-Sun: 9.30am-6pm. Adult £6, child £4, senior £6, student £6.)*

London Canal Museum

for less The **London Canal Museum** is devoted to the history of the city's canal network and is a lasting record of the often hard lives of the narrowboat dwellers. It also displays a collection of canal arts and crafts. *(12-13 New Wharf Road, ☎ 020-7713-0836. Tue-Sun: 10am-4.30pm. Adult £2.50, child £1.25, senior £1.25, student £1.25. 50% discount with voucher on page 281.)*

A colourful narrowboat at the Canal Museum

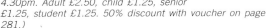

Open Spaces

Regent's Park (page 195), London's second largest open space, lies to the north of Marylebone.

Some of the splendid Georgian Squares of Bloomsbury are open to the public, with **Russell Square** an ideal place to picnic after visiting the British Museum.

The poet T.S. Eliot worked at No. 24 Russell Square in the late 1920s. On the east side of the square stands London's finest surviving Victorian hotel, the Hotel Russell, opened in 1890. The façade is a glorious mass of red terracotta, colonnaded balconies and pinnacles with two central, copper-capped towers.

Bedford Square

Bedford Square, located on the west side of the museum beside Tottenham Court Road, is perhaps the most attractive London square. It is surrounded by symmetrical 18th-century terraces.

Russell Square

Eating and Drinking

Groups of cafés and restaurants can be found on the narrow streets south of the British Museum, on Charlotte Street and further west on Marylebone High Street and around Baker Street tube station.

The **Fitzroy Tavern** *(16 Charlotte Street)* was a meeting place for literary folk in the 1920s and 1930s. The basement 'Writers and Artists Bar' is lined with pictures of famous customers, including author George Orwell and poet Dylan Thomas.

For traditional British food, try the **Creation Bar & Restaurant** (page 180) at the Kenilworth Hotel. **Mandeer** (page 181), an inexpensive vegetarian Indian restaurant, is just off Tottenham Court Road.

Traditional pubs abound in this area

Fitzroy Tavern

Mash *(19-21 Great Portland Street)* is a total contrast to the traditional pubs. This modern bar, brewery and restaurant attracts the young, fashion-conscious crowd and serves modern, funky food. The beer brewed on the premises is adventurously fruit-flavoured.

Tajine

Moroccan

7a Dorset Street
☎ 020-7935-1545

Average meal: £10-15
for less discount: 25%
VS/MC

Tajine serves delicious North African dishes. The informal restaurant is decorated in the Moroccan style. Specialities include *tajines*, stews cooked and served in a special dish.

 ## Ascot Restaurant

Modern British

Berkshire Hotel
350 Oxford Street
☎ 020-7541-3456

Average meal: £20-25
for less discount: 25%
AM/VS/MC/DC

Winner of the RAC blue ribbon award, Ascot's has an elegant, relaxed feel and a friendly, attentive service. As well as being ideal for business lunches, it's also a relaxing place to take time out whilst shopping.

 ## Glass Bar and Restaurant

European

Marlborough Hotel
7-13 Bloomsbury Street
☎ 020-7666-2035

Average meal: £15-20
for less discount: 25%
AM/VS/MC/DC

Situated on Bloomsbury, Glass is a striking contemporary restaurant with wooden floors and a collection of interesting and individual mirrors adorning the walls.

HOURS

Mon-Fri:
12.30pm-2.30pm, 5pm-10.30pm.
Sat-Sun: 5pm-10.30pm

HOURS

Mon-Fri and Sun:
12.30pm-2.30pm,
5.30pm-10pm
Sat: 5.30pm-10pm

HOURS

Mon-Fri: 12noon-2.30pm,
6pm-11pm
Sat: 6pm-11pm
Sun: closed

Aston Restaurant & Bar

Modern British

Grafton Hotel
130 Tottenham Court Road
☎ 020-7666-5430

Average meal: £15-20
for less discount: 25%
AM/VS/MC/DC

A contemporary, open plan restaurant, serving modern British cuisine in light airy surroundings. High ceilings together with a mixture of natural and state of the art lighting give a stunning effect.

Creation Restaurant & Bar

Modern British

Kenilworth Hotel
97 Great Russell Street
☎ 020-7666-2068

Average meal: £10-15
for less discount: 25%
AM/VS/MC/DC

This chic bloomsbury restaurant boasts a fabulous modern british menu. With a rich pallet of colours and fabrics the restaurant is a feast for your senses.

Caldesi

Italian

15-17 Marylebone Lane
☎ 020-7935-9226

Average meal: £20-25
for less discount: 25%
AM/VS/MC/DC

Caldesi's classic Italian menu specializes in reasonably priced fresh pasta dishes. The Victorian décor and corner tables make it perfect for a quiet dinner. In the summer, outside tables enable customers to enjoy *al fresco* dining.

Langham's Brasserie

French

**Langham Court Hotel
31-35 Langham Street
☎ 020-7491-8822**

Average meal: £10-15
for less discount: 25%
AM/VS/MC/DC

HOURS

Mon-Fri: 12.30pm-2.30pm,
6.30pm-10pm
Sat-Sun: 6.30pm-10pm

Situated within the splendid Langham Court Hotel, Langham's Brasserie serves fine French cuisine in a relaxed, elegant atmosphere. It is a tranquil escape from the bustle of the West End.

Mandeer

Indian vegetarian

**The Basement,
21 Hanway Place
☎ 020-7242-6202**

Average meal: £15-20
for less discount: 25%
AM/VS/MC/DC

HOURS

Mon-Sat: 12noon-3pm,
5pm-10pm
Sun: closed

Opened in 1967 by Ravi Shankar, Mandeer retains its 1960s feel. Its slogan is: 'Peace, love and food at groovy prices'. The self-service luncheon menu is certainly excellent value.

Bertie's Brasserie

Modern British

**The Savoy Court,
19 Granville Place
☎ 020-7408-0130**

Average meal: £10-15
for less discount: 25%
AM/VS/MC/DC

HOURS

Mon-Sun: 12noon-9.15pm

Bertie's Brasserie, with a discreet location off Oxford Street, features a host of great-value dishes throughout the day. The atmosphere is welcoming and the food excellent.

Shopping

Tottenham Court Road, which starts at the eastern end of New Oxford Street, is where people go to buy cheap computers and other electrical goods. Prices here can be well below normal high street rates, though take care not to be duped into buying second-rate equipment. Compare prices in several shops and always check the details of the guarantee. Half way up Tottenham Court Road is a major branch of the yuppie furniture store, **Habitat**.

Wigmore Street, which runs parallel with Oxford Street, has dozens of up-market shops. **St. Christopher's Place**, an alleyway near the Wigmore Street/James Street junction, has a cluster of exclusive establishments.

Tottenham Court Road

Chess and Bridge

Chess and Bridge Sets

369 Euston Road
☎ 020-7388-2404

for less discount: 20%
AM/VS/MC

HOURS

Mon-Sat: 10am-6pm
Sun: closed

This shop is an Aladdin's cave of chess and bridge boards, sets and software. It also stocks the largest collection of chess books in Europe. It is a great place to purchase a gift for the keen chess or bridge player.

Yves Rocher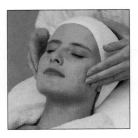

Beauty Centre

7 Gees Court
☎ 020-7409-2975

for less discount: 20%
VS/MC

HOURS

Mon-Sat: 10am-6pm
(until 7pm Wed & Thu)
Sun: closed

This modern beauty centre offers women every kind of beauty treatment. Among the services offered are manicures, facials and massages. Leg waxing and make-up sessions are also available.

Introduction. . .

Most of Bayswater was built in the 1830s and 1840s, when wealthy merchants were attracted by the easy

access to the City and property prices cheaper than those in the more fashionable Belgravia. However, the extravagant terraces and mansions, which were heavily influenced by John Nash's Regent's Park development, fell into disrepair in the early part of the 20th century.

Since the 1970s, Bayswater has undergone a remarkable period of gentrification and the majority of terraces have been fully restored to their Victorian grandeur. The best

Bayswater Road - Sunday art market

examples of the architecture are Hyde Park Gardens and the graceful curving façade at the corner of Kendal Street and Connaught Street.

Queensway is Bayswater's ever-busy hub, lined with restaurants, cafés and shops, many of which stay open very late. There are dozens of tacky souvenir shops and over-priced stores specialising in leather goods and other wares aimed at the tourist market. However, the image of Queensway has been boosted by the luxurious marble aisles of **Whiteley's**, an old department store that lay derelict for almost a decade before re-opening in 1989 as a shopping mall.

REFLECTIONS

'Westwards you enter Notting Hill, which varies almost from street to street between palatial splendour and bohemian chic, rubbing shoulders with the no less fashionable Afro-Caribbean quarter around All Saints Road, with its interesting bars, restaurants and mildly druggy music shops.' – *The Faber Book of London,* A.N. Wilson (1993)

Unfortunately, the seedy side of Bayswater has not been entirely expunged and the streets around Paddington train station are still infested with inferior restaurants exploiting the tourist trade. For better choice and quality of food, head for **Westbourne Grove** or further west into the Notting Hill area.

Bayswater and Notting Hill are two of London's most cosmopolitan neighbourhoods.

Whiteley's shopping centre

A vibrant Arab community lives around Queensway, while Notting Hill is home to a large West Indian population established in the 1950s. Forty years ago, Notting Hill was still dominated by slums, with richer residents living around the southern end of Ladbroke Grove. The proximity of wealth and poverty had always been a feature of Notting Hill, but the addition of inter-racial tensions led to riots in August 1958.

. . . Introduction

The world-famous **Notting Hill Carnival** (page 247) has its roots in this period, when West Indian community leaders decided a celebration was needed to restore the confidence of their people. Until the mid-1960s, the carnival remained a small Caribbean community jamboree. Since then, it has grown into the largest street festival outside South America. Held over three days in late August, the carnival wends its way along Ladbroke Grove and across Portobello Road.

Snaking northwards from Notting Hill Gate, **Portobello Road** is renowned for its colourful street market (page 186), held on Fridays, Saturdays and, to a lesser degree, on Sundays. The Portuguese and Moroccan communities, based around Golborne Road in the north of Notting Hill, add to the quirky mix of cultures

Crowds at Notting Hill Carnival

which made Notting Hill the most fashionable place to live in London in the 1990s.

INSIDER'S TIP

The middle day of the Notting Hill Carnival, a Sunday, has the best atmosphere.

Even public housing is done in style in Notting Hill, with the country's tallest block of flats, Trellick Tower, declared an architectural masterpiece. The bulging head of the lift shaft, which is only connected to the main structure by high-level walkways, makes the 1973 building look like a strange long-necked monster.

Many young Londoners head for Notting Hill in the evenings to drink in lively Portobello Road pubs, like the Earl of Lonsdale or the Market Bar, or to eat at one of the dozens of exotic restaurants.

However, apart from Portobello Market, there are few tourist attractions in Bayswater or Notting Hill. It is not an area in which to sightsee, but to enjoy the blend of ethnic influences, the avant-garde shops and the general stylishness of the inhabitants.

Portobello Market

Portobello Market

GETTING THERE

Notting Hill Gate tube station for southern end, Ladbroke Grove tube station for northern end.

HOURS

Sat: 8am-5pm.
Fri-Sun: smaller markets 9am-5pm.

INSIDER'S TIP

Always try haggling on the stalls; prices inflate for foreign tourists.

A Saturday stroll among the bustle, colour and street musicians of Portobello Market is one of the highlights of any trip to London.

Stretching more than a mile along the perennially trendy Portobello Road, the market offers everything from fine antiques (2,000 stalls) to bric-a-brac, with fruit, books, groovy clothing and trinkets galore in between.

The stalls get seedier further north, but beginning at the southern, Notting Hill Gate end gives an amazing insight into the diversity of the market. The specialist antique shops and stalls, some harbouring genuine bargains, soon give way to more general and affordable stalls. By the time you get to the end, there's a chance to spend just a few pence on real tat.

Dotted along the road are specialist shops selling old LPs and comics. There is even a tattoo artist, who has hundreds of photographs in his window showing the various parts of the anatomy which have been his canvas.

A number of specialist bookshops, along with several of the area's growing number of avant-garde art galleries, can be found on Blenheim Crescent. **Portobello Green**, under the flyover, is an arcade of tiny shops in which innovative designers both make and sell their wares.

There are dozens of characterful eateries and bars, with a row of pavement cafés on the northern stretch of Kensington Park Road. Café Grove, on the corner of Lancaster Road, has a terrace from which you can observe the exotic and glamorous Portobello regulars.

An artist's stall

At the far end of the market, on Golborne Road, there are a couple of very popular Portuguese cafés, the Lisboa and Porto patisseries.

Food shopping is a particular strength of the market. Applewood Farm Shop sells fresh farm produce, Garcia's offers Spanish food, and other shops sell game, fresh herbs and Caribbean fruits.

The market also operates on Friday and Sunday (when it is less lively). Many of the antique and specialist shops are open throughout the week.

Open Spaces

As many of the area's leafy squares are closed to non-residents, most locals head to Hyde Park and Kensington Gardens.

A short walk to the north-west, however, brings you to picturesque **Little Venice**. The Victorian poet Robert Browning coined the name for this triangular canal barge basin in the heart of an exclusive residential area. Many of the narrow-boats have been prettily painted, with hundreds of flower pots contributing to the colourful scene. It is a delightful place for a stroll, followed by a drink in one of the traditional, waterside pubs.

Little Venice

The **Puppet Theatre Barge**, on the Blomfield Road edge of the basin, performs weekend shows from October to May. The **London Waterbus Company** runs narrow-boat trips to Camden Lock, via Regent's Park and London Zoo. *(Little Venice, ☎ 020-7482-2550. Mon-Sun: 10am-5pm. Trips run hourly with a restricted out-of-season service. One way ticket: adult £4, child £2.50, senior £2.50, student £4. Return ticket: adult £5.50, child £3.50, senior £3.50, student £5.50.)*

Eating and Drinking

Queensway and Westbourne Grove are packed with restaurants. The northern end of Kensington Park Road has several fashionable cafés and bistros, most with pavement tables in summer.

Little Venice

There are lots of good value eateries around Notting Hill Gate, including **Malabar** *(27 Uxbridge Street)* for curries and **Manzara** *(24 Pembridge Road)* for Turkish food. The **Pharmacy**, part-owned by the controversial artist Damien Hirst, recently opened on Notting Hill Gate and is currently *the* place to be seen.

The third floor of **Whiteley's** *(Queensway, ☎ 020-7229-3844)* shopping mall is devoted to restaurants, several of which serve fast food.

Perhaps the most unusual restaurant in the area is **Veronica's** (page 189), where the menu covers 500 years of British culinary history.

The Pharmacy

Beach Blanket Babylon *(45 Ledbury Road)* is a self-consciously trendy bar and restaurant near the Portobello Road. The **Windsor Castle** *(Campden Hill Road)*, probably the most up-market pub in west London, serves delicious oysters and has a pleasant beer garden.

Ma Potter's Chargrill

Internationa|

2nd Floor
Whiteleys Centre
☎ 020-7792-2318

Average meal: £10-15
for less discount: 25%
AM/VS/MC/DC

HOURS

Mon-Sat: 9am-11pm
Sun: 9am-10.30pm

Ma Potter's serves sizzling dishes straight from its chargrill. Try the chargrilled sirloin with melted cheese and salsa. The décor is rustic, with an authentic timber barn and a raised veranda.

Tumbleweed

Tex / Mex

2nd Floor
Whiteleys Centre
☎ 020-7792-8462

Average meal: £10-15
for less discount: 25%
AM/VS/MC

HOURS

Sun-Thu: 11.30am-10pm
Fri-Sat: 11.30am-11pm

Tumbleweed - the new experience in Tex Mex dining - is situated in Whiteleys Mall. It's a lively restaurant which serves a full range of Tex Mex dishes. Fajitas are particularly recommended.

Bella Pasta

Italian

55 Queensway
☎ 020-7792-2880

Average meal: £5-10
for less discount: 25%
(present voucher on page 285)
AM/VS/MC/DC

HOURS

Mon-Sun:
10.30am-12midnight

Bella Pasta serves a wide range of Italian dishes. It's restaurants in London have excellent locations and long opening times. In this area, there is another branch at 108 Queensway.

Veronica's

Historical English

3 Hereford Road
☎ 020-7229-5079

Average meal: £15-20
for less discount: 25%
AM/VS/MC/DC

HOURS

Mon-Fri: 12noon-3pm,
7pm-11.30pm
Sat: 7pm-11.30pm
Sun: closed

Veronica's is small, beautifully furnished and serves historical English dishes. The award-winning food is light and healthy with robust flavours. Themes range from Georgian to Irish country home.

Cumberland Hotel

International / Irish / Chinese

The Cumberland Hotel
Marble Arch
☎ 020-7262-1234

for less discount: 25%
at all 4 restaurants
AM/VS/MC/DC

HOURS

Call for separate opening
times

The Cumberland Hotel has four superb restaurants offering a variety of cuisines. Try the 'Original Carvery' for English fare, 'Sampan's' for Chinese dishes, 'Callaghan's' for Irish food or the 'International Café'.

Bombay Palace

Indian

50 Connaught Street
☎ 020-7723-8855

Average meal: £15-20
for less discount: 25%
AM/VS/MC/DC

HOURS

Mon-Sat: 12noon-3pm,
6pm-11.30pm
Sun: 6pm-11pm

This elegant restaurant, part of a distinguished chain with branches all over the world, offers fine Indian food in an impressive setting. The menu includes an extensive choice of vegetarian dishes.

Shopping

The obvious place to shop in this area is **Portobello Market** (page 186), but there are also plenty of indoor shopping experiences to be had.

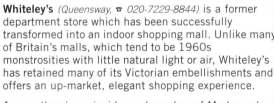

Whiteley's

Whiteley's *(Queensway, ☎ 020-7229-8844)* is a former department store which has been successfully transformed into an indoor shopping mall. Unlike many of Britain's malls, which tend to be 1960s monstrosities with little natural light or air, Whiteley's has retained many of its Victorian embellishments and offers an up-market, elegant shopping experience.

Among the stores inside are branches of Marks and Spencers and Books Etc., several expensive clothes and shoe shops and a few more affordable high street names.

An antiques shop near Portobello Market

Westbourne Grove is the place to go for stylish interiors, antiques and household gifts. **Aero** *(96 Westbourne Grove, ☎ 020-7221-1950)* and **Space** *(214 Westbourne Grove, ☎ 020-7229-6533)* both cater for the yuppie, minimalist market, while there are plenty of more traditional items on offer as you approach the Portobello Road end.

Britain's supermarkets have lately been catering for a boom in the demand for organic food, but while in Westbourne Grove visit the trend setter, **Planet Organic** *(42 Westbourne Grove, ☎ 020-7221-7171)*, a healthy supermarket complete with organic drinks section.

10500 *for less*

Hairdressing

284 Westbourne Park Road
☎ 020-7229-3777

for less discount: 20%
VS/MC

HOURS

Mon-Sat: 10am-7pm
(9pm on Thu).

The skilled stylists at 10500 will give you a whole new look or just a trim. They specialise in funky styles such as dreadlocks and braiding. A no-obligation consultation for colouring and extensions is offered.

Hyde Park

Speakers' Corner

HOURS

Mon-Sun:
5am-12midnight

INSIDER'S TIP

You can hire row boats and pedal boats on the Serpentine (Mar-Oct: 9am-7pm. £6 per hour.).

REFLECTIONS

'The parks are the lungs of London.' - Prime Minister William Pitt (1808)

The vast green expanse of Hyde Park stretches over 350 acres, from Marble Arch in the north to Knightsbridge in the south. It is a favourite place for shoppers, office workers, tourists and residents to relax, play ball games, stroll among the trees and go boating on the Serpentine.

Hyde Park

First cultivated by Benedictine monks in the medieval period, the area was one of Henry VIII's royal hunting parks. In the 17th century, it was a fashionable place for courtiers to drive their lavish carriages. Today, its association with horsemanship continues, as the barracks of the Household Cavalry lie along the south-western edge.

The park was fully opened to the public by Charles I in 1637. When the Great Plague of 1665 ravaged the City and Westminster, thousands of citizens camped in the park to escape the disease.

During the reign of William and Mary, a new royal court was established at Kensington Palace. The route through the park to the palace was known as 'Route du Roi' (King's Road), which was vulgarized to 'Rotten Row'. Horses are now exercised on **Rotten Row**, which runs along the park's southern flank.

The **Serpentine** lake was created during the 18th century. The self-service cafés are crowded and uninspiring, making a picnic an attractive alternative. Hyde Park has 10,000 deck chairs available for rental at a rate of 70p per chair for four hours.

The park's sculptures include Jacob Epstein's *Rima Monument*, whose naked goddess offended 1920s London and was twice covered in tar and feathers.

There is a century-old tradition of public speaking in the park and soap-box orators still declaim, amid witty heckling, every Sunday morning at **Speakers' Corner**.

Major festivals, like the 1851 Great Exhibition, have been held in the park and the site is still used for massive outdoor concerts.

Riding in Hyde Park

for less Apsley House

The magnificent home of the Duke of Wellington, who defeated Napoleon at Waterloo, is the last of London's great town houses to survive with its family still in residence and its art collection largely intact.

Apsley House (The Wellington Museum) stands in splendid isolation at Hyde Park Corner, one of the city's busiest traffic junctions. Its address is 'Number One London', because of its position just past a former toll gate into the capital.

Apsley House

Built in the late 18th century by the architect Robert Adam, the house was later faced with Bath stone by the Duke of Wellington. In 1832 its windows were broken by an angry mob who rioted after the Duke tried to block an

extension of the right to vote. To protect his home from further outrages, Wellington had iron shutters fitted to the windows. It is from this, not from his triumphs on the battlefield, that he acquired the nickname 'the Iron Duke'.

The 'Iron Duke'

Apsley House was presented to the nation in 1947 by the 7th Duke of Wellington. The 8th Duke of Wellington and his family still occupy the top floor and other areas, but the lower two floors are open to the public. These handsomely restored rooms have grand views of Hyde Park.

The art collection is small, but contains several important works, including Diego Velazquez's *Waterseller of Seville*, plus paintings by Franciso Goya, Sir Peter Paul Rubens and Pieter Brueghel. Canova's imposing nude statue of Napoleon stands at the foot of the mansion's ornate spiral staircase.

The most memorable exhibit is the eight-metre silver centrepiece of Wellington's Portuguese dinner service. It took two sculptors five years to make, and adorned the table at the Duke's annual Waterloo Banquet for his loyal officers.

The Waterloo gallery

ADDRESS

Hyde Park Corner
☎ 020-7499-5676

GETTING THERE

Hyde Park Corner
tube station

HOURS

Tue-Sun: 11am-5pm
Last admission 4.30pm
Mon: closed

PRICES

Adult £4.50
Child free
Senior £3
Student £3

DISCOUNT

50% discount with
voucher on page 281

Kensington Gardens

Kensington Gardens were first opened to the public in the 18th century. Queen Victoria added the **Italian Gardens**, the four stone pools at the north-eastern corner. She also commissioned the intricate 180-foot (54-metre) **Albert Memorial**, in memory of her beloved husband, who died in 1861.

Albert Memorial

HOURS

Mon-Sun: dawn-dusk

The **Flower Walk**, running from the Albert Memorial to the Palace Gate, is a haven for birds and butterflies in summer. Avenues of trees radiate out from the seven-acre **Round Pond**, where model boats are sailed.

Italian Gardens

Other highlights of the park include Sir George Frampton's **Peter Pan** statue, the **Long Water**, and the striking bronze figure entitled **Physical Energy**, in the centre of the park. The **Elfin Oak**, carved in 1930 with fairies and elves, is at the northern end of the Broad Walk. The **Serpentine Gallery** has a reputation for exhibiting controversial contemporary art. *(Beside West Carriage Drive, ☎ 020-7402-6075 for exhibition times. Admission is free.)*

Kensington Palace

for less Kensington Palace has been a royal residence since 1689. Originally a Jacobean mansion, the Palace was substantially rebuilt by Sir Christopher Wren and his assistant, Nicholas Hawksmoor. Wren added pavilions to each corner and re-oriented the building to create a courtyard on the west side.

Princess Victoria was born at the palace in 1819 and 18 years later was woken here at 5am to be told she was the new Queen of the British Empire.

Bed inside Kensington Palace

You can visit the east side, where the tour is divided into two sections: the **State Apartments** and the **Court Dress Collection**, both recently refurbished. *(The Broad Walk, ☎ 020-7937-9561. Mon-Sun: 10am-5pm (last admission 4.30pm). Adult £9.50, child £7.10, senior and student £7.70. 10% discount per person with voucher on page 281.)*

Kensington Palace

Regent's Park

Regent's Park is the second largest open space in central London after Hyde Park/Kensington Gardens. It draws tens of thousands of people every day: office workers playing ball games, visitors to the **Open Air Theatre** *(Box Office ☎ 020-7486-2431)* or the **Zoo**, families boating on the lake and couples wandering the paths that criss-cross the park.

Regent's Park

The park was laid out between 1817 and 1828 by **John Nash** for the Prince Regent, hence the title Regent's Park. Nash's original grand plan for 56 villas and a royal residence for the prince was significantly scaled down. Only eight villas and several palatial terraces were built. However, the double-circle framework has remained, preserving the boundaries of this spacious park.

Initially, access to the park was restricted to people living in the surrounding mansions and those rich enough to have carriages. In 1845, however, the public was allowed into the park on two days of the week for a small entrance fee. The park suffered severe damage in the Second World War, when troops encamped there were targeted by V2 rockets. A huge amount of bomb rubble was dumped in the park, levelling off previously undulating grassland.

The park has several beautiful formal gardens, and well-manicured flower beds stretch along the main north-south avenue. There are over 6,000 forest trees and, in **Queen Mary's Garden** in the Inner Circle, 400 varieties of rose. The main lake, shaped like a curved 'Y', has six wooded islands. The **Heronry**, with 25 breeding pairs, is on the island closest to the fork of the 'Y'. From all round the lake, you can see the golden dome of the **London Central Mosque** beside Hanover Gate.

There is a separate children's pool west of the main lake, with canoes, rowing and pedal boats for hire.

Open Air Theatre

HOURS

Mon-Sun: 5am-dusk

Queen Mary's Garden

Central Mosque

The Boating Lake

ADDRESS

Regent's Park North
☎ 020-7722-3333

GETTING THERE

Camden Town or Regent's
Park tube stations

HOURS

Mon-Sun: 10am-5.30pm
Last admission 4.30pm

PRICES

Adult £9
Child (3-14) £7
Senior £8
Student £8

DISCOUNT

20% discount with *for less* card (present at Group Sales Enquiries Office at front gate)

 # London Zoo . . .

Located at the northern end of Regent's Park, the 170-year-old London Zoo has for many years been concerned with the conservation of endangered species.

The Zoological Society of London was founded in 1826 by Sir Stamford Raffles, and the Zoological

A resident of the Mappin Terraces

Gardens opened four years later to house the society's growing collection of animals. Those from the royal collection, which had previously been housed in the Tower of London, joined the menagerie later.

Residents from the early days included Jumbo the African elephant, a four-ton hippopotamus, and the giraffes, whose coats inspired a craze for animal-print material in the mid-1830s.

Giant pandas from China were brought to the attention of the public when the first arrived at the Zoo in 1938, and their diminishing numbers in the wild have been of concern ever since.

A Sumatran tiger

During the Second World War many of the animals were evacuated to Ireland, although some unfortunates, such as the fish, had to be "sacrificed" due to the food shortage.

Today, the Zoo is home to more than 12,000 creatures, not counting the ants in the ant colony. There are almost 100 rare species, like the Arabian oryx and Persian leopard. Of particular note is the breeding programme for Sumatran tigers, of which there are only 800 left in the world.

As well as giraffes, gorillas, and rhinos, there are three Asian elephants, Dilberta, Layang-Layang and Mya,

. . . London Zoo

each of whom is brought out for a daily weigh-in.

The **Aquarium**, which was the first in the world, has several tanks including separate ones for sharks and piranhas.

The **Reptile House** is home to boa constrictors, alligators and a collection of some of the most deadly snakes in the world. There is an accompanying display about the effects of snake bites and venom.

One of the biggest crowd-pullers is penguin feeding time, which takes place at the famous **Penguin Pool**, an impressive example of modernist architecture designed in 1934 by Berthold Lubetkin.

Moonlight World is devoted to nocturnal creatures, including bats and bushbabies. The animals are revealed by special lighting.

The **Invertebrate House** has a trio of Mexican Red-kneed Bird-eating Spiders, called Sharon, Tracey and Frieda, and a variety of other creepy-crawlies including cockroaches, locusts and giant centipedes.

INSIDER'S TIP

There are various presentations and feeding times throughout the day. Pick up details at the main gate

DON'T MISS

The noisy gibbons, who signal closing time every day by hooting and howling at the tops of their voices

The Zoo remains very popular with children, partly due to the **Touch Paddock** where they can stroke sheep, goats and wallabies.

The Zoo is almost as famous for its diversity of architecture, and several of the enclosures are Grade One listed buildings. In addition as the aforementioned Penguin Pool, look out for Lord Snowdon's **Aviary**. Built in the 1960s, it is a huge, netted construction, spacious enough for the birds to fly freely inside.

Casson's unusual **Elephant and Rhino Pavilion** was also constructed in the 1960s. The newly reopened Mappin Terraces, resembling a mountainous environment, provide an authentic home for sloth bears.

Recently, modernisation of the facilities and an even greater shift in emphasis towards conservation issues has demonstrated the importance of the zoo and the vital work it does to contribute to the protection of endangered animals.

New: the astonishing **Web of Life** introduces visitors to the amazing range of animals found in the world's natural habitats, using live animal exhibits and interactive displays.

Green Park and St. James's Park

St. James's Park and Green Park well deserve their 'royal' epithet, as Buckingham Palace overlooks the tree-lined walkways of both.

Duck Island

HOURS

Mon–Sun: 24 hours a day

INSIDER'S TIP

The pelicans are fed with whole fish at 4pm daily on the lawn near Duck Island.

Constitution Arch

St. James's Park began its long royal association in 1532, when Henry VIII had it enclosed for deer hunting and built the Palace of St. James's.

James I introduced exotic animals, such as an elephant and crocodiles, given to him by foreign princes.

Pelicans in St. James's Park

Charles II, who had been captivated by the gardens of Versailles, created the first formal gardens and a half-mile ornamental canal was dug down the middle of the park.

In the late 18th century, the architect John Nash re-landscaped the park. Adopting a more romantic style, he created winding paths and a natural-looking lake. Today, it remains much how he left it.

The view from the bridge in the centre of the lake, with Buckingham Palace in one direction and Westminster in the other, is one of the finest in London. Bahama pintails, chiloe wigeon and pelicans inhabit the lake and the **Duck Island** sanctuary, east of the bridge. In summer, brass bands give lunchtime and evening concerts on the bandstand north of the bridge.

Green Park is more peaceful than its neighbour, St. James's. The benches on the long, leafy avenues are rarely full.

At the western tip of the park is the spectacular **Constitution Arch**, marooned on the traffic island known as Hyde Park Corner.

The arch is topped by the immense bronze statue *Quadriga*, depicting Peace riding a chariot drawn by four rearing horses. The size of the statue can be gauged from the fact that the sculptor, Adrian Jones, held a dinner for eight people inside one of the horses shortly before it was completed in 1912.

Constitution Arch

London by Night

Introduction

Whether you want to see a show, listen to some live jazz, watch a film at a big-screen cinema, eat at an exotic restaurant or go nightclubbing, the choice in London is huge and bewildering.

Each of the eight areas in this guide has restaurants, cinemas and clubs, but the West End is the principal entertainment district. Tens of thousands of people head to the West End every night of the week. On Fridays and Saturdays, the busiest nights, the area is overrun, and queues form outside some pubs and restaurants. Simply wandering through the streets among the crowds is an experience in itself.

Her Majesty's Theatre

The West End is a remarkably compact area, with entertainment venues of all kinds packed tightly together. Whether you have tickets for a theatre on Shaftesbury Avenue, the Strand or in Covent Garden, you will have a choice of several dozen restaurants within two minutes walk.

Legal restrictions on serving alcohol after 11pm have recently been relaxed and now many West End bars stay open later. Soho and Mayfair have the most late-night bars, though they can be difficult to get into after 11pm: try the Atlantic Bar *(20 Glasshouse Street)* or Café Boheme *(13 Old Compton Street)*. In Soho, several cafés stay open until the early hours serving food and non-alcoholic drinks, including Bar Italia *(22 Frith Street)*.

Café de Paris

Although the tube system closes shortly after midnight, night buses run at roughly hourly intervals throughout the night, starting in Trafalgar Square.

Beware of the rip-off 'strip' clubs around Wardour Street in Soho. You may pay only a modest entry fee, but compulsory drinks can boost the bill per person to well in excess of £100, with bouncers adopting aggressive tactics to extract your cash. Westminster City Council is trying to clamp down on the con-men, so inquire if the club has a current council licence.

REFLECTIONS

'The metropolis affords many amusements which are open to all; it is itself an astonishing and perpetual spectacle to the curious eye. The pleasures...are within the reach of every man who is regardless of his health, his money, and his company.' – Autobiography, Edward Gibbon (1796)

Theatres

London's renowned theatre scene is a major visitor attraction. There are clusters of theatres in three main areas: Shaftesbury Avenue/Haymarket, St. Martin's Lane/ Charing Cross Road and Covent Garden/the Strand.

Many of the theatres have colourful histories. The interiors are often richly decorated with painted ceilings and wooden carvings. Some are reputed to have ghosts. It is claimed that the **Garrick** (Charing Cross Road, ☎ 020-7494-5085) , for example, is haunted by Arthur Bourchier, the theatre's manager 100 years ago, who hated critics and is said to be trying to scare them off. The most famous theatre of all, the **Theatre Royal, Drury Lane** (page 78), is nearly 200 years old. There has been a theatre on the site since the 1660s, when Charles II's mistress, Nell Gwyn, performed comic roles.

The Garrick

In addition to the dozens of independent theatres, there are two main national companies: the **Royal National Theatre** (South Bank, ☎ 020-7452-3333) and the **Royal Shakespeare Company**.

The West End hit musical "Miss Saigon"

From December to February, several theatres stage **pantomimes**, musical comedies with lots of audience participation and absurd costumes. A trip to the pantomime is a well-loved British family tradition.

If you feel like experimenting, London is richly endowed with innovative fringe theatre. Productions are usually staged in rooms over pubs, such as the **Gate Theatre** (11 Pembridge Road, ☎ 020-7229-5387) above Notting Hill's Prince Albert, the **Grace** (503 Battersea Park Road, ☎ 020-7794-0022) above Battersea's Latchmere, and the theatre at Islington's **King's Head** (115 Upper Street, ☎ 020-7226-1916).

The Royal National Theatre

INSIDER'S TIP

In the summer months, open-air theatre is performed in Regent's Park (☎ 020-7486-2431) and Holland Park (☎ 020-7602-7856). Take a picnic and rugs to keep you warm.

The **Lyceum Theatre** (Wellington Street, ☎ 020-7656-1803), which lay derelict for eight years, has benefited from a £14.5 million restoration and is currently showing the tremendously popular Lion King. Notre Dame de Paris, a musical adaptation of Quasimodo's story, will run at the **Dominion** (Tottenham Court Road, ☎ 020-7416-6060) until at least Autumn 2000.

Lyceum Theatre

Opera, Ballet and Classical Concerts

Huge subsidies and grants ensure devotees of classical music and opera have much to celebrate in

London. There are five orchestras and two permanent opera companies, as well as a host of smaller ensembles and touring companies. Below is a brief guide to London's leading opera houses and concert halls. Also, see pages 206-208 to see where you can obtain discounts with your *for less* card.

The **Royal Opera House** has undergone major refurbishment, partially paid for by an enormous National Lottery grant (the size of which delighted British opera

Royal Opera House

lovers, but outraged just about everyone else).

London Coliseum

Sadler's Wells *(Rosebery Avenue, ☎ 020-7863-8000)* is renowned for its daring ballet productions, including a recent version of *Swan Lake* in which men were cast as swans. It plays host to several excellent touring companies, including the Gilbert and Sullivan specialists D'Oyly Carte in April and May.

The **London Coliseum** is the home of the **English National Opera** (page 206), which pulls in younger crowds with audacious productions sung in English.

The **Royal Albert Hall** *(Kensington Gore, ☎ 020-7589-8212)* hosts the Promenade Concerts from mid-July to mid-September . The 'Proms', are very British events,

Royal Albert Hall

which end with an outpouring of national sentiment during the televised 'Last Night of the Proms'. Tickets can be bought on the day of a performance, though queues form early. Other concerts and special events take place throughout the year at this historic venue (page 117).

The English National Ballet

The **Royal Festival Hall** *(South Bank, ☎ 020-7960-4242)* at the South Bank Centre hosts seasons by the English National Ballet and regular classical concerts. The RFH was built to mark the 1951 Festival of Britain.

Royal Festival Hall

The **Barbican Centre** *(Silk Street, ☎ 020-7638-8891)* is the home of the London Symphony Orchestra and is renowned for its performances of contemporary music. There are frequent free foyer concerts.

Cinemas

With more than 200 screens in central London alone, finding a film to suit your taste should not be a problem.

The Warner Village West End

Several of the biggest screens are to be found in the cinemas around Leicester Square. This is where most films tend to be premièred in Britain, where film launches lag weeks or months behind the US.

Empire Leicester Square

On the north side, is the **Empire**, proud of being Britain's most expensive cinema (£9 a seat). It has 1,200 plush seats, a massive screen, Digital Dolby Surround Sound and an opening laser show. *(Leicester Square, ☎ 0870-603-4567)*

The other big screens on Leicester Square are the **Odeon** *(☎ 0870-505-0007)* to the East and the **Warner Village West End** *(☎ 020-7437-3484)* in the North East corner.

Expect to pay £7-9 for a seat in the West End, with a soft drink and tub of popcorn adding another £3-4. Most of the large cinemas accept credit card telephone bookings.

Films are given certificates (ratings) according to minimum age limits, i.e. 18, 15 and 12, while others are PG (meaning 'parental guidance' but no age restriction) and U for 'universal' (acceptable for young children).

London has several independent art-house cinemas, which generally spurn Hollywood blockbusters and specialize instead in off-beat, cult and foreign language movies. Below is a list of the best art-house cinemas.

Barbican *(Silk Street, ☎ 020-7638-8891)*; **ICA Cinematheque** *(The Mall, ☎ 020-7930-3647)*; **Lumière** *(17 Queensbury Place, ☎ 020-7838-2144)*; **Minema** *(45 Knightsbridge, ☎ 020-7369-1723)*; **National Film Theatre** *(South Bank, ☎ 0171 928 3232)*; and **Renoir** *(Brunswick Square, ☎ 020-7837-8402)*.

The **London Film Festival** in November screens at least 100 of the world's best films from that year. There are various venues, but the National Film Theatre is the principal host.

National Film Theatre

INSIDER'S TIP

For a luxurious cinematic experience, try the more intimate surroundings of the **Curzon Mayfair**, London's smartest cinema.

Odeon cinema

Nightclubs

Staying abreast of the latest trends in London's ever-changing nightclub scene is a full-time job. A certain

club can be wildly popular one night of the week, while the next night it is deserted.

However, amid all the breathless variety and glamour, there are a few stalwarts that consistently pull in the crowds.

The dress code varies, though many places frown on jeans, T-shirts and trainers (sneakers). Most places open around 10pm and keep going until at least 3am (later at Legends, Ministry

A night on the town

of Sound and Wag). Expect to pay an entry charge of at least £10 on Friday and Saturday nights, and considerably more at the top spots. The clubs section of *Time Out* (a London magazine with extensive listings) gives details of 200 different clubs and one-nighters.

Listed below are a few recommended dance clubs.

Hippodrome *(Charing Cross Road, ☎ 020-7437-4311)*, one of London's biggest clubs, has a brilliant light show, but the décor is a little dated. It also stages a top-notch floor show that regularly springs surprises.

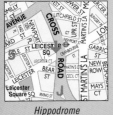

Hippodrome

Ministry of Sound *103 Gaunt Street, ☎ 020-7378-6528)* is well outside the city centre, but it is worth the trek for the astonishing energy of the young clubbers.

Stringfellows *(16 Upper St. Martin's Lane, ☎ 020-7240-5534)* has more limousines parked outside it than any other club in London. Always ahead of its time, it was the first club to introduce table dancers.

Stringfellows

Heaven *(Underneath the Arches, Villiers Street, ☎ 020-7930-2020)*, London's

Hippodrome nightclub

legendary gay club, is practically a village with its maze of bars, dance floors, shops and refreshment kiosks that are located in the cavernous vaults beneath Charing Cross Station.

Jazz Clubs

The **Jazz Café** *(5 Parkway, Camden Town tube station, ☎ 020-7916-6060)* features some of the biggest names in jazz, Latin and hip hop. Booking a table is highly recommended.

100 Club

Ronnie Scott's

Ronnie Scott's *(47 Frith Street, ☎ 020-7439-0747)* is the legendary Soho jazz club founded by the British saxophonist Ronnie Scott, who died tragically in late 1996. Book a table close to the stage for the best views. Upstairs you can dance to Jazz, Funk and Soul on Wednesdays and Thursdays and Salsa Music on Fridays and Saturdays

The **100 Club** *(100 Oxford Street, ☎ 020-7636-0933)* hosted The Who and the Rolling Stones in the 1960s, then the Sex Pistols and the Clash in the 1970s. It has now reverted to its former identity as a club for jazz and blues enthusiasts.

Comedy Clubs

The Comedy Store *(1a Oxendon Street, ☎ 020-7344-0234)*, the most famous comedy club in Britain, is where all the best stand-up comedians appear. Tickets are gold dust for the Comedy Store Players' superb improvisation shows on Wednesdays and Sundays.

A night of comedy at **Jongleurs** *(☎ 01426-944346)* involves a trip out of the centre to one of this famous club's two venues at either Battersea *(The Cornet, 49 Lavender Gardens)* or Camden Lock *(Dingwalls Building, Chalk Farm Road)*.

Oranje Boom Boom *(Macclesfield Street ☎ 020-7437-2494)* is one London's more intimate comedy spots, with highly original acts playing Wednesday nights in a crowded room over De Hems pub near Chinatown.

The Comedy Café *(Rivington Street ☎ 020-7739-5706)*, based in the City, has some of the most talented emerging stand-up comedians. The club also has the advantage of a late alcohol license until 1am on certain nights.

The Comedy Store

Live Music

London's band venues range from the huge to the intimate. Big name groups play the **Astoria** *(157 Charing Cross Road, ☎ 020-7434-0403)*, **Shepherd's Bush Empire** *(Shepherd's Bush Green, ☎ 020-7771-2000)* and **Earl's Court** *(Warwick Road, ☎ 020-7373-8141)*.

If you're in London for just a few days, you're more likely to catch a local band playing a friendly gig in a pub or bar. Try the central **Acoustic Café** *(17 Manette Street, ☎ 020-7439-0831)* or the **12-Bar Club** *(22-23 Denmark Place, ☎ 020-7916-6989)* for roots, folk, blues, indie, rock and Irish. The **Embassy Rooms** *(161 Tottenham Court Road, ☎ 020-7387-2414)* offers an eclectic range of gigs by, sometimes, pretty famous bands.

12-Bar Club

DISCOUNT

Discounts vary but are typically 20% to 50% off. Discounts are subject to availability.

West End Shows

Ticketmaster-London for less
☎ 020-7413-1436

(Telephone 24-hours a day and ask what discounts are currently available with London for less. AM/VS/MC. c.£10-50.)

Ticketmaster offers discounts off West End shows to *for less* cardholders. The number and level of discounts available will vary from time-to-time. You can also book non-discounted tickets but a booking fee might be charged.

English National Opera

London Coliseum, St. Martin's Lane
☎ 020-7632-8300

(Visit Box Office or order tickets by phone Mon-Sat 10am-8pm. AM/VS/MC/DC. £6.50-£45)

DISCOUNT

20% off tickets Mon-Thu and Sat matinées with your *for less* card. Discounts are subject to availability.

The ENO performs from September to July at the magnificent Coliseum. Formed in 1931, the ENO aims to make opera accessible to everyone. Its spectacular and innovative performances are always in English.

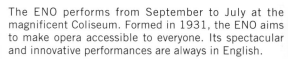

English National Ballet

London Coliseum
St. Martin's Lane
☎ 020-7632-8300

(Call the Box Office for performance times and to purchase tickets. AM/VS/MC/DC.)

DISCOUNT
25% discount off all tickets over £8. Discounts are subject to availability.

The English National Ballet is England's premier classical touring company. In December 2000 the company will perform *The Nutcracker* at the London Coliseum.

 # Almeida Theatre

Almeida Street,
Islington
☎ 020-7359-4404

(Call the Box Office for performance times and prices. AM/VS/MC/DC. £6.50-19.50.)

DISCOUNT
2 tickets for the price of 1 on day of performance only. Discounts are subject to availability.

The Almeida is one of Britain's most exciting and innovative theatres. It produces an ambitious programme of classical and contemporary plays, providing epic theatre in an intimate space.

 # Royal Philharmonic Orchestra

Royal Albert Hall
☎ 020-7589-8212

(For details of concerts call ☎ 020-7608-2381. AM/VS/MC/DC. £5-27.)

DISCOUNT
25% off all tickets over £10. Discounts are subject to availability.

The Royal Philharmonic is Britain's national orchestra. It works with the finest conductors and artists, and performs concerts at the Royal Albert Hall throughout the year.

DISCOUNT

25% off all tickets with your *for less* card. Discounts are subject to availability.

DISCOUNT

25% off all tickets with your *for less* card. Discounts are subject to availability.

DISCOUNT

Adult price reduced to £6 with your *for less* card. Discounts are subject to availability.

The London Philharmonic

Royal Festival Hall
☎ 020-7960-4242

(Call the Royal Festival Hall for performance times and prices. AM/VS/MC/DC. £5-32.)

The London Philharmonic's repertoire ranges from traditional classical music to world premières. The orchestra is resident at the Royal Festival Hall from September to May.

The Philharmonia

Royal Festival Hall
☎ 020-7960-4242

(Call the Royal Festival Hall for performance times and prices. AM/VS/MC/DC. £5-30.)

The Philharmonia is world renowned for the quality of its playing. Approximately 30 concerts are held at the Royal Festival Hall throughout the year except during July and August.

BBC Symphony Orchestra

Royal Festival Hall
☎ 020-7960-4242

(Call the Royal Festival Hall for performance times and prices. AM/VS/MC/DC. Adult £11, child £6, senior £6, student £6.)

The BBC Symphony Orchestra was London's first permanent orchestra. It has always had a special commitment to 20th century music. Seats for concerts at the Royal Festival Hall are unreserved, so arrive early.

Greater London

Hampstead & Highgate . . .

Hampstead and Highgate

One of the most fashionable of London's boroughs, Hampstead breathes an air of superiority stemming partly from its location on a high ridge overlooking central London.

A Hampstead Garden

For two centuries, Hampstead has been popular with artists, scholars and writers. Among those who lived here were the Romantic poet John Keats, whose house you can visit *(Wentworth Place, Keats Grove, ☎ 0171 435 2062)*, the painter John Constable and the writers H.G. Wells, D.H. Lawrence and Katherine Mansfield.

GETTING THERE

Hampstead: Hampstead tube station

The well-preserved Georgian village is now bristling with stylish bars, restaurants and boutiques. Yet for most Londoners, Hampstead means one thing: the glorious 800-acre wooded expanse of **Hampstead Heath**. There is an unparalleled view of London from the top of **Parliament Hill**, on the southern stretch of the Heath. A network of pretty streets runs between the Heath and Hampstead High Street, with interesting specialist shops lining **Flask Walk** and **Well Walk**. Around the corner from the tube station is **Church Row**, one of London's finest Georgian streets.

Kenwood House

Kenwood House, at the northern tip of the Heath beside Hampstead Lane, sits majestically atop a steep bank. The original 17th-century mansion was redesigned in the 1760s by Robert Adam for the Earl of Mansfield. As Lord Chief Justice, Mansfield sent more than 100 people to the gallows and was one of the most hated men of his day. Kenwood's last private owner, the Earl of Iveagh of the Guinness dynasty, bequeathed the house and his superb art collection to the nation in 1927. The **Iveagh Bequest** includes important works by Van Dyck, Gainsborough and Reynolds as well as a Rembrandt self-portrait. Adam's blue and gold library, with its richly decorated tunnel-vaulted ceiling, is the principal feature of the interior. *(8 Hampstead Lane, ☎ 020-8348-1286. Apr-Sep: Mon-Sun: 10am-6pm. Oct-Mar: Mon-Sun: 10am-4pm (10.30am Wed & Fri). Admission is free.)*

REFLECTIONS

'I have hated Hampstead for her Left-wingery, but I have loved her for her strange, secret, leafy soul. Nowhere in London are green thoughts so green, especially in rainy June, when grass grows high in her innumerable gardens tamed or wild.' – *The Stretchford Chronicles*, Peter Simple (1980)

. . . Hampstead & Highgate

Classical concerts are held on summer evenings in the huge, grassy amphitheatre below Kenwood House. The orchestra plays under a canopy across the lake from the audience. The highlight of the season is Handel's *Fireworks Music*, played on July 4 and accompanied by a fireworks show to celebrate America's Independence Day. *(Kenwood Lakeside Concerts, Jun-Sep: Saturdays only, ☎ 020-8348-1286.)*

Hampstead High Street

The Spaniard's Inn *(Spaniard's Road)*, opposite the heath on Spaniard's Road, is a 16th-century weatherboarded house. The infamous highwayman Dick Turpin stabled his horse, Black Bess, at the inn and Shelley, Keats and Byron all frequented it. Dickens used the inn for the scene in *The Pickwick Papers* where Mrs Bardell plots the downfall of Mr Pickwick. There are real fires in winter and a beautiful garden with rose bushes and plenty of picnic tables.

On the other side of the Heath, to the east, lies the equally exclusive **Highgate**. While the literati preferred Hampstead, Highgate has maintained its own prestige largely through its famous cemetery, where **Karl Marx** is buried. Most people head for the **East Cemetery**, where Marx lies beneath an enormous black bust. However, the wilder and spookier **West Cemetery**, which inspired Bram Stoker to write *Dracula*, is much the more memorable. Tours of the West Cemetery are run by the Friends of Highgate Cemetery, who have restored the grand tombs, including the **Egyptian Avenue** and a group of incredibly ostentatious mausoleums built for rich Victorian families. *(East Cemetery: ☎ 020-8340-1834, Apr-Oct: 10am-5pm, Nov-Mar: 10am-4pm. Admission £2. West Cemetery entry by tour only: Mar-Nov: Mon-Fri: 12noon, 2pm and 4pm, Sat-Sun: 11am, 12noon, 1pm, 2pm, 3pm, 4pm. Tour £3.)*

Holly Walk

GETTING THERE

Highgate: Archway tube station

REFLECTIONS

'Coleridge sat on the brow of Highgate Hill, in those years, looking down on London and its smoke-tumult, like a sage escaped from the inanity of life's battle.' – *The Life of John Sterling*, Thomas Carlyle (1851)

Docklands . . .

Docklands

The best place to view the startling modern architecture of this rejuvenated former industrial wasteland is from the driverless **Docklands Light Railway** (DLR).

Departing from Bank tube station in the City or Tower Gateway close to Tower Bridge, the DLR runs on an elevated track down through the Isle of Dogs. It passes **One Canada Square,** the 800-foot (240-metre) stainless steel-clad tower at Canary Wharf designed by Cesar Pelli. The tower symbolises the 1980s and 90s rebirth of the old docks which lie immediately to the east of the City.

Docklands' skyline

For 300 years, until the middle of this century, the **Port of London** was the key to the city's wealth. Thousands of ships would queue to unload their wares at the vast docks. In 1981, two decades after the port had moved to Tilbury, the London Docklands Development Corporation began redeveloping the area. Canadian property giant Olympia & York invested most of the money, and, after huge losses, went bust in the recession of the early 1990s.

The **London Docklands Visitor Centre**, close to Crossharbour DLR station, has a free exhibition and video presentation exploring the area's past, present and future. Close to the visitor centre is **Mudchute City Farm,** the largest urban farm in London. It has all the usual farm animals plus a llama called Gaza.

The easiest part of Docklands to explore is **Wapping**, around the corner from the Tower of London. **St. Katharine's Dock**, built in the 1820s to handle luxury goods like ivory and live turtles, is now a yachting marina with authentic swing bridges. The huge timber-framed **Dickens Inn** *(St. Katharine's Way),* though it has no connection with Charles Dickens,

Gaza the llama at Mudchute City Farm

has attractive terraces and a fish restaurant. The building dates from the 1790s, when it was a brewery. For a real Dickens pub, try the **Grapes** at Limehouse *(76 Narrow Street)* which is believed to be the model for the Six Jolly Fellowship Porters in *Our Mutual Friend*.

GETTING THERE

DLR connects with the London Underground at Tower Hill and Bank tube stations. Since 1999, the Jubilee line also goes to the Docklands.

REFLECTIONS

'The new Docklands of the 1980s show the triumph of commercial expediency over civic values. Too many mediocre buildings, and a railway suitable only for Toytown represent a feeble contribution to the rebuilding of the capital.' – HRH Charles, Prince of Wales (1989)

. . . Docklands

Purists scoff at the hotch-potch of high-rise architecture that makes up Docklands, but there are several stunning buildings. **Cascades**, on Westferry Road, is a peculiar, stepped pyramid of apartments overlooking the river.

By far the most impressive building in Docklands is **One Canada Square**, the 60-floor tower that is the centrepiece of the Canary Wharf development. The tallest building in Europe after Frankfurt's Messerturm, the tower is capped by a glass pyramid which is illuminated at Christmas with red and green lights. Two similar towers were part of the original design but were never built. For several years the existing tower remained mostly empty. Its fortunes changed in the mid-1990s,

One of Docklands' historic pubs

however, when the national press decamped to it from Fleet Street. The building has become a vertical Fleet Street, accommodating the *Mirror*, the *Independent*, the *Daily Telegraph* and

Millwall Dock

several Sunday newspapers. Unfortunately, the tower was closed to the public after the Irish Republican Army detonated a huge bomb at nearby South Quay station in February 1996, killing two people.

Cabot Square, in front of the tower, is a lush shopping mall with designer boutiques. Several local pubs have pleasant waterside terraces, including the **Cat and the Canary** (*1-24 Fisherman's Walk*). The latter has pews and a pulpit recycled from old churches and is popular with journalists from One Canada Square.

Island Gardens is the final stop on the DLR at the southern-most tip of the Isle of Dogs. The view from here across the Thames to the Royal Naval College at Greenwich was painted in 1755 by Canaletto. The scene has changed little since then.

INSIDER'S TIP

The Thames Barrier, the largest moveable flood barrier in the world, is one of London's modern engineering wonders. It is a couple of miles downriver from Canary Wharf. ☎ 020-8305-4188

One Canada Square

Greenwich . . .

Greenwich and the
Cutty Sark

GETTING THERE

Take the DLR (which
connects with the London
Underground at Tower Hill)
to Island Gardens and
cross the river to the Cutty
Sark via the Greenwich
Foot Tunnel. Return to
central London by boat
from Greenwich.

Alternatively, take the river
cruise on page 237 and
receive 20% off ticket
prices with your *for less*
card.

A day trip to Greenwich, by boat along the Thames, has
been enjoyed by generations of Londoners. The
excursion combines fine views of London with
Greenwich's superb museums and historic buildings,
most of which are associated with Britain's maritime
history. Greenwich is also the
site of the Millennium Dome,
Britain's multi-million pound
venture, which will remain in
place until the end of 2000.

The Cutty Sark

for less The **Cutty Sark** is the
world's last surviving tea
clipper – an exceptionally fast
tall sailing ship which catered
for the Victorian fashion for
the freshest tea from China.
This fully rigged ship, open to
visitors in its dry dock, was
considered a modern marvel
in the 1870s because it could
sail between China and London in as few as 107 days.
Several cabins, including the cramped but elegant
officers' saloon, are open for viewing. The main hold
contains an historical display, with a collection of ships'
figureheads. *(King William Walk, ☎ 020-8858-3445. Jun-Sep:
Mon-Sat: 10am-6pm. Sun: 12noon-5pm. Oct-May: Mon-Sat:
10am-5pm. Sun: 12noon-5pm. Adult £3.50, child, senior,
student £2.50. 50% off admission with voucher on page 283.)*

Beside the Cutty Sark is the much smaller **Gipsy Moth
IV**, in which Sir Francis Chichester broke the record
for solo world circumnavigation in 1966/7. It is likely
to be closed throughout 2001 for restoration.

Flamsteed house and the courtyard of the Old
Royal Observatory

The **Royal Naval College**,
around the corner from the
Cutty Sark, is best viewed from
the river. The view of the
buildings stretching out
towards the old observatory on
the hill hasn't changed since
Canaletto painted the scene in
the 18th century. Begun as a
palace for Charles II in the
1660s, the building was later
completed by Sir Christopher Wren as a hospital for
disabled seamen.

The **Pepys Hall** is now the **Greenwich Gateway Visitor
Centre**, a free exhibition. From here you can buy
tickets for the two impressive college buildings open
to the public. Lord Nelson lay in state in 1806 in the

. . . Greenwich

grand **Painted Hall**, and across the courtyard, the **RNC Chapel** is decorated with intricate pastel-shaded plasterwork. *(King William Walk, ☎ 020-8269-4747. Greenwich Gateway Visitor Centre: Mon-Sat: 10am-5pm. Admission to the centre is free. Tickets to Painted Hall and Chapel: Adult £3, others £2.)*

Royal Naval College

The **National Maritime Museum** celebrates Britain's long and glorious naval history. It reopened in 1999 after a major refit, and now has interactive exhibits and hands-on displays. The two existing wings and the new gallery space are enclosed under a soaring glass roof.

The past and present of nautical life are compared. Viking boats and modern seacats can be explored, as can the sunken wreck of the *Titanic*. Maritime themes such as commerce, smuggling and exploration are covered, and fascinating artefacts from the past include Nelson's bloodstained coat.

There is an exhibition of ocean-related art, sculpture and audio-visuals, showing how artists have been inspired by the sea, and visitors can access every item in the museum's vast collection using the computerised **Search Station** facility.

INSIDER'S TIP

Children will enjoy the **All Hands Gallery**, where they can try out sailors' skills.

The **Old Royal Observatory** has displays on astronomy and regular shows in the Planetarium. You can stand on the Greenwich Meridian, with one foot in each of the eastern and western hemispheres. There is a magnificent view across London from the top of the royal park's steep hill. The world sets its clocks according to Greenwich Mean Time (GMT), established in 1884 in recognition of the observatory's success in first calibrating longitude.

The **Telescope Dome** contains a huge Victorian telescope weighing over one and a half tons. The adjoining **Planetarium** runs presentations. The red timeball on top of the observatory dates from 1833, when ships on the Thames adjusted their clocks by it.

The Great Hall in the Queen's House

At the time of writing, Inigo Jones's **Queen's House** is hosting **The Story of Time**, an exploration of time measurement throughout history to herald the millennium. Future temporary exhibitions within the museum will include **South: The Race to the Pole**, the story of Captain Scott's ill-fated expedition. *(National Maritime Museum, Romney Road, ☎ 020-8858-4422. Mon-Sun: 10am-5pm (last admission 4.30pm). Combined ticket includes admission to the museum and the Royal Observatory: Adult £10.50, child free, senior & student £8.40.)*

ADDRESS

Hampton Court
☎ 020-8781-9500

GETTING THERE

Train from Waterloo
Station takes 30 minutes

HOURS

Mar-Oct:
Mon: 10.15am-6pm
Tue-Sun: 9.30am-6pm
(last admission 5.15pm)

Nov-Feb:
Mon: 10.15am-4.30pm
Tue-Sun: 9.30am-4.30pm
(last admission 3.45pm)

 # Hampton Court Palace . . .

The sumptuous interiors and beautiful gardens of Hampton Court, a few miles up the Thames from the centre of London, make it one of the most popular day-trip destinations for tourists and Londoners alike.

Cardinal Wolsey, Henry VIII's Lord Chancellor, built Hampton Court as his own palace in 1516. The extravagance of the buildings annoyed Henry, and

Hampton Court Palace

Wolsey attempted to win back royal favour by handing over the keys to his king.

Henry made substantial changes, rebuilding the chapel and extending the kitchens. Many of the great events of his reign took place at Hampton Court, including the birth of the future King Edward VI and the deaths of Edward's mother and Henry's third wife, Jane Seymour. It was here that Henry, while at mass, was told that his fifth wife, Catherine Howard, had been unfaithful to him.

During the reigns of Elizabeth I and James I, Hampton Court was the centre of the royal court's cultural life, hosting many plays and masques. Charles I was

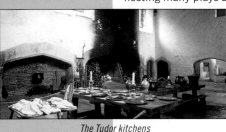

The Tudor kitchens

imprisoned here during the Civil War, after which the Lord Protector, **Oliver Cromwell**, made the palace his home.

William III and Mary II commissioned **Sir Christopher Wren** to remodel the buildings and design the new Banqueting House on the river. George III decided to turn the place over to members of the royal household and some parts still serve as 'grace and favour' residences for retired royal employees and courtiers.

A devastating fire in 1986 destroyed part of William III's **King's Apartments**. It was accidentally started by the bedside candle of an elderly resident, Lady Gale, who died in the blaze. Elizabeth II reopened the restored King's Apartments in 1992. The marvellous wall and ceiling paintings above the **King's Staircase**

. . . Hampton Court Palace [for less]

are by Antonio Verrio. The paintings represent a political allegory praising William III.

The King's Apartments are one of the palace's six thematic walking routes for visitors. Starting in Base Court, Clock Court or Fountain Court, the routes explore the public and private lives of the monarchs who lived at Hampton Court. One route explores the **Tudor Kitchens**, laid out as if a royal banquet was being prepared, while another proceeds through the magnificent Great Hall and Chapel of **Henry VIII's State Apartments**.

An aerial view of the Palace

Hanging from the walls of the **Great Hall** are priceless Flemish tapestries of the Story of Abraham, commissioned by Henry VIII in the late 1520s.

Shakespeare's *Hamlet* and *Henry VIII* were performed in the Great Hall before George I in 1718.

The **Haunted Gallery**, said to be haunted by the ghost of Catherine Howard, leads into the **Chapel**. The timber-vaulted Chapel ceiling, with its glorious blue and gold design, is the most important Tudor ceiling in the country. The great oak panel behind the altar, flanked by double columns, was carved by Grinling Gibbons in the reign of Queen Anne.

An historical guide

The **Renaissance Picture Gallery** contains the finest Renaissance works from Elizabeth II's collection, including Pieter Breugel the Elder's *The Massacre of the Innocents*.

The **Palace Gardens,** which cover 60 acres, include the famous **Maze** which dates from the 1690s. The **Great Vine**, planted in 1768, still produces an annual crop of delicious grapes. The serenely beautiful **Pond Gardens** were built by Henry VIII in 1536 as ornamental fishponds to breed edible fish for the royal table.

The maze

PRICES

Adult £10.50
Child £7
Senior £8
Student £8

DISCOUNT

10% off admission with voucher on page 283.

Windsor . . .

Windsor Castle, with its mighty medieval turrets and towers, is the oldest royal residence to have remained in continuous use by British monarchs.

Windsor Castle

Founded as a fortress by William the Conqueror in 1080, the castle occupies a naturally defendable chalk ridge 100 feet (30 metres) above the Thames. The proximity of the fortress to royal hunting grounds (now **Windsor Great Park**), encouraged Henry II to convert it into a palace in the 12th century. The greatest medieval expansion of Windsor took place during the reign of Edward III, who spent the proceeds from his military triumphs on creating a palace of chivalric splendour.

ADDRESS

Windsor Castle
☎ 01753-868-286

GETTING THERE

Direct train from Waterloo Station to Windsor Riverside (50 minutes) or train from Paddingtion Station to Windsor Central changing at Slough (35 minutes).

During the **English Civil War** in the 1640s, Parliamentary forces seized the castle and used it as a prison for royalists. Charles I was buried in the vaults beneath St. George's Chapel after he was beheaded at Whitehall in 1649. After the Restoration of the Monarchy in 1660, the new king, Charles II, initiated a grand refurbishment of the castle to assert his royal glory. Ceiling paintings by Antonio Verrio and a magnificent sequence of baroque state apartments were added.

St. George's Chapel

Windsor Castle enjoyed its heyday under **Queen Victoria**, who made it her principal palace. Her husband, Prince Albert, died here on December 14, 1861. A disued 13th-century chapel was lined with gold mosaics and inlaid marble to create the Albert Memorial Chapel.

The present queen, Elizabeth II, spent much of her childhood at Windsor. She still stays at the castle most weekends, for the whole of April and during Ascot week in June. The flagpole of the Round Tower flies the Royal Standard when the Queen is at home.

HOURS

Mar-Oct: Mon-Sun: 9.45am-5.15pm (last admission 4pm).
Oct-Feb: Mon-Sun: 9.45am-4.15pm (last admission 3pm).

On November 20, 1992, a devastating fire broke out in the **Queen's Private Chapel**, destroying the ceilings of **St. George's Hall** and the **State Dining Room**. Fortunately, few artistic treasures were destroyed as the rooms had been emptied for rewiring. The £50 million restoration programme was completed in 1998.

. . . Windsor

The visitors' entrance is on Castle Hill. The State Apartments are accessed from the north terrace. To the east of the entrance hall is **Queen Mary's Dolls' House**, with working water and electricity systems, and miniature books hand-written by leading authors of the 1920s. More than 1,000 craftsmen contributed to the 1:12 scale dolls house.

The **Grand Staircase**, lined with arms and armour, leads to the **Grand Vestibule**, where there are more war trophies. The tour continues into the **Waterloo Chamber**, where the Queen holds an annual luncheon in June for the Knights of the Garter.

After passing through several sumptuous drawing rooms and bedrooms, you come to the **Queen's Ballroom**, with its three glorious chandeliers and collection of portraits by Sir Anthony Van Dyck. The **Queen's Presence Chamber** has perhaps the finest of the surviving Verrio ceilings, framed by exquisite 17th-century wood carvings.

The Queen's Presence Chamber

St. George's Chapel is the resting place of ten sovereigns. Completed in 1528, it is dedicated to St. George, the patron saint of the Most Noble Order of the Garter, Britain's highest order of chivalry.

Make sure you save some time to explore **Windsor Great Park**, with its three-mile **Long Walk**. At the far end of the Long Walk is the huge equestrian statue of George III known as the Copper Horse.

In **Windsor Home Park**, to the south-east of the castle, is **Frogmore House**, which dates from the 1680s. It was a favoured retreat of Queen Victoria, who built an elaborate mausoleum in the picturesque gardens.

Across the river from Windsor Castle is the one street village of **Eton**, famous as the home of **Eton College**, where Britain's 'ruling class' has traditionally been educated. Charles and Diana's son, Prince William, is a pupil at the school. The highlight for visitors is the **College Chapel** (1482) with its fan vaulting and medieval wall paintings.

PRICES

Adult £10.50
Child (under 17) £5
Senior £8
Student £10.50

Prices when State Apartments are closed:
Adult £5
Child (under 17) £2.50
Senior £4
Student £5

DON'T MISS

Library of Queen Mary's Dolls' House and gold mosaic ceiling of the Albert Memorial Chapel.

The Grand Vestibule

Kew Gardens

The world-renowned **Royal Botanic Gardens** never fail to bewitch visitors with their tranquil beauty and year-round profusion of the colourful glories of nature.

ADDRESS

Kew, Richmond
☎ 020-8940-1171

GETTING THERE

Kew Gardens tube station

HOURS

Mon-Fri: 9.30am-6.30pm
Sat-Sun: 9.30am-7.30pm
Last admission 30 minutes
before closing
Glasshouses close at
5.30pm

PRICES

Adult £5
Child £2.50
Senior £3.50
Student £3.50
Includes entry to all places
highlighted in text except
Kew Palace.

Kew grows more species of flowers and plants in its 300 acres than any other garden in the world: more than 40,000, many extinct in the wild, are displayed in glasshouses, plantations and in its vast lawns.

The Palm House

As well as being a major attraction for garden-lovers, Kew is a global scientific resource which has played a key role in plant conservation for over 200 years. Captain Cook brought back some of the earliest specimens.

The **Palm House** is the most magnificent of Kew's many glasshouses. Built in the 1840s, it accommodates every main species of palm on the planet in tropical humidity. Dating from the same period is the massive **Temperate House**, with plants from every continent. It boasts the impressive Chilean Wine Palm, probably the tallest indoor palm in the world.

One of Kew's most famous vistas looks upon the 18th-century, ten-storey **Pagoda**. Kew's tallest structure, however, is the 225-foot (67-metre) flagpole hewn from a single Canadian fir tree in 1959.

The **Princess of Wales Conservatory**, opened in 1987, has ten climatic zones and includes a large collection of cacti.

The south-western section of Kew Gardens is the least visited and contains the thatched **Queen Charlotte's Cottage**, built as a royal picnic spot. The tiny **Kew Palace,** which is currently closed for restoration, is the most humble of the royal residences. It is notable for being the place where King George III was confined during his 'madness' in 1802.

Inside a glasshouse

There are two art galleries on the eastern edge of the gardens. The **Kew Gardens Gallery** has exhibitions with horticultural themes. The smaller gallery contains the work of flower painter Marianne North (1830-90).

The Freud Museum

**20 Maresfield Gardens,
Hampstead
☎ 020-7435-2002**

*(Wed-Sun: 12noon-5pm. Mon-
Tue: closed. Adult £4, child £2,
senior £2, student £2.)*

Sigmund Freud lived here from the time that he fled
Vienna until his death. The centrepiece of the museum is
Freud's study, which is preserved intact. The most famous
individual item is Freud's psychoanalytic couch.

DISCOUNT

2 for the price of 1 with
your *for less* card.

 # The Jewish Museum

**129 Albert Street,
Camden Town
☎ 020-7284-1997**

*(Sun-Thu: 10am-4pm. Fri-Sat:
closed. Adult £3, child £1.50,
senior £2, student £1.50.)*

This museum has one of the finest collections of Jewish
ceremonial art. Highlights include a 16th-century Italian
synagogue ark. The discount also applies at the other
location at 80 East End Road, Finchley.

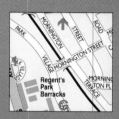

DISCOUNT

50% discount on adult
admission with voucher on
page 283

 # Ranger's House

**Chesterfield Walk,
Blackheath
☎ 020-8853-0035**

*(Apr-Sep: Mon-Sun: 10am-6pm.
Oct-Mar: Mon-Sun: 10am-4pm.
Adult £2.80, student £2.10,
senior £2.10, child £1.40.)*

This handsome red-brick villa, built c.1700, overlooks
Greenwich Park. It is best known for housing the Suffolk
Painting Collection. There is a fascinating Architectural
Study Collection in the Coach House.

DISCOUNT

50% discount on
admission with voucher on
page 283

DISCOUNT

50% discount on admission with voucher on page 283

DISCOUNT

50% off admission with your *for less* card

DISCOUNT

50% discount on admission with voucher on page 283

Chiswick House

Burlington Lane
☎ **020-8995-0508**

(Apr-Sep: Mon-Sun: 10am-6pm.
Oct-Mar: Mon-Sun: 10am-4pm.
Adult £3.30, child £1.70,
senior £2.50, student £2.50.

Chiswick House is a Palladian villa built c.1728 for Lord Burlington who was the architect of the house. Highlights are the lavish blue velvet room and the perfectly symmetrical Italianate gardens.

Dulwich Picture Gallery

College Road, Dulwich
☎ **020-8693-5254**

(Tue-Fri: 10am-5pm. Sat-Sun
11am-5pm. Mon: closed.
Adult £4, student £3,
senior £3, child free.

Dulwich Picture Gallery is Britain's oldest public gallery. The collection includes paintings by Rembrandt, Rubens, Poussin, Van Dyck, Canaletto, Gainsborough, Reynolds and Watteau.

Wimbledon Tennis Museum

Church Road, Wimbledon
☎ **020-8946-6131**

(Mon-Sun: 10.30am-5pm. Sun
2pm-5pm. Mon: closed.
VS/MC. Adult £5, child £4,
senior £4, student £4.

This museum tells the story of the history of lawn tennis. The collection includes rackets, equipment and costumes. You can stand and look out over the famous Centre Court.

Beyond London

Introduction

You could spend a month in London and hardly scratch the surface of what it has to offer. Yet it would be a shame to visit England without exploring beyond the capital. To get a true flavour of traditional English life, you must travel beyond the multicultural melting pot of London.

Victoria Station

England is remarkably compact and dozens of cities, towns and villages can easily be visited on day trips from London. The following pages contain a selection of the most interesting and popular places: the beautiful Georgian city of Bath, with its Roman spa, the ancient university of Oxford, with its fine college buildings, the famous cathedrals of Canterbury, Salisbury and York and several other outstanding places.

The cities, towns and historic sites featured in this chapter have been grouped according to their proximity to each other, to help you plan your trip. For example, an outing to Stonehenge could easily be extended to include a few hours in Salisbury or Shaftesbury. Each of the places listed, except Edinburgh, could comfortably be visited on a day trip.

Internal flights *(British Airways ☎ 0345-222111, British Midland ☎ 0345-554554)* are expensive and only really likely to be useful for getting to Scotland.

Trains *(☎ 0345-484950)* are often the best alternative. Although they can be expensive, day-return tickets are usually cheaper.

Longleat House, near Bath

Coaches *(National Express, ☎ 0990-808080)* are much cheaper, but also much slower.

Renting a car (see opposite) can be an economical way to travel, especially for a group. However, at peak times the motorways into and out of London can be severely congested. Parking is also a nightmare in some cities, especially Oxford, Cambridge and Bath.

Taking a **coach tour** is the most convenient way to cover a number of sites while learning about their history from experienced guides (see pages 238-244).

REFLECTIONS

'The lowest and vilest alleys in London do not present a more dreadful record of sin than does the smiling and beautiful countryside.'
– *Sherlock Holmes*, Sir Arthur Conan Doyle (1892)

INSIDER'S TIP

If you are travelling by train on Saturday or Sunday, buy a Second Class ticket but sit in the First Class carriage. Ask the conductor for a 'Weekend First' upgrade which costs £5-9 and enjoy the luxury of First Class seating at cut-priced rates. The ticket is a flat fee so it makes more sense the longer your journey.

Kenning Car Rental

The United Kenning Group is the largest Car and Van Rental Company in Britain. It has more branches and more vehicles than any other company and can offer you the flexibility to pick-up and drop-off at branches all over the country.

Although special offers by car rental companies might occasionally undercut these rates, *for less* rates are an average of 30% less than standard rates.

You can book your car in advance by telephone or fax by simply quoting your *for less* card number. Alternatively, go to one of Kenning's rental desks and present your card.

Drivers must be aged between 21 and 75 and have a full driving licence for at least a year (it can be your own national licence). There is a charge of £21.30 plus VAT for each extra driver per rental.

Ford Mondeo Estate

ADDRESS

London branches:
88/90 Holland Park Avenue, 1 York Way (Kings Cross), Heathrow Airport and Gatwick Airport
☎ 01246-208888
Fax: 01246-220999
e-mail: LFL@kenning.co.uk

PRICES

Rates include rental, unlimited mileage, No Penalty One Way Drop Off, Third Party Insurance, Loss Damage Insurance, Theft Protection, Insurance Premium Tax and VAT.

Prices do not include an insurance excess of £150 for which the renter is responsible.

Prices do not include the Vehicle Registration Fee of 95p per day plus VAT

Personal Accident Insurance (PAI) is an optional extra at £2.75 a day, except on multi-seaters when it is £7.50 per day.

Cars must not be taken out of Mainland Britain.

London for less daily rates:	1-6 days	7-20 days	21+ days
Manuals			
Fiat Siecento 1.0	N/A	£21.20	£20.50
Ford Fiesta 1.1	£28.00	£24.00	£23.40
Honda Civic 1.4	£32.00	£26.00	£25.50
Ford Focus 1.6	£36.00	£28.00	£27.50
Ford Mondeo 1.8	£38.00	£30.00	£29.00
Ford Mondeo 2.0	£40.00	£32.00	£31.00
Honda Accord 2.0	£44.00	£37.00	£36.00
Automatics			
Ford Fiesta 1.3	£36.00	£28.00	£27.50
Honda Civic 1.6i	£40.00	£32.00	£31.00
Honda Accord 2.0	£46.00	£39.00	£38.00
Alfa Romeo 156	£48.00	£41.00	£40.00
Alfa Romeo 166	£53.00	£46.00	£45.00
Estates			
Honda Civic Aerodeck 1.6	£40.00	£32.00	£31.00
Ford Mondeo 1.8	£44.00	£37.00	£36.00
VW Passat 1.9	£47.00	£40.00	£39.00
Multi-seater			
VW Sharan 1.9 7 seats	£85.00	£74.00	£72.00
L.D.V Minibus 15 seats	£89.00	£78.00	£76.00

Edinburgh . . .

Edinburgh Castle

No other British city apart from London exudes as much national pride and sense of its own grandeur as Edinburgh, the capital of Scotland.

The city is split into the **Old Town**, the tenements and medieval alleys to the south of the castle, and the grand terraces and crescents of the **New Town**, north of **Princes Street**. A testament to the excellence of Georgian town-planning, the New Town was laid out in the 18th century.

There's no escaping **Edinburgh Castle**, perched high on a volcanic promontory above the bustling main shopping thoroughfare, Princes Street. The rock has been a fortification for 1,500 years, but the first castle-like structure was built on it in the 11th century.

Inside the castle, the tiny **St. Margaret's Chapel** survives from this period. National treasures on display include **Scotland's Crown Jewels** and, recently transferred from London's Westminster Abbey, the **Stone of Scone**. The tartan-clad castle guides give informative and entertaining tours, telling the colourful tale of the giant siege gun **Mons Meg**. A more modern field gun is fired from the battlements at 1pm each day. *(Edinburgh Castle, ☎ 0131-225-1012. Apr-Sep: Mon-Sun: 9.30am-6pm. Oct-Mar: Mon-Sun: 9.30am-5pm. Last admission 45 minutes before closing. Adult £7, child £2, senior £5, student £7.)*

VISITOR INFORMATION

Edinburgh & Scotland
Tourist Information Centre
3 Princes Street
Edinburgh EH2 2QP
☎ 0131-437-3800

GETTING THERE

By train from London King's Cross. Trains approximately every hour; the fastest trains take four hours.

By plane from Heathrow (takes one hour).

Running downhill from the castle is the famous **Royal Mile**, which has a number of interesting buildings such as **Gladstone's Land**, a 17th-century merchant's tenement building. The Royal Mile ends at the Queen's official residence in Scotland, the **Palace of Holyrood House**. This is where Mary Queen of Scots spent six years of her reign and where her secretary, David Rizzio, was murdered. A few decades later, Bonnie Prince Charlie held court in the palace before the last, ill-fated invasion of England. Visitors can tour the royal apartments.

Gladstone's Land

The Royal Mile contains many other historic buildings, including **John Knox House**, a medieval house associated with Scotland's religious reformer. After a stern, recorded Presbyterian lecture from John Knox,

. . . Edinburgh

many visitors head for the **Scottish Whisky Heritage Centre** further along the Royal Mile.

The city skyline

Just off the Royal Mile, in Lady Stairs Close, is the **Writers Museum**, commemorating Scotland's national poet, **Robert Burns** and two great novelists, **Sir Walter Scott** and **Robert Louis Stevenson**. This spirit of intellectual excellence, which also produced the philosopher **David Hume** and the economist **Adam Smith**, is still apparent in Edinburgh, which has more bookshops per capita than any other British city.

The National Gallery of Scotland, on Princes Street, has a small but well-presented collection. The most famous exhibit is Canova's *Three Graces*, set prominently in the second of the two main aisles.

Behind Princes Street, at 7 Charlotte Square, is the **Georgian House**, a fine example of 18th century New Town architecture and one of Robert Adam's finest urban architectural achievements.

At the northern edge of the New Town lies the **Royal Botanic Garden**, 70 acres of exotic plants and perfectly manicured flower beds and lawns. Don't miss the elegant, lofty Palm House. A couple of miles west of the centre is **Edinburgh Zoo,** which houses more than 1,000 animals. The highlights are the enormous penguin pool and the well-designed chimpanzee enclosure.

The **Edinburgh International Festival,** Britain's biggest cultural extravaganza, takes place over three hectic weeks in late August and early September. Now 50 years old, the festival incorporates experimental performances in the Festival Fringe, which often threatens to eclipse the main events. Not to be outdone, the armed forces put on an impressive display in the **Edinburgh Military Tattoo** beside the castle.

The Georgian House

Edinburgh's **Hogmanay** claims to be Europe's biggest New Year's Party. It is certainly spectacular, with fireworks cascading down the castle rock, but has begun to be overwhelmed by sheer weight of numbers.

REFLECTIONS

'And so I went to Edinburgh. Can there anywhere be a more beautiful and beguiling city to arrive at by train early on a crisp, dark Novembery evening?'
– *Notes from a Small Island,* Bill Bryson (1995)

Bath

With its graceful, honey-coloured Regency buildings and surrounding wooded hills, Bath is one of Europe's most beautiful cities.

The Royal Crescent in snow

The city owes its existence to the hot springs, around which it is built. According to legend, the healing properties of the springs were first discovered 2,500 years ago when a prince bathed in the waters and was cured of leprosy.

In Roman times, Bath was known as Aquae Sulis, after the goddess Sulis Minerva. The Roman city was centred on a hot spring from which more than a quarter of a million gallons of water still flow each day.

The layout of Bath as seen today is a legacy of Georgian times, when Britain's landed gentry took houses for the 'Season'. They came initially for the healing waters, but Bath soon boasted a social whirl to rival London.

The Roman Baths

There are amazing views from the banks of the River Avon of **Pulteney Bridge**, which houses small shops in its stone buildings.

The interior of **Bath Abbey**, which dates from 1500, has recently been cleaned. Carved stones and pieces of sculpture from the earlier Norman church on this site are displayed in the **Heritage Vaults**.

There are 16 museums in Bath, the most important of which is the **Roman Baths Museum**. Set around the excavated Temple of Sulis Minerva, the museum displays Roman mosaics, coins, jewellery and the gilt bronze head of a goddess, which was found in 1727. *(Abbey Churchyard, ☎ 01225-477785. Apr-Sep: Mon-Sun: 9am-5.30pm. Aug: Mon-Sun: 9am-5.30pm, 8pm-10pm. Oct-Mar: Mon-Sat: 9.30am-5pm. Sun: 10.30am-5pm. Adult £6.90, child (under 18) £4, senior £6, student £6.90)*

The **Victoria Art Gallery** *(opposite Pulteney Bridge)* houses Bath's collection of post-17th-century British and European art, including paintings by Gainsborough and Turner.

VISITOR INFORMATION

Bath Tourist Information Centre
Abbey Chambers
Abbey Church Yard
Bath BA1 1LY
☎ 01225 477101

GETTING THERE

By train from Paddington station. Services run about every half an hour and the journey takes about 1½ hours.

York

The ancient walled city of York is remarkably unscathed by the huge influx of tourists who come to see the majestic cathedral, wander the medieval alleys and enjoy the colourful street entertainers.

The Romans established the first major settlement at York, at the confluence of the River Ouse and River Foss. Initially, the Vikings came to pillage and then founded 'Jorvik', the remains of which have now been excavated.

The best way to see York is from the **Bar Walls** which ring the city. The full circuit takes two hours at a leisurely pace, though there are plenty of access points for a shorter walk.

Perhaps the best section of the walls runs behind the 800-year-old **York Minster**, the largest Gothic cathedral in northern Europe. Built on the site of a Roman fortress, the minster is renowned for its magnificent stained glass windows. *(Minster Yard ☎ 01904-557216. Nov-May: Mon-Sun: 8am-6pm. Jun-Oct: Mon-Sun: 8am-8.30pm. Admission is free.)*

York Minster

The **Treasurer's House** behind the minster has an intriguing confusion of architectural styles, ranging from Roman to Victorian.

Another fascinating historic building is the **Merchant Adventurers' Hall** on Piccadilly/Fossgate, the finest surviving medieval guild hall in Europe. This 600-year-old timbered structure contains a collection of Elizabethan portraits, silver and furniture.

At the southern end of the walled city, on a high mound, stands **Clifford's Tower**. Originally a Norman tower constructed to help overawe the northern tribes, it was rebuilt in the 13th century by Henry III. Beside the tower is the **York Castle Museum**, which recreates Victorian and Edwardian interiors and street scenes.

Shambles and **Stonegate** are two of the prettiest shopping streets in York. Shambles, reckoned to be Britain's best-

Clifford's Tower

preserved medieval street, is still lined with craftsmen's shops which lean precariously inwards.

VISITOR INFORMATION

York Tourism Bureau
The Travel Office
6 Rougier Street
York YO1 1JA
☎ 01904-554488

REFLECTIONS

The history of York 'is the history of England'
— King George VI
(1895-1952)

Oxford & Blenheim Palace

VISITOR INFORMATION

Oxford Tourist
Information Centre
Old School Building
Gloucester Green
Oxford OX1 2DA
☎ 01865-726871

Oxford is an enticing mixture of old and new, with ancient colleges scattered across the bustling modern university town.

There are about 30 colleges, ranging from the medieval **St. Edmund Hall** to the modernist **St. Catherine's**. Each college is unique in character, some small and intimate like **Exeter**, others vast and impressive like **Christ Church**.

Oxford, city of dreaming spires

Perhaps the most impressive colleges are **Keble**, for the glorious Victorian Gothic Liddon Quad, **Magdalen** for the deerpark and cloisters and **New College**, for the fine chapel and walled gardens.

At the centre of Radcliffe Square is the magnificent domed **Radcliffe Camera**, part of the prestigious **Bodleian Library**.

The **Ashmolean Museum** on Beaumont Street is Britain's oldest public museum. There are collections of European and Oriental paintings, silver and ceramics and a bizarre collection of curiosities that includes Guy Fawkes's lantern and Oliver Cromwell's death mask.

GETTING THERE

By train from Paddington station at least once every hour and the journey takes about an 1 hour.

By coach from Victoria or Marble Arch – take the Oxford Tube or Oxford Citylink buses. Journey time is approximately 90 minutes.

Aside from the university and its history, Oxford is also a highly popular place to shop. Hundreds of independent shops specialise in books, antiques, crafts and other, more exotic wares.

Eight miles north of Oxford stands **Blenheim Palace**. One of the finest examples of English baroque architecture, it is set in 2,100 acres of parkland landscaped by 'Capability' Brown to represent the battlefield at Blenheim, the Bavarian village where the 1st Duke of Marlborough defeated Louis

Blenheim Palace

REFLECTIONS

'That sweet city with her dreaming spires, / She needs not June for beauty's heightening' – *Thyrsis*, Matthew Arnold (1866)

'I was not unpopular [at school]...It is Oxford that has made me insufferable' – Sir Max Beerbohm (1899)

XIV in 1704. It has the world's largest symbolic hedge maze, beautiful formal gardens, gilded state rooms and an exhibition devoted to Sir Winston Churchill, who was born at the palace. (*☎ 01993-811325. Mar 16-Oct 31: Mon-Sun: 10.30am-5.30pm, last admission 4.45pm. Adult £9, child (under 16) £4, senior £7, student £7.*)

Stonehenge, Salisbury & Shaftesbury

As you cross **Salisbury Plain**, the great stone circle of **Stonehenge** is majestically silhouetted against the sky. It is a sight which has inspired awe in visitors since Roman times.

The orientation of the concentric stone circles would suggest that the secret of Stonehenge is linked to the cycle of the moon and sun. Scholars, however, cannot agree whether the builders were part of a sun-worshipping culture.

Stonehenge

You can see the stones from the road or pay to walk a little closer. Visitors receive headsets with a soundtrack giving information about the site. *(Stonehenge, ☎ 01980-624715. Mon-Sun: Mar 16-May 31: 9.30am-6pm. Jun 1-Aug 31: 9am-7pm. Sep 1-Oct 15: 10.30am-6pm. Oct 16-Oct 24: 9.30am-5pm. Oct 24-Mar 15: 9.30am-4pm. Adult £4, child £2, senior £3, student £3.)*

A few miles south lies **Salisbury**, dominated by **Salisbury Cathedral**, which has the tallest spire in England (404 feet, 123 metres). Constructed between 1220 and 1258, it is the only medieval cathedral in the country to be built throughout in the same early-English style.

Salisbury Cathedral

Just to the north of the town is **Old Sarum Castle**, a massive Iron Age hill-fort which was successively occupied by the Romans, Saxons and Normans before becoming a major medieval settlement. There are sweeping views across south Wiltshire from the ramparts. *(Old Sarum Castle, ☎ 01722-335398. Apr-Oct: Mon-Sun: 10am-6pm. Oct: Mon-Sun: 10am-dusk. Nov-Mar: Mon-Sun: 10am-4pm. Adult £2, child £1, senior £1.50, student £1.50.)*

Twenty miles west of Salisbury lies the picturesque hill-top town of **Shaftesbury**. This is the northern tip of Dorset, the beautiful green county in which Victorian novelist Thomas Hardy lived and where he set most of his books.

Shaftesbury, known as 'Shaston' in Hardy's Wessex, is best known for the amazingly steep, pretty cobbled street Gold Hill.

VISITOR INFORMATION

Salisbury Tourist
Information Centre
Fish Row
Salisbury
Wiltshire SP1 1EJ
☎ 01722-334956

Shaftesbury Tourist
Information Centre
8 Bell Street
Shaftesbury
Dorset SP7 8AE
☎ 01747-853514

GETTING THERE

By train from Waterloo
station to Salisbury. Trains
run once an hour and the
journey takes 1½ hours.
(Nearest station to
Stonehenge is Salisbury)

Nearest train station to
Shaftesbury is Gillingham,
Dorset. Trains from
Waterloo station to
Gillingham run about once
every hour and the journey
time takes 2 hours.

Cambridge

VISITOR INFORMATION

Cambridge Tourist
Information Centre
The Old Library
Wheeler Street
Cambridge
CB2 3QB
☎ 01223-322640

The majestic colleges of Cambridge University line the banks of the River Cam, creating the famous **'backs'**.

The city is largely turned over to tourism in July and August, but during term time the presence of thousands of students creates an atmosphere of youthful energy and intellectual endeavour.

The origins of Cambridge date back to the Iron Age, when a Belgic tribe settled in the area, because it was the most reliable place to ford the Cam. The Romans, Saxons and Normans all built settlements prior to the first scholars arriving in 1209. The oldest surviving college, Peterhouse, was founded by the Bishop of Ely in 1284.

Trinity College

Henry VI founded the grandest of the colleges, **King's College**, with its world-famous chapel containing Rubens' *Adoration of the Magi*, in 1441. The college occupied nearly a quarter of the medieval city. Henry VIII combined two colleges to form **Trinity**, which has the largest court and a magnificent library by Sir Christopher Wren. Other Wren buildings include the chapels of **Pembroke College** and **Emmanuel College**. The latter contains a plaque commemorating John Harvard, a former student who sailed to America on the *Mayflower* in 1636 and gave his name to Harvard University.

GETTING THERE

By train from King's Cross. Services run three times every hour and the journey takes about 1 hour.

REFLECTIONS

'Oxford is on the whole more attractive than Cambridge to the ordinary visitor; and the traveller is therefore recommended to visit Cambridge first, or to omit it altogether if he cannot visit both.' – *Great Britain*, Karl Baedeker (1887)

The colleges are private, but they allow visitors to walk through the courts, visit the chapels and, in some cases, the libraries and halls. Walking on lawns is not allowed. Some colleges, including King's and Queens', charge an admission fee. Most colleges are closed for examinations from mid-April to late June.

Punting on the Cam

There are plenty of pretty towns and villages and interesting places to visit near Cambridge. They include **Ely Cathedral**, **Bury St. Edmunds**, and the stately homes of **Audley End**, **Anglesey Abbey** and **Wimpole Hall**. The surrounding, amazingly flat countryside, known as **the Fens**, often has spectacular skies and sunsets.

Canterbury

Every day, thousands of tourists follow in the footsteps of Chaucer's pilgrims to the quaint cathedral city of Canterbury.

St. Augustine and a band of 40 missionary monks arrived in Canterbury in the spring of 597, sent from Rome to bring Christianity to the British. By Christmas, Augustine had converted King Ethelbert and 10,000 of his subjects. Their first church, **St. Martin's**, is still in use and is England's oldest parish church.

Canterbury Cathedral

Within the city's surviving Roman walls is the Norman **Cathedral**, built on the foundations of an earlier cathedral established by St. Augustine. The present cathedral has a shrine to the 12th-century Archbishop of Canterbury, Thomas à Becket. He was murdered in 1170 in the north-west transept. The killers were responding to Henry II's impetuously voiced wish to be rid of "this turbulent priest". Becket was canonised three years later and Henry did public penance at his tomb. *(Canterbury Cathedral, ☎ 01227-762862. Mon-Sat: 9am-5pm. Sun: 12.30pm-2.30pm and for services. Opening times as guidance only; cathedral may close at short notice for events. Adult £3, child £2 (under school age free), senior £2, student £2.)*

Al fresco dining in Canterbury

Augustine also established a monastery, which became the country's most important seat of learning and was renamed St. Augustine's Abbey in 978. The oldest public school in England, **King's School**, grew out of the Abbey and still occupies part of the site of the original buildings. You can visit the ruins of the Abbey, which contain tombs of Saxon saints and kings, and a new interpretation centre. There is an entry fee.

The **Canterbury Tales** is a visitor attraction based on Chaucer's literary classic. You walk past life-size reconstructions from the tales, accompanied by a recorded commentary.

Canterbury is only a few miles from the pretty seaside towns of **Whitstable** and **Herne Bay**. The fairy-tale **Leeds Castle** *(☎ 01622-765400)* is also nearby.

VISITOR INFORMATION

Canterbury Visitor Information Centre
34 St. Margaret's Street
Canterbury
Kent CT1 2TG
☎ 01227-766567

GETTING THERE

By train from Victoria Station to Canterbury East. Services run twice an hour and the journey takes 1½ hours.

Frames Rickards guided coach tour to Leeds Castle and Canterbury (page 241).

REFLECTIONS

'Wel nine and twenty in a companye, / Of sondry folk, by aventure yfalle / In felawship, and pilgrimes were they alle / That toward Caunterbury wolden ryde.' — *The Canterbury Tales,* Geoffrey Chaucer (1387)

Stratford and Warwick Castle

VISITOR INFORMATION

Stratford Tourist
Information
Bridgefoot
Stratford-upon-Avon
Warwickshire
CV37 6GW
☎ 01789-293127

INSIDER'S TIP

There are admission charges to each property or you can buy a combined ticket covering them all.

River Avon

GETTING THERE

By train to Stratford from Paddington station. Services run once every 2 hours and the journey takes 2¼ hours.

By train to Warwick from Marylebone station. Services run once every hour and the journey takes 1¾ hours.

Frames Rickards guided coach tour to Oxford, Stratford and Warwick Castle (page 243)

Stratford-upon-Avon is the birthplace of William Shakespeare and home of the **Royal Shakespeare Company** (RSC). The RSC has three theatres, which concentrate on the bard's plays, but also show other works.

Shakepeare's birthplace

The Shakespeare Properties are the five historic houses in, or near, Stratford that are connected with the playwright and his family. **Shakespeare's Birthplace** has an exhibition devoted to his 'Life and Background', reconstructed wattle-and-daub walls, plus a traditional English garden. The signatures of several famous visitors are etched in the window panes.

Nash's House, owned by Thomas Nash, who married Shakespeare's granddaughter Elizabeth Hall, has a display of 17th-century furnishings. Outside is **New Place**, the site of the house where Shakespeare lived from 1597 until his death in 1616. **Hall's Croft**, home of Dr. John Hall, who married Shakespeare's daughter Susanna, has an exhibition about Elizabethan/Jacobean medicine.

There are two Shakespeare houses in villages outside Stratford. **Anne Hathaway's Cottage** in Shottery is where Shakespeare came to court his future wife. A little further from Stratford is **Mary Arden's House**, believed to be the home of Shakespeare's mother, before she married John Shakespeare. The timbered Tudor farmhouse is devoted to agricultural history, with regular displays of falconry.

Warwick Castle

Warwick Castle, eight miles from Stratford, is perhaps Britain's finest medieval castle, with gardens landscaped by 'Capability' Brown. There is an exhibition of medieval life, a dungeon and torture chamber, plus regular battle re-enactments. *(Warwick Castle, ☎ 01926-406600. Mon-Sun: 10am-5pm. Adult £9.75, child (4-16) £5.95, senior £7, student £9.75.)*

Tours

TOURS

Main bus stop: Trocadero, Piccadilly Circus

London Pride

HOURS

Summer: Mon-Sun:
9am-6pm or later
Winter: 9am-5pm

PRICES

Adult £15
Child £8
Senior £15
Student £15

DISCOUNT

20% off all ticket prices
with voucher on page 273.

The discount only applies if
you buy your ticket on a
London Pride bus. If you
go on a tour with another
bus company, purchase
the ticket from your hotel or
from another agent the
discount will <u>not</u> apply.

for less Open-Top Bus Tours

One of the best ways to get an overview of London is to take a tour on a hop-on, hop-off open-top double-decker bus.

London Pride, the largest of the open-top bus operators, offers a 20% discount to *for less* card holders.

A single ticket, which is valid for 24 hours, gives you unlimited transport on all four of London Pride's tour routes. On each of these you can jump off at any of the many stops, visit an attraction and re-board the next bus that comes along to continue your tour.

The tours allow you to enjoy great views around London and give you the flexibility to spend as long as you want at each location.

Throughout your journey, a pre-recorded commentary tells you about the places that you pass.

You can join the tour at any of the stops along the route (see below) and buy your ticket from the bus driver. Each tour is recognisable from the colour of the destination board at the front of the bus.

The Grand Tour of London (Yellow) – This very popular 90-minute tour takes you to all of the main sights. The tour follows a circular route and makes 23 stops including Piccadilly Circus (outside the Trocadero), Trafalgar Square, Green Park station, Hyde Park corner, Victoria Station (outside Thistle Hotel in Buckingham Palace Road), Westminster Abbey, Lambeth Palace, Westminster Bridge North (next to Big Ben), Parliament Street, Horse Guards, Covent Garden, St. Paul's Cathedral, The Monument, Tooley Street and Tower Hill (Tower of London).

Attractions Tour (Blue) – This 90-minute tour takes you to major attractions like Madame Tussaud's and Oxford Street. Buses leave every 30 minutes from outside the Trocadero, Piccadilly Circus.

Museums Tour (Green) – This 90-minute tour goes back and forth between the British Museum and the South Kensington Museums. Buses leave every 30 minutes from outside the Trocadero, Piccadilly Circus.

Docklands and Greenwich Tour (Red) – This 60-minute tour takes you into the heart of Docklands (page 212-213). Buses leave every 30 minutes from Trafalgar Square.

River Trips

With so many of London's most famous buildings either fronting the Thames or close to it, a river trip is a superb way to take in lots of sights without fighting through the city traffic.

Westminster Pier

One of the most spectacular trips is operated by **Westminster-Greenwich Thames Passenger Boat Services** from Westminster Pier to Greenwich. Here you can visit the Royal Observatory, the National Maritime Museum, the Cutty Sark and Queen's House (page 214-215).

Among the dozens of landmarks *en route* are the Tower of London, Tower Bridge, Shakespeare's Globe and Canary Wharf Tower. The river affords many classic vistas, including the view of the Royal Naval College which was made famous in a painting by Canaletto.

Guides provide an amusing commentary, peppered with anecdotes such as the one about the American who bought London Bridge and transferred it piece-by-piece to Arizona – thinking he was buying the more spectacular Tower Bridge. *(Westminster Pier, ☎ 020-7930-4097. Nov-Mar: Mon-Sun: 10.40am-3.20pm (every 40 minutes). Jun-Oct: Mon-Sun: 10.30am-4pm (every 30 minutes). Return fares: Adult £7.60, child £3.80, senior £6.30, student £7.60. 20% off all tickets with your for less card.)*

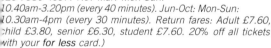
River trip on the Thames

Walking Tours

A walking tour is a good way to discover hidden London, of which most visitors, and many residents, are unaware.

Original London Walks operates 100 guided walks a week throughout the year, including explorations of Shakespeare's and Dickens's London, the Jack the Ripper walk, the Sherlock Holmes walk and the Beatles walk.

British Travel Centre

The guides, some of whom are actors and actresses, are very knowledgeable and entertaining. *(Information leaflet available from the British Travel Centre, 12 Regent Street or call ☎ 020-7624-9255 for full details. Adult £5, child free, senior £3.50, student £3.50. Adult £1 off walks, senior and student 50p off walks with your for less card.)*

Frames Rickards Coach Tours

Frames Rickards, London's premier coach tour operator, runs a large number of tours in London and

to major attractions outside the city. These luxury guided tours make sightseeing easy and enjoyable, ensuring that you do not waste time queuing for tickets, waiting for public transport or parking a car. They include all entrance prices and sometimes also lunch. On all of their tours, Frames offers substantial discounts to *for less* cardholders.

Frames Rickards luxury coach tours

Whatever your interests, Frames will have a tour to suit you. For example, if you want a one-day overview of London, take the London Experience Tour (see below), if you want to see Oxford take tour 9 (page 243) or tour 23 (page 242).

Frames Rickards' London reception

For most tours there is a courtesy hotel pick-up service available which will take you directly to and from your hotel to the tour bus. Alternatively you can catch tours at Frames Rickards' reception, located at Gate 20, Victoria Coach Station.

To obtain *for less* discounts you <u>must</u> book your tour directly with Frames Rickards by calling ☎ 020-7837-3111. If you book through a hotel, travel agent, Tourist Information Centre or other intermediary you will <u>*not*</u> obtain a discount.

Tour 29: London Experience

Mon-Sun:
8.45am-5.45pm

Adult £56.50, child £48.5▮
for less discount: 20%
(when booked on ☎ 020-7837-3111

The tour passes Big Ben and Westminster Abbey. Then watch the Changing of the Guard at Buckingham Palace or the Household Cavalry in Whitehall.

Big Ben

HIGHLIGHTS

Changing of the Guard
River Cruise (inc. lunch)
Tower of London, St. Paul's

The next stop is the City of London, where you board a river boat. Relax and enjoy the cruise, while lunch (included in the price) is served.

After lunch, you visit the Tower of London, where you see the Crown Jewels and meet the Beefeaters. The tour ends with a trip to St. Paul's Cathedral.

Tour 2: City & Tower of London

Adult £33.50, child £29.50   Mon-Sat:
for less discount: 20%   1.45pm-5.30pm
(when booked on ☎ 020-7837-3111)

On this tour you travel through the City of London, the most ancient part of London and Europe's financial centre.

You see the Bank of England, the Stock Exchange, the Mansion House (home of the Lord Mayor of London) and the Monument to the Great Fire of London.

Visit St. Paul's Cathedral and then the Tower of London, where you see the Crown Jewels and meet the famous Beefeaters, the guardians of the Tower.

Tower of London
HIGHLIGHTS
Drive through the City
St. Paul's Cathedral
Tower of London

Tour 1: London Panoramic Tour

Adult £17, child £13   Mon-Sun:
for less discount: 20%   8.45am-12noon
(when booked on ☎ 020-7837-3111)

Take a panoramic drive around the City of London and the West End, taking in all of the highlights while listening to a lively commentary.

Starting in the City, you see the Lord Mayor's Mansion House, Tower Bridge, the Tower of London and St. Paul's Cathedral.

You have excellent views over three of London's Bridges and, in the West End, you see Big Ben, Buckingham Palace and all the other big attractions.

Houses of Parliament
HIGHLIGHTS
Guided coach tour
through London

Tour 28: Ghosts & Taverns

Adult (only): £17   Mon, Wed, Fri and Sun
for less discount: 10%   6.50pm-10.30pm
(when booked on ☎ 020-7837-3111)

You are taken to crooked alleyways, ancient crumbling churchyards and gas-lit courtyards where your guide captures the shadows of times past.

You visit the site of a plague pit where 50,000 victims of the 1348 Black Death were buried in a gigantic mass grave.

Follow the Jack the Ripper trail and visit the sites of selected murders. Hear about the grisly details and the names of the suspects.

Haunted alleys
HIGHLIGHTS
Site of plague pit
Jack the Ripper trail
Visit to two London pubs

Buckingham Palace

HIGHLIGHTS

Guided tour of West End
Changing of the Guard
Palace State Apartments

River Thames

HIGHLIGHTS

Guided tour of London
River Thames cruise

Elizabethan Banquet

HIGHLIGHTS

Elizabethan banquet
Unlimited wine
Costumed entertainers

Tour BP1: Buckingham Palace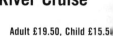

Aug 6-Oct 1 (only): Mon-Sun: £3?
8.45am-1.15pm *for less* discount: 20%
(when booked on ☎ 020-7837-3111

Buckingham Palace is open to the public in August
and September. Frames Rickards offers a tour that
guarantees admission to this popular attraction.

The morning tour includes a guided coach tour of the
West End, followed by a visit to watch the Changing of
the Guard (when available).

You finish with a tour around Buckingham Palace.
From Summer 2000 the largest room, the Ball Room,
is open to the public.

Tour 20: Sights of London
and River Cruise

Mon-Sun: Adult £19.50, Child £15.5(
8.45am-1pm *for less* discount: 20%
(when booked on ☎ 020-7837-3111

A panoramic tour of London takes in many of the
famous sights – the Tower of London, St. Paul's
Cathedral, Big Ben, Downing Street – with photo stops.
Then watch the Changing of the Guard at Buckingham
Palace (when scheduled) or the Household Cavalry in
Whitehall. Finally, there is a cruise along the Thames
from Westminster Pier on one of London's Red Fleet
boats. The tour does not include interior visits.

Tour 27: Elizabethan Banquet

Tue, Fri and Sat: Adult £5(
6.45pm-12midnight *for less* discount: 10%
(when booked on ☎ 020-7837-3111

This tour takes you to the stately home of Hatfield
House for an Elizabethan-style evening of feasting and
entertainment.

The banquet, which is served by costumed 'serving
wenches', consists of five courses of traditional
English fare and includes unlimited wine and mead.

A troupe of costumed minstrels and players perform
during the banquet. The specially printed menu
doubles as a souvenir.

Tour 6: Windsor & Hampton Court

Adult £59, Child £51
for less discount: 20%
(when booked on ☎ 020-7837-3111)

May-Sep: Tue-Thu, Sat and Sun
Oct-Apr: Tue, Thu, Sat and Sun
8.45am-6.30pm

You visit Hampton Court Palace, where you see the State Apartments, the Tudor Kitchens, the beautiful gardens and the famous maze.

From Hampton Court the tour passes the field of Runnymede where King John sealed the Magna Carta. Have lunch while cruising down the Thames to Windsor.

At Windsor Castle, a favourite weekend home of the Queen, there is a tour that includes the State Apartments or St. George's Chapel.

Windsor Castle

HIGHLIGHTS

Windsor
Lunch cruise on the Thames
Hampton Court

 # Tour 15: Stonehenge & Bath

Adult £49, Child £41
for less discount: 20%
(when booked on ☎ 020-7837-3111)

Mar-Nov: Mon-Sun:
Dec-Feb: Tue, Thu, Sat and Sun:
8.45am-7.15pm

This tour starts with the journey to Bath where you visit the famous Roman Baths, and there is also the opportunity to view the 15th century Abbey.

There is time for some independent sightseeing to enjoy the charming squares and crescents of the city, as well as taking a break for lunch and shopping.

You then travel to Stonehenge, the ancient circle of Bronze Age stone monoliths that stand in lonely majesty on Salisbury Plain.

Stonehenge

HIGHLIGHTS

Stonehenge
Bath
Roman Baths

 # Tour 14: Leeds Castle and Canterbury

Adult £47.50, Child £39.50
for less discount: 20%
(when booked on ☎ 020-7837-3111)

Apr-Oct: Wed-Mon:
Nov-Mar: Mon, Wed, Fri and
Sun: 8.45am-6.30pm

You begin with a visit to Leeds Castle. First built in the 9th century, it is set on two small islands in the middle of a lake.

Next stop is Canterbury, home of England's most important cathedral. There is time for lunch and shopping in the area close to the cathedral.

The tour continues on to Dover, where you view the famous White Cliffs. On the way back to London, you pass through Greenwich.

Canterbury Cathedral

HIGHLIGHTS

Leeds Castle
Canterbury
Dover

Tour 23: Oxford and Blenheim

May-Sep: Tue, Fri and Sun   Adult £45.50, Child £37.50
8.45am-6.30pm   *for less* discount: 20%
                            (when booked on ☎ 020-7837-3111)

First stop is the beautiful historic town of Oxford, home of the famous University. Here, you visit one of the colleges or principal buildings.

You then travel to Bladon, the burial place of Sir Winston Churchill. There is time for lunch and souvenir shopping in a beautiful Cotswold village.

Finally, the tour takes you to Blenheim Palace, the ancestral home of the Dukes of Marlborough, where you visit the State Apartments.

Blenheim Palace

HIGHLIGHTS

Oxford
Bladon
Cotswold village
Blenheim Palace

Garden Days

May-Sep: Tue-Fri & Sun: Adult £54. No children under 12
8.45am-6.15pm   *for less* discount: 10%
                            (when booked on ☎ 020-7837-3111)

The Garden Days tours are designed for the garden lover. The locations visited vary from day to day, so please enquire when booking.

The highlights include Sissinghurst Castle Garden, created by Vita Sackville-West, and the Royal Horticultural Society's garden at Wisley.

The main garden visits are complemented by trips to smaller, private gardens. Please note that cancellation fees apply to these tours.

An English country garden

HIGHLIGHTS

Visits to seasonal gardens
Specialist garden guide

Tour 5: Royal Windsor

Mon, Wed-Fri and Sun: Adult £28, Child £24
Apr-Oct: 1pm-6pm   *for less* discount: 20%
Nov-Mar: 8.45am-1.30pm   (when booked on ☎ 020-7837-3111)

Windsor Castle, the Queen's weekend residence, is the largest inhabited castle in the world. It has been a royal residence since the 11th century.

The tour starts with a guided walk through the Castle precincts, followed by a visit to the State Apartments and/or St. George's Chapel.

Cross the Long Walk, a three-mile avenue created by Charles II, and drive past the Field of Runnymede, where King John sealed the Magna Carta.

Windsor Castle

HIGHLIGHTS

Windsor Castle
State Apartments or
St. George's Chapel
Runnymede

Tour 9: Oxford, Stratford & Warwick

Adult £50, Child £42
for less discount: 20%
(when booked on ☎ 020-7837-3111)

Mar-Nov: Mon-Sun.
Dec-Feb: Mon, Wed, Fri and Sun:
8.45am-7.15pm

First stop is Oxford, the home of Britain's oldest, most beautiful and most prestigious University. A short visit is made to one of the colleges or principal buildings.

The tour moves on to Stratford-upon-Avon, the home of William Shakespeare. You visit his birthplace and a number of other buildings with which he was associated.

There is time for lunch and an opportunity for independent sightseeing and shopping. The tour is completed with a visit to Warwick Castle.

Warwick Castle

HIGHLIGHTS

Oxford
Stratford-upon-Avon
Shakespeare's birthplace
Warwick Castle

 # Tour F4: English Lakes

Adult £320 (+£65 single supplement)
for less discount: 10%
(when booked on ☎ 020-7837-3111)

Apr-Oct: Sat (only):
4 day tour
8am-6.30pm

On day 1 you visit Belvoir Castle – home of the Duke of Rutland – and Wedgewood. Then drive north to Chester, of which there is a walking tour on day 2.

Day 2 also includes a visit to Haworth in Yorkshire, home of the Brontë sisters. On day 3 the tour moves on to the Lake District to visit Wordsworth's cottage.

A circular tour of the picturesque Lakes finishes with a steamer trip. On day 4 you visit Harrogate and Cambridge on the way back to London.

The Lake District

HIGHLIGHTS

Belvoir Castle
Chester
Lake District

 # Tour F7: A Quick Look at Britain

Adult £335 (+£55 single supplement)
for less discount: 10%
(when booked on ☎ 020-7837-3111)

Apr-Oct: Sun and Tue:
4 day tour
8am-6.30pm

Day 1 takes you to the medieval city of York, where you visit the Minster on your guided walk. Later, you drive through James Herriot country *en route* to Darlington.

On day 2, you visit a Border Abbey and then travel to Edinburgh, where you have a guided tour of the city and visit the castle.

Day 3 begins with a drive through the Lake District, followed by a visit to Chester. On day 4, you visit Stratford-upon-Avon, before returning to London.

Chester

HIGHLIGHTS

York
Edinburgh
Lake District
Stratford-upon-Avon

Tour F11: Scottish Interlude

May-Sep: Fri (only):   **Adult £315 (+£70 single supplement)**
4 day tour   ***for less* discount: 10%**
8.45am-6.30pm   **(when booked on ☎ 020-7837-3111)**

On day 1, you are driven to the historic town of Edinburgh. On day 2 you travel to beautiful Loch Lomond, tour the Trossachs and visit Scone Palace.

On day 3, enjoy a guided sightseeing tour of the lovely city of Edinburgh, including the historic castle and the famous Royal Mile.

On day 4, you travel via picturesque Cheshire, the Potteries and Lady Godiva's Coventry on the way back to London.

Tour 24: Paris & Channel Tunnel

May-Sep: Tue, Thu and Sat: **Adult £150**
Apr and Oct: Sat only: ***for less* discount: 10%**
7am-10.15pm   **(when booked on ☎ 020-7837-3111)**

If you would like to take a day trip to Paris and experience the magic of the Channel Tunnel at the same time, this is the tour for you.

You are taken by coach to Waterloo Station, where you board a Eurostar Train that takes you in comfort under the English Channel to Paris.

In Paris, you go on a guided panoramic sightseeing tour of the city and go shopping before returning by Eurostar. You may need a Visa – please check.

Tour 34: Day Trip to Brussels

May-Oct: Thu: **Adult £149, child (under 12) £129**
6.15am-7.40pm   ***for less* discount: 10%**
(when booked on ☎ 020-7837-3111)

Check in at 6.15am at the BritainShrinkers desk at Waterloo Station where you will board the Eurostar train to Brussels. Journey time is 2 hours 45 minutes.

On arrival there is a guided tour of the city, finishing at the famous Grand Place with its magnificent City Hall and Guild Houses.

There will be free time for lunch, independent sightseeing and shopping, before returning to London by Eurostar. You may need a Visa – please check.

Scotland

HIGHLIGHTS

Edinburgh
Loch Lomond
Scone Palace
The Potteries
Coventry

Eurostar to Paris

HIGHLIGHTS

Eurostar Train
Paris sightseeing tour
Shopping in Paris

Grand Place, Brussels

HIGHLIGHTS

Eurostar Train
Sightseeing tour
Time for shopping

Visitor
Informatio

Calendar of Events . . .

January

London Parade, floats and aerial display. *(Jan 1. Starts in Parliament Square, ☎ 020-8566-8586.)*

Charles I Commemoration, procession. *(Last Sunday in Jan. From St. James's Palace to Banqueting House, ☎ 020-7839-8919.)*

February

Chinese New Year celebrations. *(Chinatown, ☎ 020-7431-8279.)*

March

Oxford v Cambridge Boat Race *(Date depends on tides. The Thames, Putney to Mortlake.)*

April

Chaucer Festival, music and readings. *(Early April. Southwark Cathedral, ☎ 01227-470379.)*

London Marathon *(2nd or 3rd weekend in April Greenwich to Westminster, ☎ 020-7620-4117.)*

May

Canalway Cavalcade, boat pageant. *(Usually early May. Little Venice, ☎ 020-8874-2787.)*

Notting Hill Carnival (August)

Chelsea Flower Show *(Last week in May. Chelsea Royal Hospital, ☎ 020-7630-7422.)*

FA Cup Final, England's biggest soccer game. *(Mid May. Wembley Stadium, ☎ 020-7262-4542.)*

Covent Garden Festival of Opera and Musical Arts, two-week festival of opera in shops and bars. *(Mid-May-early Jun. ☎ 020-7379-0870.)*

June

Kenwood Lakeside Concerts, classical concerts with firework displays and laser shows. *(Mid Jun-early Sep: Saturdays only. Kenwood House, Hampstead Heath, ☎ 020-8973-3427.)* See also page 210.

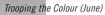

Trooping the Colour, military pageant to celebrate the Queen's birthday. *(2nd or 3rd week in Jun. Horse Guards Parade, Whitehall, ☎ 020-7414-2479.)*

Wimbledon Lawn Tennis Championships *(Last week of Jun, first week of Jul. All England Tennis Club, Wimbledon, ☎ 020-8946-2244.)*

Trooping the Colour (June)

Royal Ascot Week, famous horse racing week. *(3rd week of Jun. Ascot Racecourse, ☎ 01344-876876.)*

. . . Calendar of Events

The Proms classical concert series *(Mid Jul -Mid Sep. Royal Albert Hall, ☎ 020-7589-8212.)*

Hampton Court Flower Show *(Early-mid Jul. Hampton Court Palace, ☎ 020-7630-7422.)* See pages 216-217.

Riding Horse Parade, equestrian competition. *(1st week in Aug. Rotten Row, Hyde Park.)*

Notting Hill Carnival (page 185), live music and a million revellers. *(Last Sun and Mon in Aug. Notting Hill and Ladbroke Grove area, ☎ 020-8964-0544.)*

London Open House Weekend, hundreds of buildings not normally seen are opened free of charge. *(3rd weekend in Sep. ☎ 020-7267-2070.)*

Great River Race, 250 oared boats race from Richmond to the Isle of Dogs. *(12.20pm start. 3rd weekend in Sep. ☎ 020-8398-9057.)*

Horse of the Year Show *(Late Sep-early Oct. Wembley Arena, ☎ 020-8902-8833.)*

Punch and Judy Festival, traditional English puppeteers. *(1st week in Oct. Covent Garden, ☎ 020-7836-9136.)*

Pearly Harvest Festival, 100 Pearly Kings and Queens in costume. *(1st Sunday in Oct. St. Martin-in-the-Fields, Trafalgar Square, ☎ 020-7930-0089.)*

Opening of Parliament, Queen Elizabeth rides in procession to the Houses of Parliament. *(Usually in Nov, in-between election years. ☎ 020-7219-4272.)*

Bonfire / Guy Fawkes Night, fireworks displays and bonfires all over London to mark the anniversary of the Gunpowder Plot to blow up Parliament in 1605. *(Nov 5).*

London to Brighton Rally, veteran car event. *(First week of Nov. ☎ 01753-681-736.)*

Lord Mayor's Show, procession through the City to inaugurate new Lord Mayor. *(2nd Sat in Nov. ☎ 020-7332-3456.)*

Lord Mayor's Show (November)

Remembrance Sunday, royal family attend outdoor service on Whitehall for war dead. *(Sunday closest to Nov 11. Whitehall, ☎ 020-7730-3488.)*

Children's London . . .

INSIDER'S TIP

Try to avoid school holidays (Christmas, Easter, mid-June to early September) when queues can be horrendous.

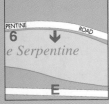

Rowing on the Serpentine in Hyde Park

Attractions – Many of the attractions in this book are ideal places for keeping children entertained, especially London Zoo (page 196-7), the London Aquarium (page 154-5), London Dungeon (not recommended for under eights) (page 152-3), Madame Tussaud's (pages 170-171), London Planetarium (page 172), the Science Museum (page 114), Natural History Museum (page 115), the Cutty Sark (page 214) and the virtual reality thrills of Segaworld, Showscan's Emaginator and the other attractions at the Trocadero (page 75).

A wax model at Madame Tussaud's

Children's museums – such as Pollock's Toy Museum (page 176) are custom-designed for kids. The Bethnal Green Museum of Childhood *(Bethnal Green tube station, Cambridge Heath Road, ☎ 020-8980-2415)* has an enormous collection of both antique and recent toys. The collection of dolls and dolls houses is worth the trip alone, though there are also displays of soldiers, model trains and planes, and a showcase of children's clothing over the centuries.

Parks and Playgrounds – All the big London parks have children's playgrounds, most with modern climbing frames and soft surfaces. There is a large and very popular playground at the northern end of Kensington Gardens. Rowing on the lakes in Regent's Park (page 195) or Hyde Park (page 192) is a traditional English family outing.

London Planetarium

Cinemas – Whiteley's (page 190) has an eight-screen cinema, popular with children because of the variety of restaurants and film selections favouring family viewing. Both the Barbican (page 202) and National Film Theatre (page 151) have special children's programmes.

. . . Children's London

Theatre – The Unicorn Theatre for Children *(6-7 Great Newport Street,* ☎ *020-7609-1800)* is the only theatre in the West End especially for young audiences.

Zoos – Apart from London Zoo (pages 196-7), there is a children's zoo in Battersea Park (a five-minute train ride from Victoria to Battersea Park), with pot-bellied pigs, monkeys and plenty of domesticated animals children can touch.

Shopping – Apart from the toy superstore Hamleys (page 89), try Beatties *(202 High Holborn,* ☎ *020-7405-6285)* for model railways and radio-controlled toys; the Early Learning Centre *(160-162 Kensington High Street,* ☎ *020-7581-5764)* for small children; or Warner Bros Studio Store *(178-182 Regent Street,* ☎ *020-7434-3334)* with its merchandise and computerised cartoon colouring station.

Theme Parks – There are several theme parks on the outskirts of London, each about an hour's journey by public transport. Legoland Windsor, a model town created out of plastic lego building bricks *(*☎ *0990-040404)* opened in 1996 and is popular with young children. Thorpe Park *(*☎ *01932-562-633)* is a water-fun theme park which has a beach and bathing lake plus thrilling rides like Logger's Leap.

Science Museum

Chessington World of Adventures *(*☎ *01372-727227)* has nine theme 'lands' and 15 rides including the Vampire roller coaster. Expect long queues.

The **Changing of the Guard** (page 50) at Buckingham Palace never fails to delight children and costs nothing. There is a ceremony every day in summer and every other day in winter, always starting at 11.27am.

Kidsline is a computerised information line with details of children's entertainment. *(*☎ *020-7222-8070, term time: Mon-Fri: 4pm-6pm, school holidays: 9am-4pm.)*

REFLECTIONS

I have regretfully come to the conclusion that the boy Auberon is not yet a suitable companion for me. Yesterday...I took him up the dome of St Paul's, gave him a packet of triangular stamps...took him to Harrods and let him buy vast quantities of toys...his mother said 'Have you had a lovely day?' He replied 'A bit dull.'– *Letters*, Evelyn Waugh (1945)

Hamleys

Visitor Information . . .

CLIMATE

The weather in Britain can be unpredictable, which makes it a popular topic of conversation. However, it does not rain as much as many foreigners are led to believe. In fact, London has lower annual rainfall than Paris and New York and, in recent years, less than Rome. Brief showers are, however, relatively common and you might want to bring an umbrella with you. See also 'When to Go' page 16.

An umbrella shop

CUSTOMS

Import restrictions on tax/duty-free goods are: **Tobacco**: 200 cigarettes, 50 cigars; **Alcohol**: Two litres of wine, plus one litre of liquor over 22% in proof; **Perfumes**: 60cc perfume, plus 250cc of toilet water; **Other Goods (souvenirs and gifts)**: to the value of £75. There are very strict laws on bringing animals into the country, with a six-month quarantine period compulsory.

ELECTRIC CURRENT

Britain uses 240 volts (50hz) electric current with a unique, large, three-pin plug. North American electrical appliances will need a transformer and an adaptor. Australasian and European appliances will only need an adaptor, which can be bought in London at airport shops and Boots, a chain of pharmacists. British hotel bathrooms nearly always contain an international two-pin electric razor socket.

EMBASSIES / CONSULATES

Australia *(Australia House, The Strand, ☎ 0207 379 4334)*; Canada *(Macdonald House, Grosvenor Square, ☎ 0207 258 6600)*; France *(21 Cromwell Road, ☎ 0207 838 2000)*; Germany *(23 Belgrave Square, ☎ 0207 824 1300)*; Ireland *(17 Grosvenor Place, ☎ 0207 235 2171)*; Japan *(101 Piccadilly, ☎ 0207 465 6500)*; New Zealand *(New Zealand House, 80 Haymarket, ☎ 0207 930 8422)*; Sweden *(11 Montagu Place, ☎ 0207 724 2101)*; United States *(Grosvenor Square, ☎ 0207 499 9000)*; Spain *(20 Draycott Place, ☎ 0207 589 8989)*; Denmark *(55 Sloane Street, ☎ 0207 333 0200)*; Norway *(25 Belgrave Square, ☎ 0207 591 5500)*; Italy *(14 Three Kings Yard, ☎ 0207 312 2200)*.

EMERGENCIES

To call for an ambulance, the fire service or the police, dial ☎ 999 from any telephone (it is a free number that operates 24 hours a day).

INSIDER'S TIP

You will find additional visitor information that will be helpful before you go to London, when you arrive, and when planning your itinerary on pages 16-21.

. . . Visitor Information . . .

Hospitals (with 24-hour casualty services) – St. Mary's Hospital *(Praed Street, Paddington, ☎ 020-7725-6666)*; University College Hospital *(Gower Street, entrance on Grafton Way, Bloomsbury, ☎ 020-7387-9300)*; Chelsea and Westminster Hospital *(369 Fulham Road, Chelsea, ☎ 020-8746-8000)*; Guys Hospital *(St. Thomas Street, entrance on Weston Street, South of the Thames, ☎ 020-7955-5000)*; St. Thomas's Hospital *(Lambeth Palace Road, South of the Thames, ☎ 020-7928-9292)*.

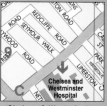

Chelsea & Westminster Hospital

St. Mary's Hospital, Paddington

ETIQUETTE

Smoking is now forbidden in many public places in London. You cannot smoke anywhere on the tube, on buses, in theatres nor in most cinemas. However, the majority of restaurants still have smoking sections and very few pubs have restrictions.

Londoners are renowned for their willingness to queue quietly and to apologise profusely for bumping into you in public places. A less accurate popular perception is that the British are cold and reserved. In fact, modern Londoners are friendly and easy going, particularly with foreigners. The best way to start a conversation is undoubtedly with a comment about the weather.

HEALTH AND SAFETY

Citizens of all EU countries are entitled to free National Health Service treatment. Citizens of other countries get free on-the-spot treatment at accident and emergency units at NHS hospitals, but must pay for all other medical services, including any admission to hospital wards. Health insurance is, therefore, advisable for visitors. Pharmacists can only dispense a limited range of drugs without a doctor's prescription.

A London policeman

London has a well-deserved reputation as a safe city. Most police do not carry guns and violent crime is rare. However, as in any other large city, you should take care of your valuables and watch out for pickpockets, particularly in crowded areas. The London police headquarters is New Scotland Yard *(☎ 020-7230-1212)*.

Report all thefts to the police (your insurance company will probably require this) and call to cancel all credit cards (see 'Useful Numbers', page 259).

LOST PROPERTY

If you lose something on a bus or tube train, try the London Transport Lost Property Office *(200 Baker Street,*

. . . Visitor Information . . .

☎ *020-7486-2496. Mon-Fri: 9.30am-2pm.).* In a taxi: Black Cab Lost Property Office *(15 Penton Street, ☎ 020-7833-0996. Mon-Fri: 9am-4pm.).* For other lost property, try your nearest police station.

LUGGAGE STORAGE

Major London train stations have left luggage facilities: Charing Cross *(Mon-Sun: 6.30am-10.30pm)*; Euston *(Mon-Sun: 24 hours)*, Paddington *(Mon-Sun: 7am-midnight)*, Victoria *(Mon-Sun: 7.15am-10pm)* and Waterloo *(Mon-Sat: 6.30am-11pm. Sun: closed).*

MARKETS

London's markets are famous both for their atmosphere and the bargains you can find. The three most famous markets are:

Portobello Market (page 186) – London's renowned antiques market. Second-hand clothes and all kinds of bizarre goods are sold from a mile-long stretch of stalls. *(Portobello Road. Notting Hill Gate or Ladbroke Grove tube stations. Sat: 8am-5pm.)*

Camden Market – A huge market selling clothes, crafts, books, records, antiques and many other items. *(Camden High Street. Camden Town tube station. Sat-Sun: 8am-6pm.)*

A post box

Petticoat Lane Market – Cheap fashion goods, odds and ends. *(Middlesex Street. Liverpool Street tube station. Sun: 9am-2pm.)*

MAIL / POST

You can purchase stamps from post offices and from most newsagents. Letters and cards can be mailed at post offices or post boxes (painted red). Post offices are generally open Mon-Fri: 9am-5.30pm, Sat: 9am-12.30pm.

Main post office close to Trafalgar Square

MEDIA

Listings – The best way to find out what's happening in London is to buy *Time Out*, a magazine that comes out on Wednesdays. It contains full listings for all London cinemas, theatres, clubs and many other forms of entertainment. *The Evening Standard* newspaper (Mon-Fri) prints listings, but they are less comprehensive.

Newspapers – A higher percentage of people reads a daily newspaper in the UK than in any other country. Newspapers are either tabloids, which are small in size and often frivolous, or broadsheets, like *The Daily*

. . . Visitor Information . . .

Telegraph and *The Times*, which are larger and more serious.

A newspaper seller

Radio – London has many radio stations catering for different tastes. The main ones are Capital Radio and BBC London Live. There are several national stations, including Radio 1 for pop music, Radio 2 for easy listening, Radio 3 for classical music, Radio 4 for current affairs, Radio 5 for sport and news and Classic FM for popular classical music.

Television – There are five national terrestrial channels: BBC1, BBC2, ITV, Channel Four and Channel 5. Many hotels have cable TV with dedicated sports and movie channels.

MONEY

Currency – The British currency is the pound sterling (£). There are 100 pence (p) in one pound. Coins come in denominations of 1p, 2p, 5p, 10p, 20p, 50p, £1 and £2. Notes are in denominations of £5, £10, £20 and £50. You may find £50 notes hard to change and they will always be checked for forgery.

Money changing – You can change money at banks or at bureaux de change. Although bureaux de change stay open longer hours, they sometimes charge much higher commissions (transaction fees).

With the *for less* vouchers on page 273, you pay no transaction fee at Travelex outlets listed in the margin.

NATIONAL HOLIDAYS

Known as Bank Holidays, because the banks are closed, most shops and attractions remain open except on Christmas Day and Boxing Day. If in doubt, please check.

New Year's Day	*Jan 1*
Good Friday	*Apr 21 (2000) / Apr 13 (2001)*
Easter Monday	*Apr 24 (2000) / Apr 16 (2001)*
May Day Holiday	*May 1 (2000) / May 7 (2001)*
Spring Bank Holiday	*May 29 (2000) / May 28 (2001)*
Summer Bank Holiday	*Aug 28 (2000) / Aug 27 (2001)*
Christmas Day	*Dec 25*
Boxing Day	*Dec 26*

TRAVELEX AMERICA INC. LOCATIONS

US airports:
Atlanta, Baltimore, Boston, Cleveland, Columbus, Detroit, El Paso, Fort Lauderdale, Fort Myers, Indianapolis, JFK (all terminals), Kansas City, La Guardia, Las Vegas, Memphis, Minneapolis, New Orleans, Newark (all terminals), Norfolk (Virginia), Omaha, Palm Springs, Pittsburgh, Portland (Oregon), Raleigh/Durham, San Diego, San Francisco, Tampa.

Heathrow:
All terminals - arrivals and departures

Gatwick:
All terminals - arrivals and departures

Central London:
142 Southampton Row. 9 Russell Square. Royal National Hotel, Bedford Way. Selfridges, Oxford Street. Imperial President Hotel, Russell Square. Tower of London. British Airways Travel Shop, Regent Street.

... Visitor Information ...

OPENING HOURS

Banks – Opening times vary. Generally, banks are open Mon-Fri: 9.30am-3.30pm, but a few stay open until 4.30pm. Some branches are open on Saturday mornings. Most banks have 24-hour cash machines, from which money can be withdrawn using credit or debit cards.

A traditional London pub

Bars, pubs and restaurants – The establishments offering discounts in this guide have their opening hours stated. The law requires a special licence for the sale of alcohol after 11pm (see page 204 for late-night bars and night clubs).

Shops – The establishments offering discounts in this guide have their opening hours stated in their entry. In general, shops are open Mon-Sat: 10am-6pm. Some shops also open on Sundays.

Sundays – Traditionally, Sunday is the day that London rests. Many Londoners leave the city at the weekend and some areas (notably the City) are almost totally deserted. However, most of the big attractions open as normal on Sundays and, although many shops close, markets such as Camden (page 252) are very busy. West End Theatres are closed on Sunday evenings.

St. Paul's Cathedral

PUB LUNCHES

Many London pubs serve cheap and cheerful lunches, usually offering traditional dishes such as Shepherd's Pie, Steak and Kidney Pie and Rhubarb Crumble. The typical pub lunch is served from 12noon to 2pm and costs about £5.

RELIGIOUS SERVICES

To find a religious service close to you, ring the relevant contact listed below.

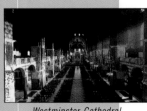
Westminster Cathedral

Baptist *(London Baptist Association, 1 Merchant Street, ☎ 020-7692-5592)*; Buddhist *(The Buddhist Society, 58 Eccleston Square, ☎ 020-7834-5858)*; Church of England (Anglican) *(Diocesan Office, ☎ 020-7932-1100)*; Jewish *(Liberal Jewish Synagogue, 28 St. John's Wood Road, ☎ 020-7286-5181, or Central Synagogue (orthodox), 36 Hallam Street, W1, ☎ 020-7580-1355)*; Moslem *(Islamic Cultural Centre, 146 Park Road, ☎ 020-7724-3363)*; Roman Catholic *(Westminster Cathedral, Victoria Street, ☎ 020-7798-9097)*.

SPECIAL TRAVELLERS

Disabled – Many London museums, restaurants and hotels have wheelchair ramps. Artsline *(☎ 020-7388-2227)* gives information about disabled access.

. . . Visitor Information . . .

Elderly – Concessions are usually available for senior citizens (women 60-plus and men 65-plus), but they may not always be advertised, so be sure to ask. You can obtain *for less* discounts, on top of senior discounts, at most major attractions.

Students – An International Student Identity Card is needed to obtain student concessions. For the cheapest accommodation, join the International Youth Hostel Federation. STA Travel *(86 Old Brompton Road, ☎ 020-7361-6161 for European flights, ☎ 020-7361-6262 for worldwide flights)* specialises in discount fares for those under the age of 26 and students. Council Travel *(28A Poland Street, ☎ 020-7287-3337)* is America's largest student/youth travel group, with a London office near Oxford Circus. You can obtain *for less* discounts, on top of student discounts, at many of the major attractions.

Gay – The Lesbian and Gay Switchboard *(☎ 020-7837-7324)* is a 24-hour helpline providing information on gay-related activities in London.

SPORT

Soccer or football is the most popular spectator sport in England, though cricket, rugby, golf, athletics and tennis events also attract huge crowds.

American Football – The London Monarchs play teams from the US and Europe at Wembley *(☎ 020-8902-0902)* in March and April. Two top US teams compete in the NFL Bowl at Wembley in August.

Athletics – There are usually a couple of major meetings every year at Crystal Palace stadium in south London *(☎ 020-8778-0131)*. Athletes can train free at West London Stadium and Regent's Park.

Cricket – International matches are played in summer at two London grounds, Lord's *(☎ 020-7289-1611)* and the Oval *(☎ 020-7582-6660)*.

Football – The season runs from Aug-May. The main London clubs are Arsenal and Tottenham (north London), Chelsea and Queen's Park Rangers (west London), Crystal Palace and Wimbledon (south London) and West Ham (east London). Tickets are available on the day for most matches.

Golf – Greater London has dozens of golf courses, though you will have to travel a few miles out of the centre of the city. There are popular public courses at

Westminster Cathedral

Lord's Cricket Ground

Wembley Stadium

Oval Cricket Ground

. . . Visitor Information . . .

Hounslow Heath (☎ 020-8570-5271) and Richmond Park (☎ 020-8876-3205).

Rugby – International matches are played during the season (Sep-Apr) at Twickenham (☎ 020-8744-3111).

Swimming – There are dozens of pools in London, with good ones at Chelsea Sports Centre (☎ 020-7352-6985) and Porchester Baths (☎ 020-7792-2919). For hardy, outdoor swimmers, there are lakes on Hampstead Heath and in Hyde Park that you can swim in.

Tennis – London has hundreds of tennis courts in public parks, including Holland Park and Parliament Hill. The Wimbledon Lawn Tennis Championships are held in late June/early July (All England Lawn Tennis Association, ☎ 020-8946-2244).

Wimbledon

Working Out – Most sports centres and large hotels have multi-gyms.

TAXES

Value Added Tax (VAT) is a sales tax of 17.5% levied on most goods (exceptions include books, food and children's clothes). VAT is included in the marked price so you will not notice that you are paying it.

Afternoon tea at the Dorchester

If you are resident outside the European Union (EU) and are staying in Britain less than three months, you can reclaim VAT on any goods that you take home with you. To do so, you must take your passport when you go shopping and complete a form in the store. When you leave the country you must give a copy to customs at the airport. Usually they will ask to see the goods so you should pack them in your hand luggage. The tax refund is later returned to you, usually either by cheque or by credit card refund. If you have the goods shipped home, the VAT should be deducted before you pay. Most major London stores, such as Harrods, Harvey Nichols and Liberty, are used to dealing with customers requiring VAT-exemption.

TEA (AFTERNOON TEA)

Many visitors to Britain will be disappointed to learn that the English now drink more coffee than tea. Nevertheless, the tradition of afternoon tea is alive and well. The best place to take afternoon tea is in one of the large, luxury hotels or department stores, most of which are located in Mayfair. Here is a selection of recommended places, most of which require

. . . Visitor Information . . .

reservations and will refuse admission if you are
wearing jeans or sports shoes:

Claridges *(Brook Street, ☎ 020-7629-8860. Mon-Sun: 3pm-
5.30pm. £19; £22 at weekends)*; Fortnum and Mason *(181
Piccadilly, ☎ 020-7734-8040. Mon-Sat: 3pm-5.15pm.
Sun: closed. Reservations not accepted. £16.50)*; Ritz
*(Piccadilly, ☎ 020-7493-8181. Mon-Sun: 2pm-5.30pm.
£27.)*; Waldorf *(Aldwych, ☎ 020-7836-2400. Mon-Fri: 3pm-
5.30pm. £18. Tea dances Sat: 2.30pm-5pm, Sun: 4pm-
6pm. £25.)*

The Ritz Hotel

TELEPHONES

Your *for less* card gives you instant access to an
inexpensive telephone service. It can be used for both
international and domestic calls from any telephone
box or hotel phone (page 8).

For calls made without *for less*, dial 100 to reach the
operator, 155 for the international operator. For
directory inquiries dial 192. Within London, there are
two codes: 020-7 for inner London, 020-8 for outer
London.

TIPPING

Restaurants – Many restaurants include a service
charge in the bill. When this is included, you are not
expected to tip. When a service charge is not
included, it is normal to tip 10-15%. We recommend
you consider tipping 15-20% on any *London for less*
discounted meal price, to ensure that the tip is not
discounted too.

Relaxing in a London pub

Pubs / bars – It is not normal to tip in London pubs,
although the habit is creeping in at certain fashionable
bars.

Taxis and hairdressers – The standard tip is 10-15%.

Porters – Tip 50p-£1 per suitcase, depending on size
and how far it is carried.

TOILETS

Public toilets may be marked as 'Public
Conveniences', 'WCs' or 'Lavatories'. Most charge 10p
or 20p. When sightseeing, museums, hotels,
department stores and restaurants are your best bet. If
you require directions, you should ask for the toilets.
In England, 'bathrooms' are places where people take
baths and the term 'restroom' might not be
understood.

TOURIST INFORMATION

The two largest Tourist Information Centres (TICs) are

*Victoria Tourist
Information Centre*

. . . Visitor Information . . .

Regent Street Tourist Information Centre

the London TIC, in the forecourt of Victoria Railway Station, and the Britain Visitor Centre on Lower Regent Street (just south of Piccadilly Circus). Smaller TICs can be found at Heathrow Airport (Terminals 1,2,3) and Liverpool Street Station.

TRAVELLING IN LONDON

Public transportation – The easiest way to get around London is on the **Tube** (subway/underground train), with trains every 3-10 minutes depending on the time of day. **Buses**, especially the upper decks of double-deckers, are a good way of seeing famous buildings and landmarks but take longer and get caught in London's infamous traffic snarl-ups.

Daily or weekly Travelcards offer unlimited travel on tubes, buses and trains and can be bought at any tube station. The daily card covering zones 1 and 2 (a large

The London Underground (the 'Tube')

area around the centre) costs £3.90, is ideal for the short stay visitor but is not valid before 9.30am. The weekend Travelcard, covering Saturday and Sunday, costs £5.80 for zones 1 and 2 and is valid all day, including before 9.30am. For information on bus and tube routes, times and possible delays, call the Travel Information line ☎ 020-7222-1234 (24hrs).

Taxi – London's metered Black Cabs, with their famous bowler-hat style shape, are clean and reliable though rather expensive. Expect to pay at least £5 for a short ride. You can hail these cabs, which display illuminated 'For Hire' roof signs when they are available. Minicabs, which must be booked by telephone, are less reliable than black cabs but are generally cheaper.

Car – Driving in central London is not recommended. Even if you know the route to your destination, prepare for heavy traffic. Parking can be even more of a problem. Cars left on yellow lines or in residents' permit areas will be swiftly clamped or impounded, with £50-150 release charges. Parking meters and car parks are difficult to find and expensive.

TRAVELLING OUTSIDE LONDON

See 'Beyond London', pages 223-224.

TRAVELLING TO THE REST OF EUROPE

Crossing the channel to France is quick and easy. You have a choice of around 20 ferry and hovercraft routes, in addition to the Channel Tunnel rail link.

INSIDER'S TIP

For more information about getting around in London see page 19.

. . . Visitor Information . . .

There are ports all along the south coast of England, but the shortest crossing is at Dover. All the main ports are linked by rail to either London Victoria or London Waterloo.

Eurostar (☎ 0990-186-186) runs trains from Waterloo International Station through the Channel Tunnel to Paris and Brussels. Motorists can take cars on **Le Shuttle** (☎ 0990-353535) trains departing from the Channel Tunnel entrance at Folkestone.

Frames Rickards offers cheap day trips to France and Belgium on Eurostar trains (page 244).

Eurostar to Paris

USEFUL TELEPHONE NUMBERS

Emergencies – Dial ☎ 999 for ambulance, fire or police.

Artsline – Information about access to arts events for disabled people (☎ 020-7388-2227).

Railway information – (☎ 0845-748-4950).

Capital Radio Helpline – General advice on London life (☎ 020-7484-4000).

Lost credit cards – American Express (☎ 01273-696-933); Visa (☎ 01604-230-230); Mastercard (☎ 01702-351-303); Diners Club (☎ 0800-460-800).

Emergency Dental Care – (☎ 020-7262-3334).

English Heritage – Information about the many historic buildings they look after (☎ 020-7973-3000).

London Transport – 24-hour information line (☎ 020-7222-1234).

National Car Parks – Information about car parks in your area (☎ 020-7499-7050).

National Trust – Information about its historic properties and gardens in London (☎ 020-7222-9251).

Sportsline – Information about sporting activities (☎ 020-7222-8000).

Time – Dial ☎ 123 for the 24-hour speaking clock.

WEIGHTS, MEASURES & CLOTHING SIZES

Britain uses both the imperial and the metric system.

Clothing sizes – In London, some clothes and shoes are sold in UK sizes and others in European sizes. To convert American women's clothing sizes to British, add 2 (e.g. an American size 8 is a British 10), for shoes, subtract 2 (e.g. an American 8 is a British 6). Men's suit and shirt sizes are the same in Britain and America, but shoes are ½ size bigger in America (e.g. an American 10 is a British 9½).

INSIDER'S TIP

To convert from Celsius to Fahrenheit, multiply the number by 9, divide by 5 and add 32.

To convert from Fahrenheit to Celsius, subtract 32, multiply by 5 and divide by 9.

Index of Discounters . . .

ART GALLERIES, ATTRACTIONS AND MUSEUMS

PERFORMING ARTS

. . . Index of Discounters . . .

HOTELS

Grange Adelphi Hotel ★★★	35	£££	SK
Amber Hotel ★★★	36	£££	SK
Millennium Bailey's Hotel ★★★★	35	£££££	SK
Barkston Garden Hotel ★★★	36	£££	SK
Beaver Hotel ★★	39	££	SK
Blakemore Hotel ★★★	46	£££	BA
Bonnington Inn Bloomsbury ★★★	40	££££	BL
Millennium Britannia ★★★★	33	£££££	MA
Burns Hotel ★★★	37	£££	SK
Comfort Inn Bayswater ★★★	43	£££	BA
Comfort Inn Heathrow ★★★	46	£££	GL
Cranley ★★★	39	££££	SK
Berjaya Eden Park Hotel ★★★	45	£££	BA
Euston Plaza Hotel ★★★★	41	£££££	BL
Generator	40	£	BL
Grange Fitzrovia Hotel ★★★★	42	£££££	BL
Millennium Gloucester Hotel ★★★★	38	£££££	SK
Haddon Hall ★★	39	££	BL
Henley House Hotel ★★	37	£££	SK
Hillgate Hotel ★★★	45	£££	BA
Grange Holborn Hotel ★★★★★	40	£££££	BL
Holiday Inn Garden Court ★★★	41	£££££	BL
Holiday Inn Kensington ★★★★	38	£££££	SK
Millennium Knightsbridge ★★★★	34	£££££	KN
Hotel Plaza Continental ★★★	39	£££	SK
Holiday Villa London ★★★	43	££££	BA
Rydges Kensington Plaza Hotel ★★★	35	£££	SK
Grange Langham Court Hotel ★★★★	42	££££	BL
London Guards Hotel ★★★	44	££££	BA
Mayflower Hotel ★★★	33	££	KN
New Linden Hotel ★★	43	£££	BA
Copthorne Tara ★★★★	34	£££££	SK
Norfolk Towers Hotel ★★★	42	£££	BA
Paragon Hotel ★★★	37	£££	SK
Quality Hotel Heathrow ★★★	46	£££	GL
Quality Hotel Paddington ★★★	44	£££	BA
Queen's Park ★★★	44	£££	BA
Grange Rochester Hotel ★★★★	33	£££££	WM
Grange Strathmore Hotel ★★★★	34	££££	SK
Wansbeck Garden Hotel	42	£	BL
Westminster Hotel ★★★	45	£££	BA
Grange White Hall Hotel ★★★★	41	£££££	BL

KEY TO ABBREVIATIONS

BA = Bayswater and Notting Hill	RP = Royal Parks
BL = Bloomsbury and Marylebone	SK = South Kensington and Chelsea
CY = City of London	SR = South of the River
GL = Greater London	WE = West End
KN = Knightsbridge	WM = Westminster
MA = Mayfair and St. James's	★ = Hotel rating category (see page 32)
	£ = Hotel price category (see page 32)

... Index of Discounters ...

SHOPS

Accessories (Gentlemen's)	Benson and Clegg	107	MA
Beauty	Cobella [Hair]	106	MA
Beauty	Hari's [Hair]	129	SK
Beauty Centre	Yves Rocher	182	BL
Candles	Violet [Gifts]	94	WE
Chess and Bridge Sets	Chess and Bridge	182	BL
Clothing (Cashmere)	Cashmere Gallery [Woollen]	130	SK
Clothing (Cashmere)	Cashmere Stop [Silk]	129	SK
Clothing (Cashmere)	Estridge [Woollen]	94	WE
Clothing (Cashmere)	House of Cashmere [Menswear]	107	MA
Clothing (Cashmere)	Supreme [Woollen]	91	WE
Clothing (Children)	Createx	128	SK
Clothing (Classic English)	London House	108	MA
Clothing (English & Scottish)	Mackenzie's	106	MA
Clothing (Leather)	Leather Classics	130	SK
Clothing (Men's)	Bellini	108	MA
Clothing (Men's)	Gallops	128	SK
Clothing (Men's)	Marmalade	92	WE
Clothing (Men's)	Paul and Shark	129	SK
Clothing (Men's)	The Face	92	WE
Clothing (Men's)	Sherry's	92	WE
Clothing (Men's)	House of Cashmere [Cashmere]	107	MA
Clothing (Men's Suits)	John Bray	108	MA
Clothing (Men's Tailored Suits)	Woollen Centre	93	WE
Clothing (Silk)	Cashmere Stop [Cashmere]	129	SK
Clothing (Women's Fashion)	Saks	91	WE
Clothing (Woollen)	Cashmere Gallery [Cashmere]	130	SK
Clothing (Woollen)	Estridge [Cashmere]	94	WE
Clothing (Woollen)	Supreme [Cashmere]	94	WE
Gifts	Piccadilly Souvenirs	93	WE
Gifts	Taylor	107	MA
Gifts	Violet [Candles]	94	WE
Hair	Cobella [Beauty]	106	MA
Hair	Hari's [Beauty]	129	SK
Hairdressing	10500	190	BA
Leather Goods	Bucci	106	MA
Make-up	Make-up Centre	130	SK
Outdoor & Camping Goods	Back Packer	91	WE
Photographic Portrait Shop	Old Time Photographers	93	WE

RESTAURANTS

American	Ed's Easy Diner	87	WE
American	Planet Hollywood	86	WE
American	Smollensky's	86	WE
American / Cajun	Old Orleans	86	WE
Asian	Bugis Street Brasserie	126	SK
Cabaret	Centre Stage	84	WE

. . . Index of Discounters . . .

RESTAURANTS (CONTINUED)

. . . Index of Discounters

RESTAURANTS (CONTINUED)

TOURS

PHOTO CREDITS

The Publishers would like to thank the following people and organizations for permission to reproduce their photographs over which they retain copyright. Any omission from this list is unintentional and every effort w be made to include these in the next edition of this publication. Debra Sweeney (principal photography), National Portrait Gallery (Andrew Putler), Westminster Cathedral 1995 Centenary Trust, Science Museum, Od Cinemas, Museum of the Moving Image, Stoll Moss Theatres, Royal Academy Of Arts (Martin Charles), Leight House Museum, Golden Hinde Educational Museum, Selfridges, Tate Modern (Marcus Leith), *Composition in R Yellow and Blue* by Piet Mondrian, purchased 1964, *The End of the Twentieth Century* by Joseph Beuys, purchased with assistance from Edwin C. Cohen and Echoing Green 1991, Tate Britain (John Webb)(Marcus Leith), *Beata Beatrix* by Dante Gabriel Rossetti, presented to the Tate Britain by Georgiana, Baroness Mount Temple in memory of her husband, Francis, Baron Mount-Temple 1889. *Ophelia* by John Everett Millais, presen to the Tate Britain by Sir Henry Tate 1894, Museum of London (Andy Chopping), MoLAS, Ministry of Sound, Hippodrome, National Postal Museum, London Transport Museum, National Maritime Museum, Greenwich, Caf de Paris, Parliamentary Copyright, House of Commons Education Unit, Segaworld, Harrods, Hamleys of Londo The Comedy Store (Jez Coulson of Insight Photography), Ronnie Scott's (David Redfern), Hard Rock Café (ID Publicity), The Savoy Group, The Dorchester Hotel, Lloyd's of London, Liberty Retail Limited, The Ritz Hotel (A Scott Associates), Tony Stone Worldwide, The London Aquarium, The Waldorf Meridien Hotel, Victoria & Albert Museum, HMS *Belfast* (Imperial War Museum), National Army Museum, The Natural History Museum (Neal Pott Associates), London Tourist Board, Gatwick Express Limited, Eurostar (U.K.) Limited, operators of the U.K. a of Eurostar, international high speed passenger service to Europe, Royal Collection Enterprises/Her Majesty Queen Elizabeth II, The National Gallery, Commonwealth Galleries, Barbican Centre (J.P. Stankowski), South Bank Centre, Courtauld Institute Galleries, The Gilbert Collection, The Wallace Collection, Joe Cornish Photographer, Imperial War Museum, English Heritage, London General House, Virgin Atlantic Airways Limited Museum of Mankind, London Docklands Development Corporation, Warner Village Cinema, London Regional Transport, Salisbury District Council (Steve Day), Southern Tourist Board (Peter Titmuss), Bath Tourism Bureau, Canterbury City Council, Warwick Castle, Warwick "The finest mediaeval Castle in England", Stratfo On Avon District Council, Cambridge Tourist Information, Blenheim Palace (Chris Andrews), York Tourism Bureau, Edinburgh & Lothians Tourist Board.

Berkeleys Hotel Connections (page 18)

Fare: Single   Circle before
                    or   boarding:
                    Return   voucher valid
                                    for either single
                                    or return

Airbus (page 18)

No. of tickets: 1   2   3   4   Circle before
                                    purchasing tickets:
                                    voucher valid
                                    for up to 4 tickets

London Pride (pages 19 and 236)

No. of adults: 1   2   3   4   Circle before
                                    purchasing tickets:
                                    voucher valid
                                    for up to 4 adults

London Pride (pages 19 and 236)

No. of children: 1   2   3   4   Circle before
                                    purchasing tickets:
                                    voucher valid
                                    for up to 4
                                    children

 **(pages 16, 19 and 253)**

Save 100% on transaction fees (commission free service) on foreign currency and
foreign currency travelers' check exchange at Travelex
branches listed on page 253

 **(pages 16, 19 and 253)**

Save 100% on transaction fees (commission free service) on foreign currency and
foreign currency travelers' check exchange at Travelex
branches listed on page 253

Berkeleys Hotel Connections (page 18)

This voucher entitles the holder of a valid *for less* card and up to 4 others to a discount of £2 off single fares or £4 off return fares on any Berkeleys Hotel Connections service between central London and Gatwick and Heathrow airports.

Airbus (page 18)

This voucher entitles up to 4 adults in possession of a valid *for less* card to the following discount on Airbus tickets from Heathrow, Gatwick or Stansted:
£2 off return fare, £1 off single fare

London Pride (pages 19 and 236)

This voucher entitles up to 4 adults in possession of a valid *for less* card to the following discount on tickets for London Pride's tours: Adult: 20% off

Valid only when tickets are purchased directly from London Pride staff.

London Pride (pages 19 and 236)

This voucher entitles up to 4 children in possession of a valid *for less* card to the following discount on tickets for London Pride's tours: Child: 20% off

Valid only when tickets are purchased directly from London Pride staff.

This voucher entitles the holder of a valid *for less* card to a saving of 100% off transaction fees (commissions) for foreign currency and foreign currency travelers' checks at the **Travelex** branches listed on page 253.
For official use only: Transaction Value:_____

Cannot be combined with any other promotional offer.

This voucher entitles the holder of a valid *for less* card to a saving of 100% off transaction fees (commissions) for foreign currency and foreign currency travelers' checks at the **Travelex** branches listed on page 253.
For official use only: Transaction Value:_____

Cannot be combined with any other promotional offer.

Westminster Abbey Chapter House (page 53)

No. of adults	1	2	3	4	Circle as
No. of children	1	2	3	4	appropriate: voucher valid
No. of seniors	1	2	3	4	for up to
No. of students	1	2	3	4	4 people

Banqueting House (page 59)

No. of adults	1	2	3	4	Circle as
No. of children	1	2	3	4	appropriate: voucher valid
No. of seniors	1	2	3	4	for up to
No. of students	1	2	3	4	4 people

Jewel Tower (page 60)

No. of adults	1	2	3	4	Circle as
No. of children	1	2	3	4	appropriate: voucher valid
No. of seniors	1	2	3	4	for up to
No. of students	1	2	3	4	4 people

Guards Museum (page 62)

No. of adults	1	2	3	4	Circle as
No. of children	1	2	3	4	appropriate: voucher valid
No. of seniors	1	2	3	4	for up to
No. of students	1	2	3	4	4 people

Rock Circus (page 74)

No. of adults	1	2	3	4	Circle as
No. of children	1	2	3	4	appropriate: voucher valid
No. of seniors	1	2	3	4	for up to
No. of students	1	2	3	4	4 people

Theatre Museum (page 78)

					Circle as appropriate: voucher valid
No. of adults	1	2	3	4	for up to
No. of students	1	2	3	4	4 people

This voucher entitles the holder of a valid *for less* card to the following discounts at the **Chapter House** (page 53):

Adult	50% off	Senior	50% off
Child	50% off	Student	50% off

Cannot be combined with any other promotional offer.

This voucher entitles the holder of a valid *for less* card to the following discounts at the **Banqueting House** (page 59):

Adult	10% off	Senior	10% off
Child	10% off	Student	10% off

Cannot be combined with any other promotional offer.

This voucher entitles the holder of a valid *for less* card to the following discounts at the **Jewel Tower** (page 60):

Adult	50% off	Senior	50% off
Child	50% off	Student	50% off

Cannot be combined with any other promotional offer.

This voucher entitles the holder of a valid *for less* card to the following discounts at the **Guards Museum** (page 62):

Adult	50% off	Senior	50% off
Child	50% off	Student	50% off

Cannot be combined with any other promotional offer.

This voucher entitles the holder of a valid *for less* card to the following discounts at the **Rock Circus** (page 74):

Adult	£1.50 off	Senior	£1.50 off
Child	£1.50 off	Student	£1.50 off

Cannot be combined with any other promotional offer.

This voucher entitles the holder of a valid *for less* card to the following discounts at the **Theatre Museum** (page 78):

Adult	50% off	Senior	free
Child	free	Student	50% off

Cannot be combined with any other promotional offer.

Theatre Royal Backstage Tours (page 78)

No. of adults	1	2	3	4	Circle as appropriate: voucher valid for up to 4 people
No. of children	1	2	3	4	
No. of seniors	1	2	3	4	
No. of students	1	2	3	4	

London Brass Rubbing Centre (page 81)

No. of adults	1	2	3	4	Circle as appropriate: voucher valid for up to 4 people
No. of children	1	2	3	4	
No. of seniors	1	2	3	4	
No. of students	1	2	3	4	

Science Museum (page 114)

This voucher does not apply to temporary exhibitions, IMAX cinema or the simulator.

No. of adults	1	2	3	4	Circle as appropriate: voucher valid for up to 4 people
No. of children	1	2	3	4	
No. of seniors	1	2	3	4	
No. of students	1	2	3	4	

Tower of London (page 136-137)

No. of adults	1	2	3	4	Circle as appropriate: voucher valid for up to 4 people
No. of children	1	2	3	4	
No. of seniors	1	2	3	4	
No. of students	1	2	3	4	

House of Detention (page 141)

No. of adults	1	2	3	4	Circle as appropriate: voucher valid for up to 4 people
No. of children	1	2	3	4	
No. of seniors	1	2	3	4	
No. of students	1	2	3	4	

Dr Johnson's House (page 142)

No. of adults	1	2	3	4	Circle as appropriate: voucher valid for up to 4 people
No. of children	1	2	3	4	
No. of seniors	1	2	3	4	
No. of students	1	2	3	4	

This voucher entitles the holder of a valid *for less* card to the following discounts on **Theatre Royal Backstage Tours** (page 78):

Adult	£1 off	Senior	£1 off
Child	£1 off	Student	£1 off

Cannot be combined with any other promotional offer.

This voucher entitles the holder of a valid *for less* card to the following discounts on self-made rubbings at the **London Brass Rubbing Centre** (page 81):

Adult	50% off	Senior	50% off
Child	50% off	Student	50% off

Cannot be combined with any other promotional offer.

This voucher entitles the holder of a valid *for less* card to the following discounts at the **Science Museum** (page 114):

Adult	20% off	Senior	20% off
Child	20% off	Student	20% off

Cannot be combined with any other promotional offer.

This voucher entitles the holder of a valid *for less* card to the following discounts at the **Tower of London** (page 136-7):

Adult	10% off	Senior	10% off
Child	10% off	Student	10% off

Cannot be combined with any other promotional offer.

This voucher entitles the holder of a valid *for less* card to the following discounts at the **House of Detention** (page 141):

Adult	50% off	Senior	50% off
Child	50% off	Student	50% off

Cannot be combined with any other promotional offer.

This voucher entitles the holder of a valid *for less* card to the following discounts at **Dr Johnson's House** (page 142):

Adult	50% off	Senior	50% off
Child	50% off	Student	50% off

Cannot be combined with any other promotional offer.

Bramah Museum of Tea & Coffee (pages 162)

No. of adults	1 2 3 4	Circle as appropriate: voucher valid for up to 4 people
No. of children	1 2 3 4	
No. of seniors	1 2 3 4	
No. of students	1 2 3 4	

Britain at War Experience (page 161)

No. of adults	1 2 3 4	Circle as appropriate: voucher valid for up to 4 people
No. of children	1 2 3 4	
No. of seniors	1 2 3 4	
No. of students	1 2 3 4	

Clink Prison Museum (page 160)

No. of adults	1 2 3 4	Circle as appropriate: voucher valid for up to 4 people
No. of children	1 2 3 4	
No. of seniors	1 2 3 4	
No. of students	1 2 3 4	

Bankside Gallery (page 159)

No. of paid admissions: 1 or 2 (please circle)

Voucher valid for number of people who hold
for less cards –
maximum 2 free admissions

Florence Nightingale Museum (page 158)

No. of adults	1 2 3 4	Circle as appropriate: voucher valid for up to 4 people
No. of children	1 2 3 4	
No. of seniors	1 2 3 4	
No. of students	1 2 3 4	

Madame Tussaud's (pages 170-171) - Code #20

No. of adults	1 2 3 4	Circle as appropriate: voucher valid for up to 4 people
No. of children	1 2 3 4	
No. of seniors	1 2 3 4	
No. of students	1 2 3 4	

This voucher entitles the holder of a valid *for less* card to the following discounts at the **Bramah Museum of Tea & Coffee** (page 162):

Adult	50% off	Senior	50% off
Child	50% off	Student	50% off

Cannot be combined with any other promotional offer.

This voucher entitles the holder of a valid *for less* card to the following discounts at the **Britain at War Experience** (page 161):

Adult	50% off	Senior	50% off
Child	50% off	Student	50% off

Cannot be combined with any other promotional offer.

This voucher entitles the holder of a valid *for less* card to the following discounts at the **Clink Prison Museum** (page 160):

Adult	50% off	Senior	50% off
Child	50% off	Student	50% off

Cannot be combined with any other promotional offer.

This voucher entitles the holder of a valid *for less* card to the following discounts at the **Bankside Gallery** (page 159):

2-for-1 admission: one free admission with each admission of equal or greater value purchased (maximum 2 free admissions)

Cannot be combined with any other promotional offer.

This voucher entitles the holder of a valid *for less* card to the following discounts at the **Florence Nightingale Museum** (page 158):

Adult	50% off	Senior	50% off
Child	50% off	Student	50% off

Cannot be combined with any other promotional offer.

This voucher entitles the holder of a valid *for less* card to the following discounts at **Madame Tussaud's** (page 170):

Adult	£1.50 off	Senior	£1.50 off
Child	£1.50 off	Student	£1.50 off

Cannot be combined with any other promotional offer.

London Planetarium (page 172) - Code #23

No. of adults	1 2 3 4	Circle as appropriate: voucher valid for up to 4 people
No. of children	1 2 3 4	
No. of seniors	1 2 3 4	
No. of students	1 2 3 4	

Dicken's House (page 174)

No. of paid admissions: 1 or 2 (please circle)

Voucher valid for number of people who hold
for less cards -
maximum 2 free admissions

Pollock's Toy Museum (pages 176)

No. of adults	1 2 3 4	Circle as appropriate: voucher valid for up to 4 people
No. of children	1 2 3 4	
No. of seniors	1 2 3 4	
No. of students	1 2 3 4	

London Canal Museum (page 177)

No. of adults	1 2 3 4	Circle as appropriate: voucher valid for up to 4 people
No. of children	1 2 3 4	
No. of seniors	1 2 3 4	
No. of students	1 2 3 4	

Apsley House (page 193)

No. of adults	1 2 3 4	Circle as appropriate: voucher valid for up to 4 people
No. of children	1 2 3 4	
No. of seniors	1 2 3 4	
No. of students	1 2 3 4	

Kensington Palace (page 194)

No. of adults	1 2 3 4	Circle as appropriate: voucher valid for up to 4 people
No. of children	1 2 3 4	
No. of seniors	1 2 3 4	
No. of students	1 2 3 4	

This voucher entitles the holder of a valid *for less* card to the following discounts off a combined ticket to the **London Planetarium** (page 172) and **Madame Tussaud's**:

Adult	£2 off	Senior	£2 off
Child	£2 off	Student	£2 off

Cannot be combined with any other promotional offer.

This voucher entitles the holder of a valid *for less* card to the following discounts off a combined ticket to **Dicken's House** (page 174):

2-for-1 admission: one free admission with each admission of equal or greater value purchased (maximum 2 free admissions)

Cannot be combined with any other promotional offer.

This voucher entitles the holder of a valid *for less* card to the following discounts at **Pollock's Toy Museum** (page 176):

Adult	50% off	Senior	50% off
Child	50% off	Student	50% off

Cannot be combined with any other promotional offer.

This voucher entitles the holder of a valid *for less* card to the following discounts at the **London Canal Museum** (page 177):

Adult	50% off	Senior	50% off
Child	50% off	Student	50% off

Cannot be combined with any other promotional offer.

This voucher entitles the holder of a valid *for less* card to the following discounts at **Apsley House** (page 193):

Adult	50% off	Senior	50% off
Child	50% off	Student	50% off

Cannot be combined with any other promotional offer.

This voucher entitles the holder of a valid *for less* card to the following discounts at **Kensington Palace** (page 194):

Adult	10% off	Senior	10% off
Child	10% off	Student	10% off

Cannot be combined with any other promotional offer.

Cutty Sark (page 214)

No. of adults	1 2 3 4	Circle as
No. of children	1 2 3 4	appropriate:
No. of seniors	1 2 3 4	voucher valid
No. of students	1 2 3 4	for up to 4 people

Hampton Court Palace (pages 216-217)

No. of adults	1 2 3 4	Circle as
No. of children	1 2 3 4	appropriate:
No. of seniors	1 2 3 4	voucher valid
No. of students	1 2 3 4	for up to 4 people

Jewish Museum (page 221)

No. of adults	1 2 3 4	Circle as appropriate: voucher valid for up to 4 people

Ranger's House (page 221)

No. of adults	1 2 3 4	Circle as
No. of children	1 2 3 4	appropriate:
No. of seniors	1 2 3 4	voucher valid
No. of students	1 2 3 4	for up to 4 people

Chiswick House (page 222)

No. of adults	1 2 3 4	Circle as
No. of children	1 2 3 4	appropriate:
No. of seniors	1 2 3 4	voucher valid
No. of students	1 2 3 4	for up to 4 people

Wimbledon Lawn Tennis Museum (page 222)

No. of adults	1 2 3 4	Circle as
No. of children	1 2 3 4	appropriate:
No. of seniors	1 2 3 4	voucher valid
No. of students	1 2 3 4	for up to 4 people

This voucher entitles the holder of a valid *for less* card to the following discounts at the **Cutty Sark** (page 214):

Adult	50% off	Senior	50% off
Child	50% off	Student	50% off

Cannot be combined with any other promotional offer.

This voucher entitles the holder of a valid *for less* card to the following discounts at **Hampton Court Palace** (page 216-217):

Adult	10% off	Senior	10% off
Child	10% off	Student	10% off

Cannot be combined with any other promotional offer.

This voucher entitles the holder of a valid *for less* card to the following discounts at the **Jewish Museum** (page 221):

Adult	50% off

Cannot be combined with any other promotional offer.

This voucher entitles the holder of a valid *for less* card to the following discounts at the **Ranger's House** (page 221):

Adult	50% off	Senior	50% off
Child	50% off	Student	50% off

Cannot be combined with any other promotional offer.

This voucher entitles the holder of a valid *for less* card to the following discounts at **Chiswick House** (page 222):

Adult	50% off	Senior	50% off
Child	50% off	Student	50% off

Cannot be combined with any other promotional offer.

This voucher entitles the holder of a valid *for less* card to the following discounts at the **Wimbledon Lawn Tennis Museum** (page 222):

Adult	50% off	Senior	50% off
Child	50% off	Student	50% off

Cannot be combined with any other promotional offer.

Bella Pasta

This voucher entitles up to 4 people to save 25% off
the total bill (including food and beverages)
at Bella Pasta restaurants.

Bella Pasta

This voucher entitles up to 4 people to save 25% off
the total bill (including food and beverages)
at Bella Pasta restaurants.

Pizza Piazza

This voucher entitles up to 4 people to save 25% off
the total bill (including food and beverages)
at Pizza Piazza restaurants.

Pizza Piazza

This voucher entitles up to 4 people to save 25% off
the total bill (including food and beverages)
at Pizza Piazza restaurants.

Planet Hollywood

This voucher entitles up to 4 people to save 25% off
the total bill (including food and beverages)
at Planet Hollywood (page 86).

Donuts and Company

This voucher entitles up to 4 people to save 25% off
the total bill (including food and beverages)
at Donuts and Company (page85).

Not valid in conjunction with any other offer. Voucher should be presented with bill before paying or discount cannot apply. Not redeemable for cash.

 Not valid in conjunction with any other offer. Voucher should be presented with bill before paying or discount cannot apply. Not redeemable for cash.

 Not valid in conjunction with any other offer. Voucher should be presented with bill before paying or discount cannot apply. Not redeemable for cash.

 Not valid in conjunction with any other offer. Voucher should be presented with bill before paying or discount cannot apply. Not redeemable for cash.

 Not valid in conjunction with any other offer. Voucher should be presented with bill before paying or discount cannot apply. Not redeemable for cash.

 Not valid in conjunction with any other offer. Voucher should be presented with bill before paying or discount cannot apply. Not redeemable for cash.

Customer Response Card

We would like to hear your comments about *London for less*
so that we can improve the book. Please complete
the information below and mail this card.
No stamp is required, either in Britain or overseas.

) Name:...

) Address:...

) Telephone no:...

) Where did you purchase your book?....................................

) What is the reason you chose *London for less*?....................

....

....

) How many days were you in London?.................................

) Please circle discounts used:
   Attractions ~ Performing Arts ~ Tours ~ Hotels ~ Shops ~
   Restaurants ~ Nightclubs ~ Currency Exchange

) What was the total of the discounts that you received? £..........

) On a scale of 1 to 5 (where 5 is the best) how would you rate
ondon for less?
   1   2   3   4   5

0) Would you recommend *London for less* to a friend?..................

....

....

1) What did you like most about the book?................................

....

....

2) What would you like to see improved?..................................

....

....

....

....

NE PAS AFFRANCHIR

NO STAMP REQUIRED

By air mail
Par avion

IBRS/CCRI NUMBER: PHQ-D/2560/W

RÉPONSE PAYEE
GRANDE-BRETAGNE

Metropolis International (UK) Limited
222 Kensal Road
LONDON
GREAT BRITAIN
W10 5BR